RETURN OF THE VIKINGS

A momentous journey from administration to rugby league's
top tier

RETURN OF THE VIKINGS

A momentous journey from administration to rugby league's
top tier

Mike Healing

WIDNES VIKINGS

To my wife Lynn

For her unfailing support and encouragement throughout this project

Cover Photographs
Front cover, top: Ben Kavanagh, Mark Smith, Iain Morrison, Kevin Penny and Richard Fletcher celebrate 'ticking the box'.

Front cover, bottom: Widnes Vikings 2012.

Back cover: Mike Healing (left) in conversation with Denis Betts.

First published in Great Britain in 2013 by DB Publishing, an imprint of JMD Media Ltd

ISBN 978-1-78091-202-8

Printed and bound by Copytech (UK) Ltd, Peterborough

Contents

Acknowledgements

I must record my thanks to the many people at Widnes Vikings who have come to my assistance throughout the writing of this book. Special thanks go to Steve O'Connor, Paul Cullen, Denis Betts and former head coach Steve McCormack for giving their time so freely.

Valuable assistance was also forthcoming from the Operations and Media Departments of the Rugby Football League, and my wide range of contacts throughout the rugby league world, of whom there are too many to mention.

I am also grateful to Ste Jones of KT8 Photography, *Runcorn and Widnes Weekly News*, *Runcorn and Widnes World* and Widnes Rugby League Museum for allowing the use of their images, which greatly enhance this publication.

Thanks are also due to London League Publications for allowing the use of extracts from *A Dream Come True* – by Doug Laughton & Andrew Quirke.

Photograph Credits

Front cover, top: Mike Boden – *Runcorn and Widnes World*
Front cover, bottom: Ste Jones/KT8
Photo 1: Stuart Bogg – *Runcorn and Widnes Weekly News*
Photo 2: Ste Jones / KT8
Photo 3: Mike Healing
Photo 4: Ste Jones / KT8
Photo 5: Ste Jones / KT8
Photo 6: Ste Jones / KT8
Photo 7: Ste Jones / KT8
Photo 8: Ste Jones / KT8
Photo 9: Ste Jones / KT8
Photo 10: Ste Jones / KT8
Photo 11: Ste Jones / KT8
Photo 12: Ste Jones / KT8
Photo 13: Ste Jones / KT8
Photo 14: Ste Jones / KT8
Photo 15: Ste Jones / KT8
Photo 16: Ste Jones / KT8
Photo 17: Stuart Bogg – *Runcorn and Widnes Weekly News*
Photo 18: Widnes Rugby League Museum
Photo 19 Widnes Rugby League Museum
Back cover: Mike Healing

Foreword

The Widnes Vikings story has been a roller coaster in the Super League era!! Originally left out of the plans in 1996... they've been in and out of the headlines – and the competition – ever since.

IN Super League under Neil Kelly – OUT a few years later. INTO administration and then OUT – rescued from oblivion by a man who has definitely put his money where his mouth is, and now under Steve O'Connor they are building again to get back INTO the position where they once were – the undisputed Kings of the Rugby League.

Whether they will ever win a World Club Challenge again and recreate their Wembley and Championship successes of the past remains to be seen but it won't be for the want of trying.

You can only admire a bloke like Steve – a hugely successful local businessman doing his best to put something back into the local community – risking his life's fortune to give Widnes Vikings a fighting chance of rekindling their former glories.

There is much to be admired – and the story is a fascinating one.

Enjoy Mike Healing's second book on the Vikings – it's obviously a Labour of Love for him too!

Eddie Hemmings
Sky Sports

Introduction

'WHAT A SHOCKER'…

With these opening words, the then Leader of Halton Borough Council, Councillor Tony McDermott MBE summed up the feelings of Widnes supporters everywhere when he, along with chairman Steve O'Connor, addressed the Widnes fans from the pitch when the Vikings entertained Dewsbury Rams just five days after the Rugby Football League [RFL] had announced the results of its inaugural Licensing process.

Those results had been made public on 22nd July 2008 when Richard Lewis, executive chairman of the Rugby Football League, had announced the names of the 14 clubs who had been successful in their Licence applications for an expanded Super League competition from 2009.

Councillor McDermott, surrounded by the club's backroom staff who had worked so diligently on the club's outstanding Licence application, explained: "this pitch invasion today is to show that we are together – the Council, the Club, the Supporters – in taking things forward. We want to prove the Rugby League wrong". In a direct reference to the Administration saga of autumn 2007 Councillor McDermott reminded fans that "we have had worse days than this" and paid tribute to Steve O'Connor for saving this former giant of the rugby league world.

Taking over the microphone Steve O'Connor described the range of emotions that he had felt since the shock of the announcement made just days earlier. Maybe concerned that his measured and dignified reaction to the news that the Vikings faced another three years away from the top flight might indicate "that we don't care" O'Connor said that he had shared "every emotion that the fans have experienced this week from sadness and anger to bitterness". However, it was his conclusion that all thoughts of retribution should be put to one side while concentrating on rebuilding the club and forging a new relationship with the RFL.

O'Connor concluded his address by stating that "we accept their decision, we don't agree with the decision, we don't agree with the reasons," before saying "the licensing process is the right way to make rugby league a more sustainable game. We were unfortunate, we are not comfortable with the reasons, but I think what you need to hear from me is that over the next three years I am determined to stay and determined to make something happen".

The shockwaves of disappointment and incredulity were not only felt in WA8. As the days rolled by this was amplified by a groundswell of similar reactions being expressed by respected figures within the game, fans from a host of other clubs and many sections of the national rugby league media.

A siege mentality grew among everybody with connections to the club, but the club's reluctant but dignified acceptance of the situation espoused by O'Connor demonstrated that the owner had identified what he felt was the most productive way forward for his, and our, club.

The future of Widnes Vikings had already begun to take shape before Councillor McDermott led that 'pitch invasion' as O'Connor and his management team immediately began planning for the next round of licensing applications and beyond.

Before the outcome of that next round of Licence applications was determined there were to be many changes taking place at Widnes Vikings. While the greater part of the fans' attention was naturally centered on the playing side, the more significant changes were taking place within the infrastructure of the club. The stadium, referred to as 'adequate' by the RFL's assessment panel in 2008, had the benefit of further upgrading to make the facilities for fans and players alike the envy of most within Super League.

The condition of several antiquated stadia within the top flight was to become the subject of much concentrated attention by the rugby league media, and a hot topic among fans, as the RFL intimated that it was finally running out of patience with clubs who had continued to ignore the state of their grounds. The 2012-14 Licences would, apparently, only be issued to clubs who had taken serious and demonstrable steps towards upgrading their tired stadia or building new facilities.

In rejecting the 2008 application the RFL had also drawn attention to the fact that it felt that Widnes was lacking in the production of 'home grown' talent which was progressing into the senior side. The Widnes hierarchy set in train, at not inconsiderable expense, a total overhaul of the club's youth structure which was to bear fruit as it became recognised as one of the best in the game.

Less visible, but nonetheless vital, changes were also being made behind the scenes as the club put in place structures and protocols that were to form the bedrock of key elements of the application to be submitted for the 2012-14 Licence. Supported by nigh on 4,000 readers of the *Widnes Weekly News* signing up to the 'Back the Bid' campaign, the club's formal application was handed in at RFL Headquarters by Anthony Thackeray and young fan Adam Blinston, who had travelled across the snow-covered Pennines in a Stobart truck.

Also under consideration were bids from Halifax and Barrow Raiders, but decision day, Thursday 31st March 2011 was destined to be a day that will live long in the minds of Widnes fans whether they were gathered at the Stobart Stadium, watching on television at home or 'surfing the net' thousands of miles away!

It is from the elation of this emotion-charged day, and the events that subsequently unfolded, that we now look back, over 982 frustrating and painful days, to consider the vast strides taken by Widnes Vikings since an equally emotional, but distressing, 22nd July 2008.

CHAPTER ONE
No Strangers to Adversity

To fully appreciate where Widnes Vikings are today, and the not inconsiderable strides that it has taken in recent years, it is necessary to understand where it has come from, both as a professional rugby league club and a business.

Widnes Rugby League Club has long been regarded as one of the leading lights of the 13-man code, despite having only sporadic successes until 1975, when the Challenge Cup success of that year saw the start of a period of almost unbroken success until 1991. While also picking up Championship trophies, the then 'Chemics' earned a reputation as the 'Cup Kings' – which included becoming the first 'official' World Club Champions by beating Canberra Raiders at Old Trafford on that magical night of 4th October 1989. This was backed up with regular successes in the Challenge Cup as well as other knockout competitions such as the Lancashire Cup, John Player Trophy and the Floodlit Trophy, while recent history shows the Northern Rail Cup (NRC) residing in the Vikings' trophy cabinet in 2007 and 2009. That 2009 victory was to prove vital to the club's future and its importance is discussed later in this book.

In many ways the sustained period of success during the '70s and '80s was all the more remarkable as, since becoming an inaugural member of the Northern Union in 1895, the club had regularly been beset by a variety of financial problems which threatened its future. It says much for the dedication, resilience and loyalty of the people of Widnes that their club overcame each obstacle that was put in its path to ultimately rise to the pinnacle of rugby league achievement at club level on that night at Old Trafford.

The humble beginnings of this now world famous club could not be further removed from the so-called Theatre of Dreams as it led a nomadic existence within the town – firstly on unfenced fields on what is now Ross Street – before finally making the current site on Lowerhouse Lane its permanent home. But this home was subsequently to be at the centre of the first of many obstacles faced by the club down the years – the most serious of which was to come with the Administration saga of 2007.

In 1926 the club had faced a serious threat to its continued existence when the Widnes Town Council slapped a Compulsory Purchase Order on the land owned by the Widnes club, which by this time had been its home for some 30 years. The Council's intention was to use the land for housing development, but this was averted after discussions with Central and Local Government officers resulted in the rugby club being awarded a five year lease. This stay of execution allowed the club the time and opportunity to raise the funds necessary to buy the ground back from the council and secure their immediate future. Finally, in August 1932, after many fund-raising initiatives the Ground Purchase Appeal Fund – the brainchild of club secretary Tom Naughton – reached its target of £3,250 and the ground was back in the ownership of Widnes Rugby League Club.

Typical of the uncertainties that had surrounded the club through most of its existence was a clause in the contract of sale that allowed the council to buy back the ground at the same price. This understandably affected the desire of the club to commit significant sums towards making any major improvements to the ground during the 40 years that the clause remained in place. Amazingly amid all this uncertainty the team of 1929-30 found a vein of form that took them all the way to Wembley where they lifted the Challenge Cup for the first time. However, while this run of success put extra funds into the coffers the financial position of the club was to remain difficult for some time.

As the club continued to experience periods of financial difficulty, ownership of Naughton Park alternated between the Council and the club for many years until the local authority took full ownership in January 1999.

However, during the nineties the minds of everyone associated with the club were exercised by two major issues, either of which could have led to the demise of professional rugby league in the town. At the beginning of the decade bankruptcy was a real possibility, while 1996 was to see the switch to 'summer rugby' with the creation of the Super League competition and the political in-fighting that accompanied it.

The first of these concerns, the threat of bankruptcy, ironically followed closely on the heels of the club's greatest achievement – that success against Canberra Raiders in the World Club Championship in 1989. For much of its existence the Widnes club had relied, with some justification, on the rich seam of local talent at its disposal, but by the early nineties the growing demand for continued success had seen several 'imports' wearing the famous black and white. The likes of Welsh trio Jonathan Davies, John Devereux and Paul Moriarty as well as Emosi Koloto, Alan Tait and Martin Offiah were by then an integral part of the team, and that obviously came at a significant cost. Quite simply the success of the 1980s came at a cost that the club's income could no longer support, a fact demonstrated by the balance sheet for the 1992-93 season. Despite making a Wembley Challenge Cup Final appearance and a 'top four' finish in the league, an operating loss in excess of £300,000 was recorded, although this was offset to some extent by the sale of the bowling club. One significant factor had been a steady decline in attendances which had seen an average 'gate' of 8,600 in 1989 fall to 5,400 in 1993 with a resultant loss in revenue of £250,000.

The club's precarious financial situation was obvious to all by this stage and to balance the books several players were transferred to other clubs, and the ground was once again sold to the council. While the exodus of players made a significant reduction in the club's operating costs and provided a much needed injection of capital in the short term, the long term effect was a resultant drop in playing fortunes which in turn led to a downward spiral of lower match-day attendances and gate receipts. Having just lived through the 'thick' of a period of unrivalled success it was perhaps understandable that fans had become blasé about supporting their team through the 'thin'.

It is a double-edged sword for all professional sport that income from all sources is directly linked to performance on the pitch. Widnes were now to witness first-hand that it is an unhappy fact of life that in these circumstances, when the need for a boost in income is at its greatest, that it is most difficult to generate or reinvigorate that interest among fans and sponsors.

However, worrying as the situation was for Widnes supporters, putting things into the context of the bigger picture it should be noted that Widnes were by no means the only rugby league club experiencing financial difficulties at this time.

In the light of current issues within the game it is worth taking time here to consider evidence submitted by the Leisure Industries Research Centre (LIRC), in 1999, to a House of Commons Inquiry into the future of professional rugby league. It showed that the game as a whole was facing some serious challenges.

LIRC drew attention to the fact that a financial analysis carried out during 1991-93 had shown that the professional clubs had lost a total of £8.8 million, and that 17 of the 31 clubs examined were in fact technically insolvent. This was exacerbated by a 10% increase in players' wages while gross income only showed an improvement of 3% over the same period.

In addition to financial analysis LIRC also carried out a detailed analysis of attendance figures in the first three seasons of the Super League era. This clearly demonstrated that compared to the last full season (1994-95) under the old structure 419,000 spectators had deserted the game by 1998.

It is also pertinent to note that the main conclusions of the LIRC report have more than a passing resonance with many of the opinions expressed by rugby league fans of today, and some sections of the media. They concluded that:

'This decline in attendance figures and the number of people actually watching the sport on television highlights potential problems for the future:

- Super League was introduced in order to solve the crisis that the game found itself in. However, not only has this been unsuccessful, but the crisis remains and is even worse than before.
- The fact that only a small percentage of the population can watch Rugby League on television affects the promotion of the game.
- The decline in attendances, compounded by the continuing increase in the average age of the rugby league supporter – the majority being within the 40-60-year-old age bracket – suggests that the ageing spectators are not being replaced by new young fans.
- This emphasises the danger of lack of television exposure by BSkyB to the younger generations as there will not be the future generations to not only support the game, but to provide its future stars. Rugby League needs to be regarded by youngsters as a major team sport, with which they want to be involved.
- Rugby League is in competition today with so many other leisure and sporting pursuits that if exposure is lacking, then as a game with an ageing supporter base, its future seems precarious.'

To be fair the RFL had already produced a document designed to reverse this trend as they presented *Framing the Future* – which described the financial state of the game as a whole as 'in crisis' – to member clubs for consideration in August 1994. The report was endorsed by the RFL Council in October 1994 and as a result certain changes to the structure of the game were implemented including:

i)   The creation of the Super League structure
ii) The move to a summer playing season
iii) An £87m deal with BSkyB for broadcasting rights
iv) The introduction of the salary cap

Hindsight shows that the financial windfall alone was not the panacea that many had hoped it to be. In some ways it merely fed the ills that bedevilled the game – driving up players' wages while at the same time many clubs turned a blind eye to their ageing and progressively decrepit stadia. Thus *Framing the Future* was a missed opportunity as many clubs continued in the time honoured fashion of living beyond their means, while taking a short-sighted view of the future. In more recent times the impact, financially and otherwise, of a flawed expansion programme and an embryonic licensing system, have hardly helped to stabilise the sport, especially below Super League level.

Against this backdrop Widnes had, by the time '*Framing the Future*' was endorsed by the clubs in October 1994, already taken the first steps towards a more secure future, and adopting a more business-like approach, when they became a 'limited company' through incorporation on 20th May 1993. The initial company name of 'Giventime' was later changed to 'Widnes Rugby League Football Club Limited' by special resolution on 29th June 1993.

Having been a members' club for over 120 years the Widnes club took the first steps to become a limited company when, at an Extraordinary General Meeting in August 1993, the committee's proposal was passed with just one dissenting vote. Considered by the committee to be the only way to safeguard top class rugby league in the town, 'PLC' status was sought in a bid to avoid calling in liquidators, such was the dire state of the club's finances. Over the previous two years expenditure had outstripped operational income by a sum in excess of £700,000 while the projected deficit for the current financial year was a further £300,000.

With a total potential share issue of one million £1 shares available to existing club members the club set about raising the necessary funds through a combination of that share issue and borrowings. With its declared aim of maintaining Widnes as a 'top of the table' club the committee identified the following six objectives:

i)   Raise enough finance from members so that the club can borrow sufficient funds to cover the shortfall in expenditure.
ii) Reassess players' contracts and wages to financially reward success.
iii) Increase income from gate receipts, sponsorship, ground and programme advertising, lotteries and shop and bar sales.
iv) Reduce administration costs wherever possible.
v)   Achieve better communication with 'members'.
vi) Incorporate a 'limited liability' company to take over the club's assets in exchange for assuming responsibility for the existing financial obligations.

Once the new company was formed the existing committee members became directors for an initial three-year term. Nearly £90,000 was pledged by committee men and other members but Tom Fleet, chairman of the finance sub-committee, conceded that it was 'unreasonable and unrealistic' to expect to raise the £350,000 needed through the share issue alone. 'We can only do this through a combination of sale of shares to members and the sale of more assets', Fleet explained. As the only remaining assets held by the club were its players this would inevitably lead to another downturn in playing fortunes, in the short term at least. The danger was that the club would then spiral out of control again as revenue from all sources fell away. However, it is plain that the club had to take this somewhat risky step in order to survive, and hopefully prosper in the future. Fast-forward to 2007 and the Administration saga shows many parallels with the dilemma faced by the club's committee, and fans' fears, in 1993.

It is now a matter of record that the new company moved the club forward and, in association with the local authority, aided by a contribution from the National Lottery Fund, resolved to implement a re-development programme which would transform the spartan surroundings of Naughton Park. Thus the all-seater Halton Stadium began to evolve which, in addition to being the home of Widnes Vikings, also provided a multi-purpose complex for the benefit of the wider community comprising a social club, and recreational, conference and banqueting facilities.

It was about this time that Tony Chambers had joined the board of directors, later to become chairman. During his long association with the club, which lasted until he left the board in 2006, Chambers' leadership was integral to the club surviving the turmoil that surrounded it in the early '90s, and to its ultimate return to the top flight in 2002. Along the way he played a vital, but largely unseen, role which was central to the success of the development programme mentioned above, but while Chambers may not have had the financial resources of the current incumbent, he certainly had the club's future at heart during his tenure as chairman.

In an interview with the *Black & White* (the club's matchday programme) in April 1994 Chambers explained: "Having married a Widnes girl I moved to the area some 20 years ago from the West Midlands, and having followed the club to Wembley in 1975, I was hooked." In the same article he is credited with adding the phrase 'Widnes – Twin Town Wembley' to a road sign on Norlands Lane!

It was certainly this love of the club together with his business acumen that prevented the club from disappearing without trace during very turbulent times.

As mentioned earlier *Framing the Future* had spoken of a game in financial crisis, yet still in recent years several clubs – including some in Super League – have entered Administration, while many others have been walking a financial tight-rope, and indeed Blackpool have gone to the wall. Again with the benefit of hindsight it is plain to see that, with the game still facing many of the problems of the nineties, and more, the RFL's policy of revolution rather than evolution was one doomed to failure.

The key recommendations of *Framing the Future* – a 16 team (subsequently 14 and ultimately 12) top tier, club mergers, introduction of a salary cap, and a wholesale updating of grounds – had been adopted much sooner than many in the game could have anticipated. These proposals led directly to levels of turmoil and controversy that the game had not previously experienced, culminating in supporters' demonstrations and rallies in grounds and town-centres across the rugby league heartlands.

So, having beaten off the threat of bankruptcy the next challenge to Widnes' existence was, surprisingly, to come from within the game itself! The RFL's decision to introduce a new competition and all its ramifications, as a key element in their strategy for the game's development and financial viability, led to another period of uncertainty and confusion descending upon the Widnes club.

The RFL's headlong rush to set up the new competition had, perversely, come about as a direct consequence of a battle over television rights in Australia. When Rupert Murdoch's News Corporation lost out to Kerry Packer's Channel Nine, Murdoch immediately set his sights on setting up a worldwide competition excluding the Australian League. His offer of £77 million to the British clubs was the first stage in this media battle.

The process gained almost indecent momentum when RFL chief executive Maurice Lindsay attended a hastily convened meeting, on 4th April 1995, with representatives of BSkyB in London. It was only three days later that club chairmen were presented with the outline for Super League at a meeting in Huddersfield, with the deal being approved by the clubs the following day at a further meeting held at Central Park, Wigan. With the promise of £77 million to be ploughed into a near-bankrupt sport over five years it is hardly surprising that the clubs voted unanimously to accept the deal. Thus the concept of Super League was born.

The RFL's announcement of the 14 member clubs (See Appendix I) on 8th April 1995 spawned another chaotic period for Widnes during which the club was 'out', 'in', then 'out' again before the abortive proposal that it merge with Warrington saw it finally excluded from the new competition. To rub salt into the wounds Paris St Germain and London were effectively given byes into the top tier – in the name of expansion – and Widnes were 'relegated' to the second tier of the professional game. Further, it became apparent that the Super League clubs were each to receive a total of £5 million over five years while clubs in the First Division were to receive a single payment of a mere £100,000.

It is hard to comprehend that the RFL did not foresee the furore that would follow their proposals. Club mergers involving 15 senior clubs, 'invitations' being extended to London, Paris and Toulouse in the name of expansion, and the disparity in the distribution of Murdoch's millions were a certain recipe for unrest in boardrooms and on the terraces. It is a further irony that the issue of expansion is still a very large thorn in the side of the RFL today as it was then.

However, over the next few days the deal struck between the governing body and the clubs began to disintegrate as the shock of the proposed mergers sank in. While supporters feared the end of 'their' club, and the Players' Association was concerned about players' contracts and the probability of redundancies, Members of Parliament expressed alarm at the prospect of the sport being sold lock, stock and barrel to a private media company. In the midst of this – on the 14th April – there was a collective sense of relief in Widnes as the proposed merger with Warrington was abandoned, as the French Federation had decided to enter only one club, thus opening the door for both clubs to take their places in Super League. One by one the plans for other proposed mergers began to unravel and following a further meeting between the clubs and the RFL, on 30th April 1995, the merger proposals were withdrawn and a return to three divisions, with a 12 team Super League (See Appendix II), was agreed along with a further £10 million from BSkyB.

It was Lindsay who proudly announced that "the revisions take account of the concern raised over the last three weeks. I believe that we have now been able to allay the fans' fears over club mergers and the loss of the game's traditions. We have taken these steps after a great deal of thought. Now is the time for everyone involved in the game to pull together."

While there is no trace in the public domain of the criteria used to select the original 14 members of Super League, the revised membership of 12 clubs was apparently based on final placings in the 1994-95 league table. Exceptions to this rationale were made in the cases of the London and Paris clubs who were arbitrarily invited to join the top 10 from 1994-95! Thus it was on this basis that Widnes were finally excluded from the inaugural Super League competition, having been told that they were 'in' just 16 days earlier. It was no great surprise to learn that Widnes were the only club to vote against the revised proposals, and subsequently initiated unsuccessful legal proceedings against the RFL. On the 26th May 1995 Mr Justice Parker determined in the High Court in Manchester that the vote taken at the meeting of 30th April, of 32-1 in favour of the proposals, was legally valid leaving the club rooted in Division One and with legal costs of approximately £50,000.

As a result of the revised structure, and the additional £10 million from Murdoch's News Corporation, the financial distribution became somewhat more equitable. Each of the 12 Super League clubs would now receive £900,000 for each of the next five years, while First Division clubs would each collect between £200,000 and £700,000, on a merit scale, for each season. Those clubs in the Second Division would be richer by £150,000 per season over the same period. However, the gap between the 'haves' and 'have nots' would continue to grow year on year – a policy that may well have exacerbated the financial plight of smaller clubs, many of whom continue to struggle to this day.

As already mentioned Widnes' own financial situation was far from healthy at this time which had put the club into a vicious circle of selling their best players, struggling on the pitch and falling attendances. The financial implications of being cut adrift from Super League, having been assured that they had been included, added yet more strain to the purse strings at the club. It was to the eternal credit of chairman Tony Chambers and his board of directors that the club survived this body blow, regrouped and worked towards regaining top flight status for the club just six years later.

While Chambers and his board were considering their options to overcome the Super League fiasco and the attendant financial implications, to take the club forward, added impetus for their plans arrived from an unexpected source. Thus in late 1996 came a new dawn in the club's history which merits documenting here.

Widnes Rugby League Club had since its formation thrived on a very close bond with the town and local community, drawing many of its players from the local chemical industry in the early years. It was natural then that for the majority of its recorded history the club had been universally referred to as 'The Chemics'.

It therefore came as something of a shock to die-hard supporters when in 1996 a change of name – in line with the trend of the time – seemed to signal the death-knell of 'The Chemics'. On the back of missing out on a place in the inaugural Super League competition the club's board of directors were looking for fresh impetus and ideas to promote and market the club. At the same time 17-year-old Frodsham High School student, and avid Widnes fan, Helen Baxter was looking for a suitable subject for her A-level Design course, and chose the club as the topic for her 'Marketing and Promotion' project. Citing a lack of marketing initiatives Helen commented at the time that "I think the club can make so much more of itself", adding "We've got a new generation of players, a new stadium and we should be looking to create a new image for the club".

With the club receptive to Helen's approach, initial discussions were held with directors Tony Chambers and John Hodgson with regard to looking at the way in which the club marketed itself. At the time the club's promotional activity centred around basic posters scattered around the town advertising the next home match. Helen's vision was to produce a range of promotional and marketing initiatives to attract fans in greater numbers, especially families and young children. During these early discussions common ground was found as the forward thinking club was already looking to produce a package of initiatives to reinvigorate the club. However, when it became apparent that the club was already actively considering a name change – to 'Widnes Wizards' – the main thrust of Helen's project switched to identifying a new name which would also generate marketing and promotional opportunities.

It was agreed that any new name must reflect the combative nature of rugby league, offer marketing opportunities, and have a fun element in addition to local connotations. So where better to start than with the name of the town, with Helen's research leading to the original Danish name of 'Vid-noese', and the Viking presence on the north bank of the River Mersey. It was a natural progression to thoughts of viking warriors doing battle as our 10th-century Danish 'Widnesian' counterparts took on the Saxons based in Runcorn. Having identified 'Widnes Warriors' as the best-fit option Helen moved on to draw up marketing proposals and designed a comprehensive range of merchandise to support her recommendation, which ranged from toys and pens to hats, scarves, flags and T-shirts. The opportunities presented by the combination of name-change, merchandising and marketing proposals were then put to directors Tony Chambers, John Hodgson and Ernie Bate who in turn presented them to the full board for approval.

At this point the Rugby Football League made the club aware that Whitehaven were already planning to adopt the 'Warriors' moniker and Widnes were asked to consider an alternative. As Helen's design work had focused throughout on viking warriors – along with a new club mascot 'Chemik the Viking'– the obvious alternative, giving a nod to the town's history, was 'Widnes Vikings'. Although 'Chemik' was so named to provide a natural link to the longstanding nickname and the heritage of both the club and town, it was later amended to what was considered a more marketable 'Kemik'.

So having gained boardroom approval Helen's recommendations were implemented on 27th November 1996 when the club became officially known as Widnes Vikings, coinciding with the opening of a club shop in the Greenoaks Centre and the launch of the club's own informative but short-lived newspaper – the Viking Flagship. At the launch chairman Tony Chambers commented: 'It's not just a change of name. It signifies the club's change of approach.'

The historic final match in which Widnes were officially known as 'The Chemics' took place on 25th August 1996 when they went down by 25-16 at Dewsbury. The line-up on that day was: Broadbent; Hunter, Myler (D) (2g), Kendrick (1t), Smith (P); Cooper (1t), Charles; Makin, Donno, Hansen (L) (1t), Myler (P), Cunningham, Cassidy. Subs: Pechey, Hansen (S), Ashton, McCurrie.

Some five months later the 'Vikings' took their official bow, in a Challenge Cup third round tie at home to Clayton, on an equally notable 26th January 1997, when they ran out victors by 56-2. The history-making team that did duty on that day was: Broadbent; Kendrick, Myler (D), Nelson, Smith (P); Waring (3t), Lythe (8g); Makin, Cassidy (3t), Hansen (L) (1t), Harrison, Myler (P), Cunningham (1t). Subs: Bloem (1t), Collier, Mills, Connor (1t).

The final piece in the jigsaw came on 9th March 1997 when 'Kemik' made his debut in the home match versus Workington. He had completed the transformation from Helen's initial sketches and hand-made doll to a living, breathing club mascot entertaining fans young and old.

Looking back recently Helen commented that 'while many clubs appear to have chosen a name at random it is nice that the club has a story to tell about where its name came from. It is part of the heritage of the club. The fact that I am a fan is quite a special thing – and it was not just a corporate decision. I was astounded that something I was doing for a piece of school work was actually used. It was amazing really'.

Thus a 17-year-old Frodsham schoolgirl has left her indelible mark on the history of her club.

Returning to the theme of the continuing financial battles, the club, having regained that top flight status in 2002, was again staring further troubled times in the face with the very real threat of relegation at the end of the 2004 season. This was despite their first season in Super League seeing them finish a creditable seventh and just missing out on the play-offs. While the fans looked forward to further progress in 2003 the club were unable to make any significant investment in the playing staff and the team slipped to ninth, followed by a desperate 2004 when Super League survival was not secured until the final day of the season.

As it was if Castleford had beaten Wakefield and Widnes had suffered a heavy defeat at Hull, the Vikings could have been relegated on 'points difference'. In the event both teams lost their final match and Castleford were relegated.

In an interview with the *Widnes Weekly News*, published just days before that final match at Hull, Vikings' chairman Tony Chambers explained the consequences of possible relegation. While the club's future at this point still remained in their own hands Mr Chambers announced that the financial cost of relegation would see a shortfall of at least £1 million in the club's budget:

'It's a million pound game. We currently get £700,000 from Sky television and good gate receipts and if we get relegated, then we would have to operate on a budget that is lower at £400,000 instead of £1.4 million. It's a massive game for the club – it's like the NFP Grand Final in reverse'.

Admitting that there was no fallback plan Mr Chambers added: 'We will have a meeting on Sunday to discuss whatever situation we find ourselves in. There will have to be a 'Plan B' if the worst happens but we don't think it's right [at this time] to be discussing a plan for failure.' While the club did maintain its top-flight status, and avert an immediate financial disaster, it was plain that it was leading a 'hand-to-mouth' existence.

Relegation did in fact follow just 12 months later, as in 2005 two teams were to be relegated in order to accommodate French club Catalans Dragons, in addition to promoting a club from the second tier of the domestic game. Although knowing 10th position was the minimum target from the start of the season Widnes fans felt that they were again the sacrificial lamb for yet another French experiment. Paris St Germain had in most people's eyes been given Widnes' rightful place in Super League in 1996, only to disappear from the scene after just one season. In what was seen as another controversial move by the RFL, no doubt keen to avoid a repeat of the 'Paris' embarrassment, the Dragons were given an amnesty against relegation for three years and a seemingly unlimited quota of overseas players! The combination of these exceptional circumstances caused widespread concern throughout the game as the Dragons were able to build a squad based largely on antipodeans while guaranteeing them three years of Super League rugby. Coincidentally promotion and relegation was a thing of the past by the time that amnesty had lapsed!

The fans' fears that relegation could be the death-knell for the club were heightened by the news that Pete Barrow, the club's financial controller, had identified that the club had serious financial problems and had been running with a significant deficit in its trading operations for some time. And so it was in 2006, against another gloomy financial backdrop, that the club again set about regaining its place in Super League. The task was not made any easier by major changes in the boardroom as Stephen Vaughan replaced the out-going Tony Chambers as chairman and majority shareholder. This lack of continuity was to some degree off-set by the arrival of a new, young and ambitious coach in Steve McCormack, who narrowly failed to take the club back to the top in each of his first two seasons at Widnes.

To a large extent fans, apart from those with close connections to the club, were blissfully unaware of the depth of the continuing struggles behind the scenes as they, naturally, enjoyed the upsurge in fortunes on the pitch. Thus, ignorant of the severity of the club's problems, the events which followed defeat to Castleford in the 2007 Grand Final came like a bolt out of the blue to the vast majority of us who had been at Headingley.

CHAPTER TWO
A Near-Death Experience

The most recent and potentially most threatening issue was that of the club entering Administration in October 2007. While this was discussed in *Dreams To Reality* I feel it merits revisiting in the context of the club's recent history and achievements.

With the benefit of hindsight it is an easy conclusion to draw that, following relegation from Super League in 2005, Administration, or worse, was an accident waiting to happen. Former chairman Peter Knowles' summary of the immediate aftermath of relegation highlights the gloomy portents for the club's future:

"We had a difficult start to 2006 but the performances on the field improved as the season progressed and Steve McCormack started to put together his own squad. But in the end we were no match for Hull KR and were beaten in the play-off Final, while off the field the financial problems continued.

"The attendances we were getting were disappointing and this combined with the low level of sponsorship we were attracting, and the costs of playing at the stadium, were resulting in us continuing to trade at a significant loss.

"Stephen Vaughan took over from Tony Chambers as chairman, appointing Pete Barrow as chief executive, and the new chairman started to bankroll the club. Ultimately Chambers, Tom Fleet, Alan Gregson and Graham Ashton resigned from the board.

Mr Knowles added that "We went in to the 2007 season with some optimism, believing that we had a stronger squad than 2006 and believed we had an excellent chance of winning the play-off Final and gaining promotion to Super League. We also had, in Stephen Vaughan, a wealthy chairman who was supporting the club financially.

"Considering that we started the season so successfully and were playing some excellent football it was disappointing that attendances were lower than 2006; sponsorship was also very disappointing and therefore we were still trading at a significant loss".

It is plain therefore that the two major income streams – sponsorship and 'gate receipts' – had not been providing adequate levels of income to support the operating costs of the club, giving some validity to the fans' oft-mentioned criticism of the club's commercial and marketing operations. Certainly with Widnes' high level of exposure, especially from Sky's live coverage of the National Leagues, it was reasonable to expect a greater level of sponsorship and advertising revenue to be forthcoming.

Head coach Steve McCormack had certainly earned his corn by putting together squads that reached successive Grand Finals in 2006 and 2007 playing, in the main, attractive rugby.

It was therefore difficult to understand both the inability to attract the required level of sponsorship, and the apparent apathy displayed by the population of this 'rugby town'. Generally speaking fans will turn out in high numbers to watch their team, in any sport, as long as it is winning. It was cause for concern then that a team not only winning, but winning in style was, as Mr Knowles pointed out, pulling in less paying customers than in 2006.

However, on the back of a very successful and enjoyable 2007 – including an impressive Northern Rail Cup Final victory against Whitehaven – the team qualified for the National League One Grand Final, to face not only the considerable challenge of Castleford Tigers, but the potentially serious implications of another major change to the structure of the sport. Having seen their top flight status arbitrarily removed by the governing body in 1996 and relegated in 2005 the Vikings knew that victory in that Grand Final of 2007 would be the last opportunity for them to regain that status by automatic promotion. The RFL had decided to abandon promotion and relegation in favour of aping the Australian system of awarding Licences to allow clubs to play in the top tier. Thus defeat at Headingley would consign Widnes to the vagaries of the new, and unproven, Licence application process for future 'promotion' to Super League.

Defeat was indeed the outcome of the Grand Final. It brought with it an unwelcome side-bar to the evolving financial situation when some elements, searching for a way to excuse the defeat, pointed accusing fingers at a team who 'didn't try' either because they were leaving or they knew that the club was facing possible extinction. These accusations of disloyalty were put to bed by head coach Steve McCormack who confirmed that "six or seven had indeed signed contracts elsewhere because we weren't in a position to offer them contracts;" and that while "no one actually said that if we lose we will go into Administration I did know there were massive problems. I kept it to myself and had conversations with a few people within the club in the week leading up to the Grand Final. Not the best build up from my point of view but hopefully that didn't get through to the players.

"To say that those players didn't try or put 100% in for Widnes is a scathing comment which the players didn't deserve, and couldn't be further from the truth. At the end of the day we were beaten by a far better side on the day."

Returning to the financial repercussions of losing to Castleford I think it is true to say that very few of us would have expected the announcement that came out of the Halton Stadium offices just two days later:

> Following Sunday's disappointing defeat in the National League 1 Grand Final the Board met at length on Monday and Tuesday to discuss the current financial position of the Club.
>
> After these meetings the decision was regrettably taken to put Widnes Rugby League Football Club Ltd into administration with effect from today, Tuesday 9th October, 2007.
>
> The Board took this decision following independent advice received from Jonathan Avery-Gee, Senior Partner of Kay Johnson Gee, Chartered Accountants, who was appointed as the Administrator.
>
> This decision will hopefully allow the Administrator the opportunity to achieve a sale of the Club and with it the potential to keep professional rugby league alive in the Borough where it has been an integral part of many people's lives for five generations and given great enjoyment.
>
> It is a very sad time for all concerned within the Club and the Board would like to thank everybody who has contributed to its success over the years at whatever level.
>
> The Administrator is now responsible for all matters concerning the Club. He will be seeking offers for the Club and already members of the Board have confirmed their intention to put together a package to take the Club forward into 2008 and beyond.
>
> Pete Barrow
> Chief Executive

Virtually the whole season had been played out against a backdrop of financial insecurity, with various parties making claim and counter-claim as to the root cause, but the Widnes faithful were naturally shocked and very concerned about the future of their club following the dramatic announcement from the chief executive. It is doubtful, however, that anyone outside the boardroom was aware that financially it was a case of 'Super League or bust' as we took our places at Headingley.

So while the club had been taking major strides forward on the pitch, these were counter-balanced by the ongoing and growing problems behind the scenes, which were exacerbated by the mid-season resignation of Stephen Vaughan as chairman. Indeed the loss of Vaughan's financial backing prompted discussion within the boardroom as to whether they should have taken the decision to enter Administration at that point. This was averted thanks to an undertaking made by directors Jim Quinn and Sam Evans to support the club financially until the end of the 2007 season. The revised board of directors therefore elected to keep the club going until the end of the season with the hope that promotion to Super League would enable them to develop a new business plan which would make the club sustainable through new investors, increased attendances, and improved levels of sponsorship in addition to the money from Sky television.

Aware of the implications of defeat the directors arranged a board meeting for the Tuesday following the Grand Final to determine the best way forward for the club. However, they were overtaken by events when, shortly after 9am on Monday 8th October, a 'fax' was received from Her Majesty's Revenue & Customs in which they suddenly reversed an offset arrangement that had been in place for over a year, and demanded an immediate settlement. Failure to comply would result in a winding up order against the company.

As chairman Peter Knowles commented this was "the final nail in the coffin. We had no alternative but to seek advice from a senior insolvency practitioner. We met the adviser, Jonathan Avery-Gee, on Monday 8th October and when he examined the situation he told us that legally we had no alternative but to go into Administration with immediate effect".

Of immediate concern to the fans was the fact that once the club had entered Administration it was unable to make contract offers to players and the vultures began to hover over an uncertain Widnes playing staff. In the immediate aftermath fans took solace from the lack of instant departures but this proved a false dawn as within a few days other clubs slowly but surely began to proudly announce their rich pickings from the Vikings.

While most fans had feared that Mark Smith would be among the first to leave the club the popular skipper told the *Runcorn & Widnes World*: "It is a very worrying situation. Last season I had a number of clubs interested, but I have not had anything this year – even from Widnes. By this time next week I could be signing on the dole and I have a wife and child to think about. I feel for them more than myself." Demonstrating the closeness of the squad he added "It would be nice to see the club offer a bit of something to the lads so they can still have a life in rugby league. I have never played with such a good bunch of lads. There were no cliques and we all got on really well." Smith went on to speak in defence of the club's directors by adding "I cannot fault the Board and I know they will be doing this for the right reasons."

Among the first to comment publicly on the news was Terry O'Connor who had finished his playing career with his home-town team just 12 months previously. "Absolutely gutted" was O'Connor's heartfelt reaction adding that it was "shocking to see the way the club has gone. Losing again in the Grand Final for the second year in a row was bad enough, but this just adds to the misery of everyone at the club." Echoing the thoughts of many fans he added that "the town is known for its rugby league… there were times when every lad was playing rugby at night."

"I thought getting relegated was the lowest point of my career, but this isn't far off. Being a Widnes lad, there is nothing more heartbreaking. I am absolutely gutted."

What followed was a truly desperate time for news-hungry fans as they explored every possible source, and rumour mill, for any clue as to what was happening to 'their club'.

The protocols of Administration meant that technically the club ceased to exist from 9th October 2007 and an obvious lack of news emanating from the Halton Stadium, with fans naturally becoming more and more frustrated as time wore on without any sign of progress or official comment. The harsh truth of the situation was that while the Administrator was charged with the responsibility of finding new owners for the club all rugby related activity was put on hold.

However, on 17th October, the Administrator announced that he had received expressions of interest from two parties with regards to the purchase of the club. The speculation and concern about the ownership issue – and indeed the survival of the club – was to rumble on for a seemingly inordinate amount of time. However, when the new owners were finally announced on 1st November 2007, it should be remembered that this was just 23 days after the club had entered Administration – a quicker than average conclusion.

During that period there was further worrying news as head coach Steve McCormack resigned and took up a post with Hull KR. Within 24 hours record points scorer Mick Nanyn had also decamped, to Oldham. While at this point there were still some members of the 2007 squad who had not signed for other clubs, there was now great fear among supporters that the departure of the head coach and the talismanic Nanyn would finally lead to the floodgates opening. As it turned out the majority of players understandably moved on to pastures new to secure their futures but a small, but key, nucleus did remain.

While the club battled for its very survival the thorny question of launching a successful bid for a Super League Licence for 2009-11 continued to occupy many people's minds, with recent events polarising opinions. On the one hand opinion was that Administration, and the belief that Celtic Crusaders and Salford were virtually 'shoo-ins' for the anticipated two additional places, had destroyed any hope of gaining a Licence. In contrast there was a school of thought that a financial 'clean sheet' might in fact strengthen the bid. Those of the latter persuasion were encouraged by the fact that amid all the speculation the club had re-iterated its intention to pursue a Licence bid after new owners had been identified.

Then, on 25th October, a tantalising hint of positive news came from the Halton Stadium when club chief executive Pete Barrow announced that "the Administrator expects to make a decision on new owners in the early part of next week".

The fans' increasing appetite for positive news was eventually satisfied on 1st November when, in what some would call typical Widnes fashion, the hearts and minds of those fans were first tossed into turmoil, and then within hours shown the light at the end of the tunnel. Against the ever-present background of speculation and rumour two announcements were made via the official club website. During the morning came the announcement that, following a meeting with Halton Borough Council, the bid for the club led by former directors Jim Quinn and Sam Evans had reluctantly been withdrawn, and the Administrator continued discussions with other interested parties.

It appeared that we were back to square one but as the day unfolded this apparent setback gave way to anticipation that there would finally be a definitive announcement later in the day. And so it proved when at 8pm the statement that all Widnes fan's had been longing for appeared on the website to herald a new era for Widnes Vikings:

Widnes businessman Steve O'Connor has purchased the assets of Widnes Rugby League Club Ltd from the Administrator.

Mr O'Connor mounted a rescue operation to save the ailing club after it narrowly failed to win promotion to the Super League this season.

Crippled by debts and with an exodus of star players, the historic club's future looked bleak as it was placed into administration.

But now Mr O'Connor, in partnership with Halton Borough Council, has devised a business plan that guarantees the future of rugby league in Widnes.

Mr O'Connor and Halton Borough Council chief executive David Parr immediately set about a complete overhaul of the entire operation to ensure the long-term future viability of the club. In addition they met senior officials at the Rugby Football League headquarters in Leeds to outline their short-term proposals for the club and their longer-term vision.

With the local authority holding a 15% stake in the new company (later confirmed as Widnes Sport Company Ltd), Leader of Halton Borough Council, Councillor Tony McDermott MBE added:

Over the past few weeks we have spent many hours talking to a variety of consortiums to try and find a solution. We were very impressed with the proposal submitted by Steve O'Connor. His proposal offers a substantial cash injection and impressive long-term vision – but at the same time recognises the short-term challenges required to put Widnes Vikings back together again.

We are now working in partnership with Steve to ensure that the future of Rugby League in Halton is secure and Widnes Vikings can once again challenge for Super League status.

The new Vikings owner later added that a "corporate strategy would be put in place, together with realistic goals and objectives, and fallback targets". In a peculiar way talk of 'fallback targets' was seen as a positive indicator by the majority of the club's supporters as this indicated that not only did Mr O'Connor have a 'Plan A' but there was also a 'Plan B'. There would be no boom or bust approach to reawaken this 'sleeping giant'!

With the club safely out of Administration a representative of the Manchester based Chartered Accountants Kay Johnson Gee – the club's Administrators – provided the following insight to the process:

Following the Grand Final defeat, the resultant loss of £800,000 potential income from Sky Television, and the subsequent demand from HMRC, Mr Jonathan Avery-Gee was asked to carry out an independent assessment of the financial situation of the club. His conclusion was that the club 'were unable to meet their liabilities when they were due'.

At the Board Meeting held on Monday 8th October 2007 the Directors considered the advice of Mr Avery-Gee, and explored all options open to them for the continuance of the club. The main thrust of Mr Avery-Gee's advice was that the club had significant debts with little or no assets with which to offset those liabilities. Widnes Rugby League Club Ltd had liabilities approaching £1.5 million, with the major creditors and approximate amounts being:

HMRC (VAT and Inland Revenue)	£590,000
Halton Borough Council	£329,000
Directors & Shareholders	£337,000
Trade & Expense Creditors	£143,000
Staff holiday pay	£50,000

The company's assets were identified as:

Exercise & Medical equipment
Fixtures & Fittings
Motor Vehicle
Computer equipment
Residual Club Shop stock

With the liabilities far outstripping the assets there was no 'book value' for the club and in fact the most valuable, or saleable, part of the club was its 'Goodwill'. This left only two possible outcomes – Administration or Liquidation – for the company (club), particularly as there was a real possibility of HMRC seeking a winding up order against the company. The Club's Board of Directors therefore took the only practical option and voted to place the company into Administration. The necessary documents were sworn at 6.30pm, and lodged with the Manchester District Registry on the morning of 9th October 2007. From that point the club was effectively being run by the Administrator.

The understandable lack of detailed information in the public domain fuelled speculation that the club could have survived without taking such drastic action. However, with the purpose of Administration being 'to find a better realisation than if a company is wound up' (liquidated), I would suggest that there were two compelling reasons to support the move into Administration:

i) 'Winding up' orders cannot be instigated against a company that is in Administration.

ii) A company that has been 'wound up' immediately ceases trading, and is therefore a much less attractive proposition to any prospective purchaser.

The obvious benefit of the first is that it forestalls any likelihood of the second taking place, at least until the Administrator has exhausted all possibilities of selling the business as a going concern. If Widnes Rugby League Club Ltd had in fact ceased trading it would have been much more difficult to find a saviour such as Steve O'Connor, and therefore more difficult to satisfy the requirements of Halton Borough Council and the RFL. The likely scenario would most probably have been the end of professional rugby league in the town!

So, given that the club was insolvent the Administrator's task was to achieve the following:

1) rescue the company as a 'going concern'.

2) achieve a better result for the company's creditors as a whole than would be likely if the company were wound up (without first being in Administration).

3) realise property in order to make a distribution to one or more secured or preferential creditors.

Once potential owners had been identified the Administrator then held meetings with each of the interested parties to assess the viability of their bids, based on cashflow and business plan projections, before submission to Halton Borough Council and the RFL for approval. In this case Halton Borough Council (as landlord), and the RFL (as the governing body who issue the Licence to compete) set a condition that the club should not be sold to any person(s) who had been involved in the previous management of the club, effectively ruling out former board members.

As we now know the sale to Steve O'Connor was approved and he was granted a Licence to run the club for three months, while it technically remained in Administration. Once approval had been received from the RFL Mr O'Connor would be able to assume full ownership, and the Administrator move to discharge the Administration Order and dissolve the old company.

The club had been in limbo since entering Administration on 9th October with the fans desperate for a saviour as it appeared to lurch towards possible extinction. In little more than three weeks the future of the club had been safeguarded by a dynamic owner with what many saw as the dream ticket – strong business credentials and an allegiance to the local community.

With their club safeguarded fans could now look to the future with some degree of optimism. Quite what that future held was still unknown – but at least there *was* a future. As events unfolded, and the new owner showed himself to be both positive and decisive, the dark clouds over WA8 faded away as quickly as they had gathered and we had a glimpse of what that future was to be like.

CHAPTER THREE
Back from the Brink

The staff, remaining players and fans of Widnes Vikings who had spent 23 days in the wilderness of Administration, with doubt and uncertainty the only constants, now had a future to look forward to. And, listening to the early sound-bites emanating from the club, that future appeared to be a promising one.

Having saved the club from extinction Mr O'Connor commented via the club's website:

I fully understand the passion, commitment and desire of the supporters who want to see this rugby club move forward and I want to see their wishes fulfilled.

I appreciate the public will want to know all the details about our plans. However, we have had to move extremely swiftly to complete this deal and it is too soon to talk publicly in detail about our long-term proposals.

At the moment it is important to reassure the people who work behind the scenes at the club, those players we are looking to bring to Widnes Vikings and the fans that the club's future is in safe hands.

Much work needs to be carried out to put a management structure in place for the forthcoming season and to develop a strategy to ensure our place in the Super League by 2009.

As soon as we are in a position to give more details, the dedicated fans of Widnes Vikings will be first to know.

The decisive nature of the new owner was clearly demonstrated, within 24 hours of him assuming control of the Vikings, by an ambitious determination for the club to hit the ground running in 2008. While it is true to say that his first act did not meet with universal approval among the club's supporters it did, however, show that there was a decisive man at the helm.

The eventual departure after the club entered Administration of Steve McCormack had prompted a good deal of speculation as to his replacement, with fans' front-runners being Karl Harrison and Ian Millward, while some hankered after the return of Neil Kelly. McCormack was a man in demand and received approaches from two National League clubs and, with a young family to support, he had lengthy discussions with one of them. Ultimately he didn't take either job "because I wanted to stay at Widnes and there were two or three sets of people wanting to buy the club". Just days before Steve O'Connor took control of the club McCormack received a call, while he was preparing his Scotland squad for a World Cup qualifier, from the Hull KR chief executive, Paul Lakin. He was offered the job of assistant coach to Justin Morgan, a post which he eventually accepted and was "really looking forward to although I was sad to leave Widnes".

The day that O'Connor completed his takeover he immediately attempted to set up a meeting with the club's former head coach with a view to inviting him to return to the Halton Stadium. However, having just made a "firm commitment to Hull KR", McCormack's first reaction was to say "no" but he did eventually agree to drive down from the Scotland team's training camp at Inverclyde to meet the Vikings' new owner at the Thistle Hotel, Haydock. Straightaway McCormack was taken with O'Connor's enthusiasm and ideas for rebuilding the club. "Surprised and humbled" by the subsequent offer to return as head coach he was aware of leaving himself "open to criticism from press and fans and the possibility of being seen as a mercenary". But such was his commitment to the Widnes club "having put my life and soul into the club for the three years I've been here," and "feeling I owed them (the club) a bit for giving me the chance to come from Whitehaven," McCormack finally agreed to return. Just nine days after leaving the Vikings he walked back into his old office again as the club's head coach.

In announcing the return of McCormack, Steve O'Connor had managed to completely wrong-foot the media and fans alike. Describing his head coach as 'driven' and 'very bright', and having the 'respect of players' Mr O'Connor cited the need for stability and the fact that in 2007, against all the odds, McCormack had put together 'a very successful side'.

Widnes' new owner added that "Steve McCormack has done a tremendous job at Widnes over the past couple of seasons in very difficult circumstances. I'm convinced he's the right man to take the club into the Super League and we will provide him with the resources necessary to challenge for the very top honours. Steve knows the club, is popular with the fans and has the ability and experience to make this club great again. Steve's appointment is just the first important step to secure the future of this club. I'm working around-the-clock to develop our business plan and intend to share my vision with the Vikings' greatest asset – our supporters – over the coming weeks."

McCormack commented: "I'm absolutely delighted to be back with Widnes and to have the opportunity to take the Vikings on to even greater success in the future. When I recently announced my reluctant departure from the club it came at a time when I genuinely felt I'd taken them as far as possible under the Vikings' existing structure.

"With the change of ownership – and the new financial structure of the club – I believe this is a fantastic time to be involved with the Vikings. Knowing the many strengths of the club, the unrivalled devotion of its fans plus the commitment shown by Steve O'Connor, I just couldn't resist the opportunity to get back."

Having been given the green light to a recruit a 'full-time' playing staff McCormack added: "The Co-operative National League is a fiercely competitive and highly intensive championship. To compete successfully at this level it is important the team is run on a full-time basis which helps me immensely in attracting the right calibre of experienced players to the club, and within minutes of the announcement of my appointment as head coach, players from England and overseas were ringing me expressing interest in joining Widnes Vikings… already you can sense the buzz of excitement and expectation and everyone is now looking forward to the new season."

So, with the head coach safely in place Mr O'Connor was able to turn his attention to the vital meeting with the RFL and gaining their approval of his vision and proposals for the future of the club. This was the beginning of a process through which the club re-applied for membership of the governing body and to be readmitted to National League One for the coming season.

Supported by Vikings' chief executive Pete Barrow and the leader of the council, Councillor Tony McDermott, Mr O'Connor was later reported as finding the initial talks "encouraging", and being "hopeful the RFL Board will agree to our membership quickly so we can then concentrate on instigating the numerous ideas contained within the business plan to rebuild the Vikings."

In making their decision the RFL Board were charged to exercise 'due diligence' in regard to the following:

i)   Any new owners of a club will safeguard the future of that club and promote rugby league at all levels in that particular area.

(This is designed to guard against speculative acquisition of a club and its assets, which may later be stripped for purely financial gain on the part of a new owner).

ii) The submission of a robust Business Plan that demonstrates that the club is sustainable.

iii) An appropriate Staffing structure exists.

iv) The club is seen as part of, and involved in, its local community.

v)   A positive and realistic vision and projection for the future of the club.

Although this process was conducted in private and away from the glare of TV cameras it bears a striking resemblance to the award of Super League Licences that was to follow in July 2008 and March 2011. Certainly the level of nervousness among supporters was of equal proportions.

Recognised as having one of the best stadia in rugby league, in addition to an award winning community programme, world class scholarship programme, and top class academy, the club could now add a robust commercial background to its CV. It was hoped that the impressive combination of these factors would make readmission to the RFL little more than a formality. However, it was not until 19th November that Widnes' membership of the RFL was confirmed through the following press release from Red Hall:

The RFL Board of Directors have today readmitted the Widnes Vikings club to the co-operative National League One competition from 2008 onwards.

In accordance with the RFL Operational Rules, the Vikings' membership of the competition was suspended after the club undertook an act of insolvency and the ownership of the club changed hands at the conclusion of the 2007 season. Also in accordance with the RFL Operational Rules the club will be deducted nine competition points with effect from the start of the 2008 co-operative National League season.

On finally being readmitted to the Rugby Football League chairman Steve O'Connor commented: "We're obviously disappointed to be docked points for the start of the season but accept this as being the RFL's normal course of action following a club being placed into administration. However, we're confident we can establish a squad that can overcome this hurdle and take Vikings on to great success." He added that: "We must now move on and concentrate on our long-term plans for the revival of Widnes Vikings and to secure success in National League 1 which can act as a springboard for a successful Super League Licence application."

In the interim period there had been much speculation regarding the possible penalty for entering Administration. Convincing, but ultimately erroneous, arguments were put forward for no penalty, a six point deduction, and even relegation to National League 2. While those championing the case for no penalty were basing their argument on the fact that the club had completed the season prior to entering Adminstration, the 'six point' campaign was citing the recent adjudications in the cases of Doncaster and Swinton as precedents.

In fact the RFL does not differentiate between clubs who become insolvent during the season and those who find themselves in that position during the close season. With regard to the comparison with Doncaster and Swinton I was informed at the time by the RFL that their penalties were calculated under the old points system of two points for a win, as they "did not *enter* Administration during 2007". In all three cases the penalty is equivalent to the points gained for winning three matches. However, there is scope under the RFL's guidelines to vary the penalty handed down according to the circumstances of each case. This 'flexibility' would later be highlighted in 2011 when both Crusaders and Wakefield were only docked four points while Whitehaven suffered a deduction of six points for the same breach of rules!

So ultimately all was well as the Vikings were cleared to play in National League One for 2008, although they would have to overcome a nine point penalty to achieve their immediate target of qualifying for the end of season play-offs. With Steve McCormack at last able to begin to put his squad together the nucleus was made up of the ever-popular skipper Mark Smith, and team-mates Bob Beswick, Gavin Dodd, Dean Gaskell and local boy Paul Noone.

Having remained loyal to the club during its darkest days – and now affectionately known as the 'Famous Five' – these players achieved instant cult status for their loyalty to the cause and re-signing for the club as soon as RFL rules permitted it.

Beswick and Noone moved on at the end of 2008, but it must have been a great source of pride for 'Smithy', 'Doddy' and 'Deano' to play their part on the day that the Vikings 'ticked the box' with their Northern Rail Cup Final victory against Barrow on 12th July 2009. That victory meant that the club had met the on-field criterion, which in turn gave them the right to apply for a Super League Licence in 2011.

While waiting for the green light from Red Hall Steve O'Connor had begun his task of rebuilding the club by issuing a challenge to the people of Halton to come out and support the Vikings. Citing the average attendance in 2007 of 3,300 Mr O'Connor commented "This just isn't good enough. We are now up against the wall – we need to be very clear – you use it or you lose it."

Mr O'Connor emphasised that "the final piece in the jigsaw is in the hands of the people of Halton. I hope that if any good at all can come out of the club being forced into administration, it is that it is a wake-up call for the whole town not to take things for granted. We want to fill the stadium on match days and create a unique atmosphere. The fans are an absolutely vital ingredient for success and I hope they will catch the mood of what I want to achieve here. I absolutely would not be involved with the Widnes Vikings if I didn't think the club had a successful future."

As if to demonstrate his continuity of thought the Vikings' chairman was to issue a similar challenge to the local populace, albeit from a more secure footing, when he took to the pitch to launch the innovative 'Vikings Stronghold' in April 2011.

Having survived the tension of the Administration process, the fans' optimism was soon on a steep upward spiral as the new owner was making very positive comments about the future of their club. Buoyed by this new-found positivity supporters were enthusiastically waiting to hear details of Steve O'Connor's plans.

The opportunity to see the 'flesh on the bones' of those plans soon arrived when on 6th December 2007 Mr O'Connor shared the platform with fellow board member David Parr (chief executive of Halton Borough Council), Alex Bonney (chief executive of Widnes Vikings), and head coach Steve McCormack at a Fans Forum. Such was the level of interest generated that within 24 hours of its announcement it had been made an all-ticket event.

Since the announcement of O'Connor's successful bid for the club there had been much discussion among fans, based on his business connections, about possible new sponsorship deals. Indeed this was the first question to be answered, in emphatic style, as fans approached the stadium that evening. The sight of a fully liveried 'Eddie Stobart' vehicle outside the main entrance instantly made those attending feel that they were now part of something substantial and tangible. And once inside the air of professionalism was all-pervading.

Not only was it confirmed that the Stobart Group was to be the shirt sponsor for the Vikings, but also that the internationally-renowned logistics company had secured naming rights for the stadium. For the next five years the former Naughton Park, which had 'morphed' into the AutoQuest Stadium and then Halton Stadium, would be known as The Stobart Stadium Halton.

With the Stobart Group, which was seeking to create up to 1,200 local jobs, having seemed to have burst into the local community in a business sector that was not universally popular, O'Connor felt it would be valuable for the logistics giant to demonstrate a stake-holding within the local community. An approach was made to William Stobart and it was agreed that a link with a sport which shares the same values as the company would be of mutual benefit and the long-term partnership was born.

Having demonstrated in words and deeds that the short term future of the club was secure, the club's new chairman again underlined the need to improve match attendances when he pointed out that this would be one of the main criteria that the RFL would consider when awarding Super League Licences for 2009.

Mr O'Connor had learned from the RFL, that there would be five key areas to the Licence application:

- the stadium
- community initiatives
- playing strength and academies
- a sound business plan
- the fan base

Confident that his management team would put a powerful business proposition to the RFL he went on to say that "I believe four of these are achievable, through professional people, with the energy and enthusiasm of a driven management team… [but] at the end of the day it's the fans who will decide if that Super League application is successful."

Highlighting a cost of up to £1 million to put the club in a position to win a Super League Licence, Mr O'Connor added that it would be an essential part of any successful Licence application that the club could demonstrate that attendances were on an upward spiral, towards a level that could support a Super League club.

Explaining the need, and desire, of all parties to succeed in this venture the chairman pointed out that neither he, nor his partners from Halton Borough Council "can afford to be involved in this if it fails. I don't want to be associated with a business that fails. I would only have got involved if I thought we could make a success of it. We are very clear what the objectives are and what the milestones are to achieve a Super League Licence."

"We have a short window of opportunity to prove to the Rugby League that we're very serious about an application. I'm very confident that, with the support of the fans, we will deliver a very professional Super League Licence application".

Underlining the amount of work to be done Mr O'Connor stressed that "for a successful bid this has to be a business that is capable of a £4 million turnover and 10,000 people coming to the game every week. Not necessarily 10,000 people in this league – but 10,000 people to watch Super League. That's the be all and end all. If this club cannot generate 10,000 fans to watch Super League, it wouldn't be viable to make that bid. However, I'm sure we can deliver more people than historically have been coming here over the last 12 months at an average of 3,300 per game which is a long, long way from enabling us to satisfy the payroll for the business we need for next year.

Having said that, if we really struggle to hit the numbers, we might need a plan B and that seems to be what has been missing. Plan B is that we build for 2011 and that we build a successful club that is successful in applying for a Licence next time around. It's not the first aspiration but we have to be realistic and not have a boom and bust mentality that it's that or nothing. It would be folly, I think".

It was plain to see, from Mr O'Connor's words throughout the evening, that the club was going to be run as a 'business', on business principles. "The days in which sports clubs can be run on blind faith are long gone" said the Vikings chairman. He went on to announce a major reduction in the price of season tickets and match day tickets for the 2008 season but warned: "The business cannot afford not to sell its product. It's a chicken and egg. We need a demonstration of people who are committed to the club. We are hoping to charge less to encourage more people to come in."

Adding weight to his chairman's comments, David Parr, Halton Borough Council chief executive commented: "Halton is a rugby league borough and the Vikings are a very important part of the community that is Widnes, that is Halton. They are at the heart of the community and certainly, when I've spoken to people, it's been pretty clear that the town needs a successful team.

"There is a lot of evidence that successful sporting clubs bring a lot of success within a town, within a borough. Certainly from the discussions I've had with local politicians, local businesses and local people there was a big desire to ensure the Vikings survived".

Returning to the theme of attaining Super League status Mr O'Connor reiterated the need to "demonstrate that something dramatic has happened at Widnes since the end of last season. We have a black mark against us financially because we look like an organisation that is not sustainable. So we need to fix that. When we deliver our presentation it will be such a sensational change, if we can demonstrate an improvement in the number of people coming to the games, that they will find it very, very difficult to resist our application".

"As much as possible, I will put the financial commitment in; I will put the professional commitment in but it is absolutely down to the fans whether or not we win that application".

Mr O'Connor added: "We are looking at every aspect of the Vikings' operation to ensure the long-term future of rugby league in Widnes. This is a fresh start for the club and we wanted to develop a new, modern look in keeping with the demands of the 21st century. Widnes has a fantastic heritage and that's a great foundation to build upon. Now our aim is to bring financial stability to the club and use that as a springboard to seek a return to those glorious days, not that long ago, when the town boasted the best club side in the world".

While there had been much talk of 'business principles' there was equal reference to the need for the club to be 'up to date' and to embrace the benefits of modern technology. The first evidence of this was the change of the club logo from the familiar 'Viking head' to a more simplistic image based on a Viking longboat, and the launch of a new website. While it is true that there was some resistance to the introduction of the 'on-line' purchasing of tickets and merchandise, and the new logo, they were to become more readily accepted with the passage of time, as fans became used to the dynamic style of the revitalised Widnes Vikings.

At the end of the evening the expectant mood of fans entering the room had been replaced with one of confidence about the future of their club as they left. This was underlined in the days and weeks that followed as Mr O'Connor continued to build his management team, while modifications to the existing office accommodation and the construction of a new fitness suite under the North Stand underlined the new approach at the Stobart Stadium.

Among the first appointments were the key roles of chief executive and commercial manager, taken by Alex Bonney and Mike Banks respectively.

Bonney arrived from the Stobart Group in what could be described as the club's first 'Dual Registration' signing, long before the RFL came up with the concept! The former financial director of the O'Connor Group was working full-time on the handover to Stobart while also holding down the position of the Vikings' chief executive. Having also worked in the 'rag trade' for a zip manufacturer – with a sideline in bodybags(!) – before joining the O'Connor Group the role with Widnes represented another quantum leap, into the realm of professional sport.

Six months down the line, as the handover between the O'Connor and Stobart companies was finalised, Bonney's role with Stobart diminished while that with the Vikings grew considerably and he became the club's permanent CEO for a further two years.

Prior to joining the Vikings Banks had gained a wealth of experience from senior positions in a variety of top-flight sporting organisations, including The Jockey Club, Everton FC and Sale Sharks. At the time of his appointment Mr Banks said "I'm very excited and this is a fantastic opportunity. There's a lot of work to do but with my background I'm very confident I will make a tremendous difference. I am absolutely sure we can increase gates week on week." However, in September 2009 Banks moved on to become chief executive of Rochdale Hornets.

Just days after these appointments came news of the return of two former favourites. While it had long been rumoured that John Stankevitch would be returning to the club, in one coaching capacity or another, the appointment of Terry O'Connor took people by surprise as it involved a new position in the structure of the club. As explained on the club's website he was appointed to the new position of sporting director, and would be responsible for a wide range of administration duties including player recruitment, player welfare, community initiatives through schools and youth groups while continuing his work with Sky Sports.

Following his appointment former skipper O'Connor echoed the optimism of the fans when he said: "There's obviously a tremendous amount of work to be done to transform the fortunes of the Vikings and I'm thrilled at being given the chance to help. Since Steve O'Connor took over, people within rugby league are all talking about the professionalism he has brought to Widnes. There's a genuine excitement in the town that big things are going to happen and I'm delighted to be able to be a part of it.

"I'm really looking forward to working with my great friend Steve McCormack. I'm hoping I will be able to take a lot of pressure off Steve's shoulders by looking after all the off-field activities involving the players, their welfare and offering practical support to them, leaving Steve free to concentrate all his energies on the playing side and developing a successful team."

Chairman Steve O'Connor said: "At the outset I made it clear we would transform this club by introducing experienced business professionals to work alongside talented and successful people from the world of rugby league. Terry O'Connor is ideally placed to help us achieve our goals of securing the long-term future of this club and mounting a successful campaign to win one of the coveted Super League Licences."

On the same day it was also announced that the popular John Stankevitch would be returning to the club as assistant to Steve McCormack. 'Stanky' had built a strong reputation as a coach with the Widnes Senior Academy squad before leaving to take up the head coach position at Doncaster in June, a position from which he had resigned in November.

As a demoralising 2007 gave way to an optimistic 2008 there was a tremendous groundswell of support for the revitalised Widnes Vikings, under the dynamic leadership of its new owner. With the benefit of hindsight Steve O'Connor made the valid point that "going into administration may have been the best thing for the club to do at the time. It wouldn't have felt like it at the time but it acted as a catalyst for change".

However, it should not be forgotten that if Peter Knowles and his interim board of directors had not elected to keep the club afloat, following the resignation of Steven Vaughan, there may not have been a club for Steve O'Connor to rescue.

A measure of the interest in the reborn club came from the new website which had been launched at the fans' forum. The capacity on the club's new-look website had to be dramatically increased following an incredible response from fans with more than 50,000 individual visits in just 16 days since it had been launched. Furthermore within hours of the 'on-line' shop going live the website was bombarded with thousands of hits which crashed the server putting the site out of action for 24 hours.

Vikings' chief executive Alex Bonney said: "Naturally we apologise for any inconvenience caused to our fans. However, it is really encouraging that so many people are taking an interest in the new website which is going to be the focal point for accessing information about the club, purchasing match tickets and shopping for merchandise."

CHAPTER FOUR
Inside Steve O'Connor

So what do we know about the human 'phoenix' who enabled Widnes Vikings to rise from the ashes of Administration?

The announcement issued by the club at the time of the change of ownership included the following:

> Mr O'Connor, a familiar and respected figure in the Halton business community, recently sold his shares in his highly-successful Widnes-based rail freight and logistics company, O'Connor Group, to Stobart Group in a multi-million pound deal. He is now responsible for developing the Stobart's brand across the North West.
>
> Initially he has pledged £250,000 to guarantee the immediate future of the club, which will trade as a new company, on top of a five figure sum he paid to secure the rights of the Widnes Vikings' brand.

Widnes-born Steve added at the time "I would be the first to admit that football is my first love rather than rugby league but ultimately I am fiercely passionate about sport and I'm equally passionate about business and the community where I was brought up".

That love of his local community dates back to the days he attended St Bedes and St Joseph's schools in the town before moving on to Penketh High School. His early sporting interests were firmly in place by the time the family moved from Widnes when he was 11 years of age, and he continued to play in the Widnes Sunday Football League until the age of 16.

It can be no surprise that, growing up within a family haulage business, a regular adventure in his early years was a day out in a lorry – so much so that the mischievous young Steve was often known to hide in one in an attempt to avoid going to school – on one occasion only revealing himself when halfway to Scotland. Demonstrating a liking for adventure another favourite pastime of the young O'Connor and his friends was to cling on, for as long as possible before being discovered, to the buffers of the shunting engines which ran along the now defunct line superceded by Watkinson Way.

This liking for adventure may well have been passed from father to son as Steve's father, after eight years service in the Royal Navy, had in the mid-sixties become a pioneer of the road haulage routes to the Middle East. It was from the success of this venture that the family business was established in 1971 when he set himself up as an 'owner-driver' in the haulage business. Interestingly during his naval service O'Connor senior had been a veteran of the nuclear testing on Christmas Island, telling his son that "when the bombs went off we were told to face the other way with our hands over our faces. And when the bombs went off we could see our own skeleton!"

Despite the constant distraction of the family trucks Steve completed his education at Penketh High School, and as he grew older had aspirations to be a writer or an architect. However, his first job offer, at the age of 16, came from a Warrington firm offering him a position as a draughtsman. But the dye was cast for his future career when, as he says, "I sold myself for £3", and declined that offer in favour of accepting an administrative position in his father's haulage business for the extra £3 per week.

From the humble beginnings of that administrative job O'Connor learnt all about the haulage and logistics business and became the dynamic leader of the very successful O'Connor Group, which had been transformed from his father's single vehicle business into a successful multi-million pound operation. So successful were his efforts that in early 2007 he received an approach from the Westbury Property Fund – who were seeking to diversify from their property portfolio – for the O'Connor Group. Some six weeks after agreeing the sale of his own business he became aware that Westbury had completed a 'reverse takeover' of the logistics giant Stobart Group and rebranded themselves as 'Stobart'. The result was that the O'Connor Group was now effectively part of the Stobart Group, one of the best known brands in Europe. This in turn led to O'Connor becoming a member of Stobart's Executive Board with responsibility for the Ports Division, a position which remained his 'day job' until part-way through 2012.

It is indeed fortunate for all connected with the Widnes club that O'Connor was handsomely rewarded for the growth of his business, as it gave him the freedom to do something tangible for his town, his community, later in 2007.

Having sounded out Halton Borough Council O'Connor discussed his plan with his wife Clare, who told me that "Steve was very grateful to the Widnes community for the success of his business and he liked the idea of giving something back to that community. He has pride in his community." After mulling it over for a week or so, and with the full support of his wife, he decided to go ahead with his rescue package for the Vikings. Indeed Mrs O'Connor expressed her pleasure that her dynamic husband "had something to get his teeth into. A new challenge to stimulate him following the sale of his business." From that day a love affair with rugby league began for both the new owner and his wife, whose previous sporting affiliations were restricted to Liverpool and Blackburn Rovers respectively.

Feeling embarrassed with the way that the club was viewed within the sport and the community, just 18 years after lifting the World Club Championship, O'Connor felt that he was in a position to try to change that perception. He had begun by having those talks with the council to see what help he could offer to put the club back on a firm footing.

At the time he commented: "Originally I was just looking to make a donation or set up a trust and hoping some people might come out of the business community who might want to lead this forward.

"As it turned out, there wasn't anybody else that came along and it became fairly obvious that in order to safeguard that sort of investment, I would probably need to be involved over a longer period of time.

"We've done very well out of the town of Widnes and we're very fortunate we're in a position to make this investment without affecting our own security. And I suppose it's a way of giving something back."

The new owner, who admits to climbing over the perimeter fence to gain entry on his occasional visits to Naughton Park as a young boy, went on to say: "What has happened to Widnes Rugby League Club over recent years is a tragedy. It's a fantastic institution which should be competing at the very highest level. I firmly believe that, with the support of Halton Borough Council, I can put together a team of experienced individuals from the world of business to work alongside talented and successful rugby people to ensure we can bring the glory days back to Widnes.

"My goal is to use my wealth and expertise to help put strong foundations in place where Widnes Vikings can flourish and take their rightful place in the Super League elite where they belong."

It became patently clear that the new owner was not one to indulge in the 'boom or bust' approach and under his stewardship, the club would be looking beyond a short-term fix. He spoke clearly and bluntly highlighting that if Super League status was not achieved in 2008 that there had to be a fallback plan to re-group and try again in 2011. This in itself was a welcome change of direction. However, no matter how powerful the business plan put to the RFL it would still need greater support from the public. Mr O'Connor warned:

"People think in this particular league there's a £400,000 salary cap, so we've got £400,000 wages to find. The business plan that we've put together suggests we've got more than £750,000 of a wage bill connected to our football activity by the time we look at the professionals behind the scenes: the physio, doctor and coaching staff to maintain the academies.

"There's a great deal more expense and there are some very simple 'maths' that I would like people to think through about a business that's got a payroll of three quarters of a million pounds, while it only has 12 opportunities to raise any finance – the games it is guaranteed to host. We need to achieve more than three quarters of a million pounds of revenues from somewhere."

Just five months after Steve O'Connor assumed control of the club the application for a Super League Licence for 2009-11 was handed in to the RFL's offices in Leeds, on 31st March 2008, by operations manager Pat Cluskey.

The chairman who, "simply could not stand by and watch this club, with all its fantastic heritage, die" commented at the time: "We are one step closer today to realising our dream. We have been working tirelessly behind the scenes on our application and we all hope we achieve the result we want. I am overwhelmed with the support we have had and hope we won't disappoint our supporters."

It transpired that shortly after 10am on July 22nd 2008 it was in fact the Widnes fans who were to be disappointed as the two additional Licences were, somewhat controversially, awarded to Salford City Reds and Celtic Crusaders.

Although obviously disappointed at the way the decision making process went, O'Connor remained dignified in admitting: "I get the sense that if I was in the RFL's position, and trying to be objective about why our bid was not successful, I think that they thought that we were just a little bit 'hit the ground running and turn something into a deliverable' type of application.

"They always had the way out that we had been in administration – that was always a very genuine concern.

We would have been quick to seize upon that if it had been another club."

Demonstrating a 'we are all in this together' approach the Vikings chairman had spurned the opportunity of advance notice by refusing to open the e-mail from the RFL. The man who had used his personal wealth to save the club would find out the club's fate at exactly the same moment as the fans. Like the rest of us he was plainly shocked at the outcome but quickly confirmed his long-term commitment to the club.

Speaking on Radio Merseyside shortly after the announcement a bullish O'Connor re-affirmed his intention to see the job through to a successful conclusion. "I intend to be here for the long run and I'm determined that we'll take the club into Super League. It's obviously going to be harder than I thought and we will push on."

Looking to the future he added: "I'd like to think that I'm an objective sports fan and I absolutely know that you have to have the bad days to recognise the good days. We'll be successful in the league that we play in and we'll provide an irresistible addition to Super League in the future."

By the time that he addressed the fans from the pitch on 27th July O'Connor's self-confessed anger had, through several sleepless nights, been transformed into a dignified determination to ensure that the club went one stage further in 2011.

The Widnes faithful showed that they were at one with their chairman when he set out the way forward during his half-time address during the match with Dewsbury. He was at pains to point out that the calm nature of his public reaction to missing out on a Super League Licence belied his inner feelings and the affinity that he shared with the fans.

He admitted that he had "felt every emotion that all the fans have felt this week from sadness and anger to bitterness, but eventually we need to reach acceptance. I didn't sleep from Tuesday until Friday. I was still fighting on Thursday night and planning for retribution but woke up on Friday and decided that any time, effort and money should be spent in rebuilding the club. Over the next three years I am determined to stay and make things happen".

O'Connor's reaction to the disappointing news later drew this comment from Ray French: "No whingeing, no shrieking at imagined persecution or unfair treatment, and no negativity – only a chairman and his club standing tall and determined to play their part for not only Widnes but rugby league itself."

Following his dignified acceptance of the situation O'Connor set about rebuilding frayed relationships with the governing body and learning more about how the RFL saw the profile of a successful applicant for Super League in 2011.

Much work had gone on behind the scenes by the time I next spoke to the Widnes chairman in February 2009. The long-term commitment to the Vikings cause was evident as he said "it would do no good if all I do is stand this club up until we get back to Super League. I need to teach it that if I don't put money in after a certain time it learns to do it itself. It's far too easy at the moment to come to me. From the beginning my role was to teach a starving man to fish, and ultimately it is easier to fish if we get into better waters."

O'Connor was also quick to point out that the successful rebuilding of the club is also in a large part due to Halton Borough Council, – which has a 15% stakeholding in the new company – David Parr and Tony McDermott as "without their support we would have a non-starter". The fact that the club has its home in a "sensational genuine community stadium" is due to the Local Authority acting promptly on the recommendations of the 'Framing the Future' policy document issued by the RFL in 1994.

Following that disappointment of missing out on a Super League Licence at the first time of asking O'Connor showed his resolve by ensuring that he and his management team did everything possible to ensure success in 2011. However, for the next round of Licence applications the RFL had decided to revamp the system and had included playing criteria into the mix. In order to be allowed to make an application for 2012-14 a club must first meet those criteria by either winning the Northern Rail Cup or appearing in a Grand Final in the 2009 or 2010 seasons. Thus the first target was to win the Northern Rail Cup in 2009 and relieve the pressure on the club as soon as possible.

Ironically that pressure was immediately increased as the team fell to a home defeat to Oldham in the opening match of the group stages of the Northern Rail Cup. The fallout was seen within days as the Vikings' chairman not only displayed his determination to succeed, but also showed that he was prepared to make the tough decisions when he felt it appropriate. So much so that fans were genuinely shocked when it was announced that head coach Steve McCormack was to leave the club. Further evidence, as if it was needed, that O'Connor was his own man came when McCormack's successor was eventually announced.

Very quickly after McCormack's departure the internet forums were identifying Paul Cullen as a serious candidate for the post, and fans were queuing up to vow that they would never again watch the Vikings if the ex-Warrington man was appointed. With O'Connor believing that "you appoint the best man for the job" and not being weighed down with "the baggage about Paul Cullen's background" Cullen was given the task of taking Widnes to Super League.

Just three months later O'Connor's decision to appoint Cullen was vindicated as they celebrated together on the Bloomfield Road pitch having defeated Barrow to lift the Northern Rail Cup and 'ticked the box'. "It was a huge monkey that is now off our backs" said O'Connor after the victory that confirmed the club's right to apply for a Super League Licence for 2012-14. He paid tribute to his head coach who had "galvanised our team and found a format that is working", adding that "you can't underestimate the part the fans played". A further benefit identified by the chairman was that the club could now afford to rely less on the experienced players and give youth its head.

Looking back O'Connor added "I think we have had a reasonably successful season, but I'm disappointed as we budgeted to reach the Grand Final. We would've enjoyed another battle at Halifax, but we satisfied the silverware requirement and there have been success stories like the emergence of Paddy Flynn and Ben Kavanagh."

With the pressure off as far as 'qualifying' for the Super League application process was concerned the 2010 and 2011 seasons were seen by many as 'dead rubbers'. Not so for Mr O'Connor who wanted to "earn the right to be in Super League by being the best club outside of it, on all levels from our rugby to our matchday experience.

"We want to add value to the community, develop a winning culture and if we don't have six or seven fine young Widnes athletes in our team by 2012 then our investment in youth development will have been a huge failure."

As time moved on the Vikings chairman was in regular contact with the governing body regarding the minimum criteria for entry into Super League in 2012. In December 2009 he was so confident that the club would meet those minimum criteria that he told fans "You have nothing to worry about. I know we will be in Super League in 2012.

"We're in a group of clubs that has aspirations for 2012 but there's a feeling that there will be a positive announcement in spring 2011. If other clubs are struggling then I have sympathy with them. We don't take any pleasure in seeing other clubs struggle as we want to join a vibrant league. Let's create a winning culture and hope that we are better equipped when we do go up."

With 'D-Day' just weeks away O'Connor repeated his faith in the licensing system, and confidence that Widnes would be successful but, reflecting on the 2008 disappointment, added this note of caution: "That experience ensures that we won't count any chickens."

Despite having had to bear a further three years in the Championship, and desperate to see his dream for the club and town come true through this nerve-wracking process he told Andy Wilson of *The Observer.* "The principle of licensing is a fabulous way to avoid dealing with the boom and bust that had previously accompanied promotion to and relegation from Super League.

"After misunderstanding last time around what the RFL were looking for, we've spent the last three years trying to tick every box, especially in areas like youth development where we've got a crop of under-16 and under-18 players, mostly Widnes lads, who we hope could form the nucleus of a successful team for years. We are convinced that we can add the most value to the Super League competition, and that's what licensing is all about."

Underlining his commitment to the Vikings cause the man who saved the club in its darkest days added: "I'm a Widnes lad who grew up watching football and supporting Liverpool, but I've been seduced by the game since I got involved. It's got great integrity and family values, but I think it undersells itself."

Further evidence of his new-found love of the game came when he told Alan Jackson of *Radio Merseyside*: "My school motto was 'perseverance' – you keep going, you don't give up – and I felt there was job to do. Maybe I thought three years ago I could get us to Super League, hand it over to somebody and they would move forward with it. But I'm really, really excited about being around."

As we now know the licensing decision went in favour of the Vikings on 31st March 2011, justifying the considerable expenditure of time, effort and money by Steve O'Connor and his staff.

While it is fair to say that most fans prefer the concept of promotion and relegation, O'Connor took the opportunity to speak out in favour of the licensing system, having seen off the challenge of Barrow and Halifax, to secure the club's readmittance to Super League. Repeating comments made to me in that interview in February 2009, he told the club's official website:

"I was always a fan of the licensing system. It's the right way to go. There are elements that other sports can learn from. I think the club going up and taking all the players from the club coming down was destined to fail, and promoting a team in October doesn't give them time to recruit. You can't nurture talent in that sort of environment and we have some very exciting talent here and it will be great to allow them to play on the top stage. The licensing system allows us to experiment a little bit more. If we were in a simple promotion and relegation scenario it would be very difficult to blood some of those youngsters."

It was plain to see from the chairman's comments that while a fair array of senior players would be recruited from home and abroad the current, and future, crop of home-grown talent will be a feature of the Widnes approach under O'Connor's stewardship.

Speaking on Boots 'N' All just hours after Widnes had been granted a return to Super League a visibly relaxed O'Connor told Eddie Hemmings: "I was reasonably confident that we had a bid that was the most robust bid of the three applicants and I was very comfortable until about 48 hours ago. Then I started to get a little bit spooked, a little bit uncomfortable, and I'm just glad that the whole process is over now, and we can move on".

The man who takes great pride in his community hoped that the club's success would create a sense of inclusion and a boost for the whole town. "I want to try to take people on a journey. My intention is to get a whistle out and everybody comes and follows me!"

That Steve O'Connor felt he had another journey, or journeys, in him was music to the ears of all Widnes fans. In his programme notes just three days later he wrote: "I made a commitment to the fans three and a half years ago and I could easily walk away into the sunset now, but I'm not going to do that as I'm enjoying it." The man had made his mark on Widnes Vikings and the game of rugby league, but it had obviously been reciprocated.

Some four months after the Vikings had secured that Super League Licence the remaining 13 successful clubs for 2012-14 were announced, leaving Halifax and Crusaders as the odd men out. Having suffered the same fate some three years earlier the Widnes chairman was quick to show an understanding of their plight.

Via the club's website he demonstrated his wider appreciation of the RFL's decision by commenting: "I'd like to offer my empathy to the supporters of both Crusaders and Halifax RLFC, two clubs with their own history and tradition, who, for differing reasons, will not be involved in the game's elite competition for the next three seasons.

"I appreciate only too well how devastated both groups of supporters must be now their fears have become a reality. To learn that your immediate future lies outside the game's top-flight is devastating and once that initial shock passes, the realisation of the huge task ahead and the re-building involved is a massive challenge for any organisation with an aspiration of achieving Super League status."

With Widnes' place in Super League secured Dennis Betts and Paul Cullen were able to concentrate on the recruitment of a Super League squad, while O'Connor turned his attention to making the club a stable and sustainable organisation.

Rebuilding the club off the pitch had been a complex and long-term, task. Indeed in his first message to Widnes fans following his purchase of the club O'Connor had commented that "much work needs to be carried out" to put in place the structures and strategies that would be required to take the club forward. While there were varying short and medium term objectives the long-term aim of the new owner was that the club would be self-supporting and not need to rely on a benefactor.

Central to that long-term sustainability was to be the 'Viking Stronghold'. Addressing supporters at the home match against York just days after the Licence announcement the chairman launched the innovative scheme, where supporters become 'members' in return for a monthly membership fee, instead of the traditional lump sum cost of being a season-ticket holder. While the club benefits from a constant cash flow and easier financial planning, the club's members would be entitled to a variety of benefits in addition to admission to matches.

Mr O'Connor said: "I made a commitment back in 2007 to develop a sustainable, robust and successful Super League club here at Widnes. The Viking Stronghold demonstrates an innovative and creative approach aimed at engaging the whole community. In order to commit to 2012 expenditure, it is vital for the club to understand our potential revenue."

The new initiative was well received by fans and speaking to the *Liverpool Daily Post* some four months later the Vikings' chairman was able to comment that "the early figures for our Viking Stronghold are extremely encouraging and this number is steadily increasing week on week".

Such is the commitment of Steve O'Connor to the Vikings' cause it is easy to forget that he still had that 'day job' as director of the ports division of the Stobart Group. Despite spending many hours each week on club business O'Connor did still have that role to fulfil, a major part of which was the Mersey Multimodal Gateway project, a facility that has already created thousands of new jobs for the region. Indeed in recognition of both his track record in business, and for driving the development of the multi-million pound transport hub O'Connor received the *Liverpool Daily Post*'s DLA Piper Business Person of the Year Award in May 2010.

In accepting the award Mr O'Connor commented: "It's a very humbling experience to be among my peers, my family and my friends and to receive this award. A night like this gives you a phenomenal opportunity to reflect – and to look ahead. I don't really feel worthy of this accolade. We just keep getting on with our job."

'Just getting on with our job' could well be the mantra that describes the Widnes club's professional approach under Steve O'Connor, as it was initially saved, stabilised and rebuilt in order to reclaim its place among the sport's elite on 31st March 2011.

The position of the club in the summer of 2011 was light years away from that in which Steve O'Connor found it in October 2007. It is safe to say that under his stewardship the club has continued to move forward on a more business-like footing so that it is now in a position to support top flight rugby league.

It was, in a way, typical of the man that having saved Widnes from extinction four-and-a-half years previously, O'Connor made a gesture that took the rugby league world by surprise in March 2012, when he came to the aid of a rival club facing a similar fate. The Vikings' chairman had built a reputation within the sport as a clear-thinking, innovative and determined leader but the crisis at Bradford Bulls allowed him to demonstrate his generosity of spirit and empathy with another member of the oft-mentioned rugby league family. Despite an inauspicious start to Widnes' return to Super League O'Connor found it within himself to be among the first to respond to the Bradford appeal for help. The Widnes chairman not only made a five figure personal donation, but he also sanctioned the donation of ticket receipts, from the Bradford fans attending the Easter Monday fixture at the Stobart Stadium, to the appeal fund.

Peter Hood, chairman of Bradford Bulls, commenting on O'Connor's "heartfelt and extremely generous contribution" explained: "Steve spoke eloquently at length about the rugby league community and how we are all in this together. He talked of the outstanding contribution that the Bradford Bulls have made to the game and he wants that to continue."

Back at Widnes O'Connor and his management team consistently reminded fans that the long-term sustainability, and success, of the club is in their hands. So, if the innovative Viking Stronghold continues to grow, along with increased numbers of 'walk up' supporters, and other successful commercial initiatives, Steve O'Connor will surely be able to say that he has indeed "taught a starving man to fish".

CHAPTER FIVE
Licensing – A New Phenomenon

As discussed in *Dreams to Reality* the 2007 Grand Final was the last chance for Widnes Vikings to reclaim their place in Super League through the traditional route – their efforts on the field of play. The fact that they failed to grasp that opportunity not only led to the saga of Administration but also consigned them to the vagaries of a new licensing system to determine which teams operated at the highest level of professional rugby league. Clubs in the second tier who wished to be considered for 'promotion' therefore had to take part in a paper chase to convince the mandarins at Red Hall that they deserved a crack at Super League.

It is in the DNA of every follower of sport – amateur or professional – that the status of their team or club is determined on the field of play. At least it was until the RFL took our sport down the same road as their Australian counterparts, with the declared aim of improving standards across the game. It was felt that the process of awarding three-year 'Licences' to clubs operating in Super League would bring an end to the 'boom and bust' approach as clubs fought to avoid relegation or gain promotion. There was indeed evidence that clubs hovering near the drop zone, or pushing for promotion, would throw money at expensive short-term signings in an attempt to achieve their goal. In many cases such 'short-termism' indicated the lack of a well thought-out business plan by which such clubs could grow and survive at a higher level.

The argument proffered by the RFL was that a three-year Licence would give clubs the opportunity to establish themselves without the fear of relegation and the ensuing loss of income. This period of stability would allow clubs to not only build up their playing strength, including investing time in the progression of young players, but perhaps more importantly direct funds to address the sorry state of many stadia and facilities without fear of losing their status in the meantime.

The governing body went to great lengths to emphasise that, in their view, a 'three-year period with no threat of relegation should ensure that clubs don't take short term decisions to avoid the drop, which have often been at the expense of bringing young talent through the system.' They put forward the following rationale:

'Licensing should result in clubs investing in longer term objectives such as facilities and youth development. Currently every spare pound and every ounce of management for some clubs is spent avoiding relegation.'

It was also suggested that at international level the home countries would all benefit in the long run through the greater investment in youth.

Ironically the RFL cited 'the disparity between the funding of the two leagues' as a reason why 'promotion and relegation doesn't work'. If one looks back to the deal, struck with some haste, between the RFL and BskyB in April 1995 it is possible to see the origins of that scenario.

This laudable benefit of the licensing system – saving clubs from themselves – was however, only one side of the argument. It was seen in many quarters as 'pulling up the drawbridge' and looking after the 12 so-called elite clubs. The great fear expressed by many was that it would render the competitions below that level almost meaningless and lead to the possible extinction of some of the oldest clubs in the country. Without anything tangible to play for it was feared that attendances and sponsorship would fall leading to serious reductions in revenue.

The Process

While promotion and relegation remained in place between the two National Leagues it was only every third season that clubs in National League 1 could attempt to improve their status. And that was to be done, in the main, by submission of business plans, assessments and financial reports, with what seemed only a passing reference to the actual game of rugby. In theory a team could finish bottom of National League 1, be relegated but start the following season in Super League!

Thus for the inaugural round of licensing in 2008 the RFL published the following criteria against which an Independent Board would assess each application:

- Potential to consistently attract healthy crowds
- Strong financial turnover
- On-pitch performance
- Good facilities – stadia/capacity/training ground
- Well run financially and administratively
- Business plan
- Production of professional players and youth development

Applications were to be invited from clubs who felt that they met the criteria provided that they were competing in the Super League or National League 1 during the 2008 season. But in addition there was a wild card entry route for clubs not based in the United Kingdom. Those with affiliations to Widnes were understandably concerned at this development as they were plainly unable to be judged against the same criteria as the British clubs – a fact fully recognised by the RFL.

Alarmingly to many Widnes fans there had been much publicity surrounding an application from the French club Toulouse and this raised fears of missing out, in the name of expansion, yet again. In 1996 Widnes had missed out on the original Super League due to the experiment with Paris St Germain, and were the additional club to be relegated in favour of admitting Catalans Dragons in 2006. To be excluded in favour of another French team in 2008 would have been an unpalatable hat-trick.

However, with the decision to increase Super League to a 14-team competition from 2009 there were to be at least two new Licences awarded. By the time the application deadline of 31st March 2008 arrived 19 hopeful clubs had submitted applications hoping to be among the list of successful clubs to be announced on 22nd July 2008.

Whichever clubs made the final cut the sport would be entering a new era where those who had missed out would be facing a period of three years with no hope of promotion to Super League. With many fans passionately opposed to the whole concept of licensing there was a real fear – shared by officials of some clubs – that clubs in the National leagues could be facing extinction.

The process began with the RFL writing to all professional clubs inviting applications from interested parties. Once those who did not meet the minimum criteria had been eliminated the remaining clubs were assessed against the criteria detailed above, and given an A, B or C grading depending on how well they met those criteria.

Speaking in April 2008 the RFL Chief Executive, Nigel Wood, claimed that the licensing process had already had a beneficial effect "as clubs have undergone their own searching assessments" to identify areas they need to strengthen. He added that the successful applicants will "need to demonstrate that they will deliver across all aspects, producing quality teams containing substantially home produced players, in 21st century facilities for supporters".

In reality several of the clubs who were eventually awarded Licences in 2008 had still seemed to continue to turn a blind eye to the issue of ground improvements by the time the next round of licensing took place in 2011! This is all the more remarkable as the concept of *Framing the Future* had by now been around for 17 years. It can also be said that some of the successful clubs did little to further the cause of home grown players.

In the run-up to the licensing process in 2008 there had been debate in the media about the 'scoring' process by which clubs would be graded. With a lack of clarity or transparency from the RFL the best guess was that clubs would be awarded a point for each of the 10 criteria that they met. This system seemed to open up the possibility of several clubs ending up on the same score, with those of us with a suspicious nature left to wonder how such a photo-finish would be resolved.

This widespread concern was crystallised in an article written by John Lawless in the *Viking Storm* in March 2008. He observed that under the heading of 'player strength' a club would be awarded a point if they had averaged eighth position or better in the last three years. He further noted that "Harlequins/London Broncos get the same number of points for coming sixth, seventh, and ninth as St Helens get for coming first, first and first!"

The vagaries of the system were hammered home as Lawless added in regard of stadia "the problem is you can only win 1-nil. So you can have a fully up-and-running modern facility…and only get one point more than somebody who has had a portacabin delivered to a field".

There was certainly concern among fans about the scoring system in place, as it appeared to leave great scope for subjective rather than objective decisions. With the likelihood that several clubs could achieve the same 'score' there was a fear that it would not simply be about taking a detached assessment of the criteria, as outlined by the RFL. Conversations on the terraces, in pubs and clubs, and on internet messageboards centred around the unknown nature of the 'tie-breakers'. The conspiracy theorists were having a field day, and understandably so.

Despite the confusion and concerns expressed in many quarters about the whole process the RFL were at pains to point out that "any club who isn't granted a Super League Licence in 2009 should not be downhearted," adding as if by way of consolation that "although it is anticipated that Super League in 2009 will have 14 teams there is no upper limit on membership".

There was, however, the nebulous caveat that the league could be further expanded if "it makes financial sense for all clubs involved in the league to accept a new member. However, this should not be detrimental to quality and player supply". The reality of the situation was that it would be highly unlikely that clubs who had already seen their central funding reduced by the addition of two new clubs to Super League would vote for a further reduction in that income.

So with the existing 12 clubs in Super League odds on to retain their status the seven potential newcomers – Celtic Crusaders, Featherstone Rovers, Halifax, Leigh Centurions, Salford City Reds, Toulouse Olympique and Widnes Vikings – were challenging for two places.

In many quarters Widnes were among the front runners as, despite the Administration issue, the club would meet the majority of the criteria, and had a strong tradition within the sport. Based on sound-bites attributed to Red Hall the biggest threat was deemed to come from the 'expansionist' clubs with several high profile commentators espousing the causes of Celtic Crusaders and Toulouse, while strangely, Salford City Reds were often mentioned in the same sentence. It is interesting to note that as far back as 2005 the embryonic Crusaders website was reporting that "promotion and relegation will remain in place for the next four seasons but then potential new clubs are likely to come from London, Wales or France."

Of these three clubs the greatest threat to Widnes' chances was thought to be the 'Welsh bid' of Celtic Crusaders. Although it could easily be claimed that they were inferior to Widnes in most areas of the assessment they did have what appeared to be one trump card – location. There was certainly a strongly held belief across the rugby league community that there was a desire by the governing body to move into new territory. The Welsh outfit, who were only admitted to the professional ranks of National League 2 in 2006, were to be based at the Brewery Field in Bridgend, South Wales, the spartan home of Bridgend Ravens RUFC and Bridgend Town FC. In June 2005 the Crusaders website reported Richard Lewis, the RFL executive chairman, as welcoming the new club saying "The Crusaders come into professional Rugby League playing out of the excellent Brewery Field Stadium in Bridgend and having lodged a robust business plan with the RFL". I think those fans who have travelled to Bridgend will find Lewis' description somewhat bizarre, and with the benefit of hindsight it would also seem that the business plan was less than robust.

There was another marked contrast with the Widnes club which was commented upon in many quarters. In much the same way that it used to be said of Newcastle United that they simply shouted down the pit and another star footballer appeared, the Vikings are based in a town long renowned for its own sporting production line. Given that the RFL saw the award of three-year Licences as a means to promote the development of young British talent it was strange that the Welsh bandwagon had gained so much momentum. With no history of professional rugby league in the principality, of any standard, it seemed extremely optimistic that this would be reversed during the course of one or even two three-year Licences being awarded to the Crusaders. Widespread concerns about this were highlighted when Andrew Kirchin of *Rugby League World* commented in May 2008 that "the current [Crusaders] squad is made up of 9 Australians, 2 Welsh qualified Australians, 1 Tongan, a French-Canadian American footballer, 8 players with very little Super League experience and six players from the Summer Conference". This was compounded by the coaching appointments who, with the exception of former Warrington player Kevin Ellis, all came from overseas.

There was also strong support for another French team in Super League. Having previously been overlooked in the battle for 'preferred bidder status' by the French Federation, in favour of Union Treiziste Catalane (later known as Catalans Dragons), Toulouse Olympique were adopted as the 'French candidate' in 2008.

The flourishing club could already claim to be following the Super League 'model' with its off-field structures and had the advantage of having its home in a large and prosperous city. Although Olympique did not have a permanent home at the time – they had the choice of the council-owned Stade de Minimes, Stade Ernest Wallon, and Stade Benchidou at Colommiers – they did have solid financial backing from both the private and public sectors.

In the run-up to the announcement their excellent publicity machine made much of the benefits, for French rugby league, of having two clubs in Super League. However, from a distance, it seemed that their achilles heel may be the ability to attract the desired fan-base and the availability of sufficient French players to support two Super League clubs. Indeed this proved to be the case on their subsequent admission to the Co-operative Championship in 2009. As with their Welsh counterparts there were a high proportion of antipodean passport holders in the dressing room and matches were played in front of modest attendances. Again hindsight tells us that Super League would have been a step too far for the amiable French club as they opted to return to the domestic French league in 2012.

While the expansionist campaign for a Welsh or French addition to Super League took on a life all of its own there was, surprisingly, a similar campaign under way to convince all and sundry of the 'benefits to the game' of a top tier club in Greater Manchester. The fact that Salford were hoping to move to a new stadium was also causing great excitement with some commentators as it was seen as a sure fire way of increasing their attendances.

Now to the best of my knowledge the city of Salford has always been within the urban sprawl of Greater Manchester. Likewise the Salford club has had the benefit of being within the Greater Manchester conurbation since it was originally founded in 1873, and since then has consistently failed to attract all but a relatively small hard-core following.

The arguments being put forward, by people in authority outside the Salford club, were tantamount to the City Reds being touted as a way for rugby league to 'expand' into another new area. I have to ask why would the populace of Greater Manchester suddenly flock to watch rugby league in great numbers when it had resisted the temptation for so many years? And why would 'neutral' people continue to repeat the notion in support of the Reds' cause?

While all 19 clubs who submitted applications would, I'm sure, be content to be judged on the chosen criteria, the sudden presentation of Salford City Reds candidature on an 'expansionist' ticket must have been seen as a curve ball, particularly by those hoping to break into the top tier.

So everybody's attention was on the announcement to be made by RFL chairman Richard Lewis, live on Sky television, on 22nd July 2008. At the end of his announcement the 14 successful clubs to compete in Super League for 2009-11 would be known.

The majority of Widnes fans that I had spoken to in the run-up to that announcement believed that, despite the merits or otherwise of the various applications, Celtic Crusaders had long been regarded as certainties to be awarded a Licence.

If this was true the Vikings were left to target one additional place along with the other clubs – thereby reducing the chance of being successful. The ghost of the Administration saga raised its head again, to dim our confidence, despite supposed assurances that it would not be a determining factor. Like the fans of all clubs we 'knew' our club was 'better and more deserving' of a place in Super League than some others, but that 'knowledge' and confidence became less assured as the clock ticked by. Fans gathered in large numbers in and around the stadium, or anywhere else that they could watch Sky's coverage of this momentous decision, aware of the haunting fact that for the first time ever failure to gain this 'promotion' could not be rectified on the pitch next season. It would be three years before another paper chase could begin and application submitted!

In any event everything that could be done had now been done. The application had been submitted and the dye cast.

The Widnes faithful had put their trust in Steve O'Connor and the team responsible for compiling the bid document. Despite the arguments in favour of expansion we were confident that there could not be 14 better applications submitted to the RFL. All that was left to do was wait until the announcement was made by Richard Lewis.

As D-Day approached the Widnes chairman used his programme notes for the Batley match on 11th July to deliver one last rallying cry – with a side order of realism.

"Our next home game against Dewsbury Rams will either be a cause for major celebration or an occasion where we have to deal with the undoubted disappointment."

While "hoping and praying" that Widnes would not be one of the five unsuccessful clubs O'Connor stated that "should the result go against us I want to assure our fans that we will not be giving up on our dream. Far from it! We will continue our efforts to prepare Vikings for Super League with a strong team capable of competing at the very highest level supported by a sound and financially viable business".

Citing the "dramatic transformation" that had taken place at the club since he took over in November 2007 O'Connor drew attention to "a powerful business with excellent facilities, a strong supporter base and a fantastic community and commercial operation with a growing number of sponsors. It is an attractive package that would, in my opinion, be a massive asset to the Super League brand".

He concluded by adding that "I believe that we have made a compelling application to be awarded one of the coveted Super League Licences and have done everything we possibly could to demonstrate that we deserve a place in the top league. Win or lose there is still a massive amount of work to be done to make this club a major power again. I am fully committed to Widnes Vikings for the immediate future – be that in Super League or National League One".

Batley were duly dispatched on that Friday evening before the Vikings played out a draw against Halifax at The Shay just two days prior to the announcement. To some extent those games passed by as if we were in a trance as all thoughts were focused on 22nd July 2008.

The Bid

Just five months after the club was saved from extinction operations manager Pat Cluskey handed in to RFL headquarters the application for admission to Super League in 2009. Although, as Steve O'Connor later confided "the document was put together at pace, and we were on a steep learning curve", it is arguable that not many – if any – clubs would have produced a bid document that matched that of the Vikings for substance and quality.

The club was already unrecognisable from that which fell into Administration in the previous October and the governing body may have been wary of a club that could appear to have come so far in such a short space of time.

So what were the key elements of the Vikings' bid?

The following pages give an insight into how the club presented itself to the governing body in an attempt to get that Super League Licence.

In his foreword to the application O'Connor spoke of the achievements already made and the future targets of his administration. The list of impressive achievements – in addition to a raft of senior staff appointments – included:

- Developed the relationship with Halton Borough Council
- Introduced the world-renowned Stobart Group as sponsors
- Rebranded the club with a dynamic new logo
- Refurbished facilities for players and staff
- Begun a refurbishment programme of spectator facilities
- Introduced electronic ticketing and access system
- Introduced a review of community activities

With further supportive comments from both local and central government the club could clearly demonstrate its role within, and on behalf of, the community within which it lives. While Leader of the Council Tony McDermott MBE spoke proudly of the partnership of the club with the local authority, highlighting the many benefits to the community, local MP Derek Twigg paid glowing tribute to the work done by the new regime. Indeed Councillor McDermott went on record at the time as saying "I have never been so confident in the future of the club, and I'm convinced this business case will take it to greater things".

Another high profile individual to commend the application to the RFL was journalist Colin Myler who, coincidentally, was chief executive of the inaugural Super League. Having grown up in Widnes Myler, now editor in chief of the *New York Daily News*, has followed the fortunes of his home-town club for over 40 years and shared the relief of all fans when Steve O'Connor rescued the club. Impressed by the progress made in such a short time he was hopeful that "the officials at the Rugby League HQ will see that Widnes will be a great asset to Super League".

While the licensing process was necessarily about the future plans and targets of the club, on and off the field, the bid document justifiably made reference to the club's illustrious past. From being founder members of the Northern Union in 1895 the club had enjoyed periods of great success culminating in becoming the first official World Club Champions in 1989. Along the way championships had been won in addition to regular success in competitions such as the Lancashire Cup, John Player Trophy, and more latterly the Northern Rail Cup. A particular high point was the heady days of the '70s and '80s when they made the journey to Wembley for seven Challenge Cup Finals (being victorious on four occasions) in a 10-year span, becoming known as the 'Cup Kings' along the way. It is on this rich canvas that the achievements and successes of the O'Connor era will surely be painted.

While reference to the club's past gave context to the bid for Super League status it was very much a forward-looking application that was handed in to the RFL. In addition to highlighting the business credentials of Steve O'Connor the 98 page bid document, put together by PR specialists Paul Smith Associates on behalf of the club, clearly demonstrated the structure and quality of the management team that the Vikings' chairman had put in place.

While Steve O'Connor paid tribute to "a succession of well-meaning enthusiasts who have tried to rescue the club", I believe it is doubtful that the club has ever been supported by such a professional and business-like structure. By the very nature of the licensing process, and the attendant assessment criteria, the bid document concentrated more on the business side of the club than on the playing side. The success of this area of the operation was largely in the hands of the senior management team who, alongside the chairman, comprised Alex Bonney (chief excecutive), David Parr (director) and Sue O'Connor (company secretary).

As mentioned earlier Bonney came to the club having gained great experience in fulfilling similar roles with both the O'Connor and Stobart Groups while Parr brought the benefit of over 20 years managerial experience in local government. Currently Halton's chief executive he has a vital role in the partnership between the club and local authority, who own the stadium and 15% of the new company. Sue O'Connor, a Vikings season ticket holder, had become the Group Legal Director with the O'Connor Group after spending 14 years as a claims director in the insurance industry in the United States.

The commercial department, at the time of the submission, was in the hands of the experienced Mike Banks who had fulfilled similar roles with a variety of leading sporting organisations. Banks was to head up a department charged with promoting the club across the region and maximizing the commercial and marketing opportunities that were produced. The bid document outlined the key areas of responsibility as:

- Increasing match attendances
- Sponsors and Partners
- Fund raising including a new Lottery
- Merchandising and Ticketing initiatives
- Public relations and fan liaison

There had been much talk about successful clubs needing to demonstrate a capability of attracting average attendances of 10,000. Ultimately this was replaced by a 'potential to consistently attract healthy crowds', no doubt due to the fact that very few clubs could realistically achieve that target. There were certainly several 'heartland' clubs currently in Super League who would not achieve that target, never mind the expansion clubs! Nonetheless Widnes were committed to building their fan base to a level that could support a Super League club. With the benchmark of a 3,442 average attendance at the Halton Stadium in 2007 the average 'gate' for the six matches staged at the Stobart Stadium by the time the application was submitted was 3,916 – a healthy increase of 14%. Mike Banks had declared in the bid document that "the aim is to increase fan numbers game-on-game" while he was "targeting a 20% increase on the 2007 figures". While much of the early increase was probably due to the new-found 'feel good factor' surrounding the club the end of season average of 4,146 actually represented an on-target growth of 20.45%. Within these figures the club was also able to claim an increase of 25% in season ticket sales from 1,968 in 2007 to 2,471 for 2008.

It seemed as though the club was well on the way to being able to demonstrate that it could 'consistently attract healthy crowds'.

Further evidence that the dark days were behind them, and that they should be considered as serious contenders for a Super League Licence, came with the significant strides made with finding new sponsors and partners. However, a vital building block was the continued, and formalised, relationship between the club and the local authority. With a failed 'joint venture' company, and a sometimes strained landlord/tenant arrangement behind them, the club's landlords now had a 15% stakeholding in the club, and a representative on the club's board of directors. Such an arrangement could surely only serve to underline the long term viability of Widnes Vikings in the eyes of the RFL.

With no disrespect to those companies, organisations and individuals who had supported the club financially in previous years the headline grabbing arrival of the Stobart Group raised the club's profile immeasurably. The huge logistics group, known throughout the UK and beyond, and the local O'Connor Group had both agreed deals to invest in the future of the club for five years. Part of the Stobart commitment came in the form of a five year naming rights deal for the stadium struck with the council. Not only would Halton Borough Council, and indirectly the club, benefit financially from such a deal, but the Vikings arguably had the highest profile club sponsor in the sport. In addition to these headline deals there were a series of partnerships with other high profile companies including Nike, Carlsberg UK Ltd, Lookers, Hattons Solicitors and Domino's Pizza.

Also highlighted in the bid was the excellent work of the 'Vikings in the Community' scheme under the guidance of the vastly experienced Pat Cluskey. Established in 2002, through funding from both Central and European governments, the community department had expanded from one member of staff to five, and the club took the decision to safeguard its future by forming a Trust, which would allow access to funding available to 'not-for-profit' organisations. Thus the Valhalla Foundation was set up with Cluskey as its chief executive officer in addition to his role as operations manager of the rugby club.

Using players as role models the aim of the community department was to encourage participation in sport while also promoting healthy lifestyles and good citizenship. In partnership with Halton Borough Council, Cheshire Constabulary, Halton Primary Care Trust, Halton Education Department and Riverside College, the Foundation aimed to deliver sporting services to the wider community. This included such activities as helping amateur clubs with fundraising, improving facilities and staff training.

Working across the borough of Halton the Community Coaches were responsible for delivering core-skill sessions to pupils of local Primary schools. As the children developed their skills they progressed to taking part in curtain-raiser matches at the Stobart Stadium, which in turn introduced them and their families to the world of rugby league, and Widnes Vikings in particular. Immediate beneficiaries of the scheme are the local amateur clubs, as children with an aptitude for the sport are directed to them by the community coaches. The benefits to grass-roots rugby league were evidenced by teams from as far afield as Weaverham, Telford and Manchester taking part in the curtain-raisers.

Away from the game of rugby league the Foundation also undertook educational projects with children from nursery to sixth form levels. Key among these were presentations to the borough's secondary schools on topics such as drug awareness, diet and exercise. The club also ran a 'Get Working' initiative which gave valuable advise to students on job searches, writing a CV, completing job application forms and interview techniques. Further work carried out with Primary age pupils presented a novel way of addressing numeracy and literacy. Questions prepared in the classroom were put to a Vikings player with the interview then being written up for submission to the match-day programme. Similarly when the pupils were invited to a match they submitted their own match reports.

Mention was also made of the Vikings Against Bullying project which was another community based initiative carried out in conjunction with schools and the local authority. This new venture saw community staff, players and coaches visiting schools to demonstrate the negative effects of bullying through workshops and assemblies led by the Vikings players.

Complementing the work of the community department was a partnership struck between the club and its near neighbour the Riverside College. Through the partnership under-19s and first team players were able to study for qualifications such as National Diplomas and NVQs in sport. This would allow them the opportunity to go on to university, undertake coaching courses or other careers related to rugby. Courses at the Riverside College Rugby Academy were open to any student, also providing an opportunity for non-players to seek a career in rugby league.

The headline catching sponsorship deal concluded with the Stobart Group certainly caught the imagination of Widnes fans far and wide. It is probably also true that the capture of such a high profile partner, on an initial five year deal, by a club that had only just emerged from Administration raised a few eyebrows outside the immediate area – not least at the RFL headquarters in Leeds.

Described in the bid document as 'one of the world's leading brands with a turnover in excess of £170 million', the logistics giant had already established strong connections with the local area and only served to add weight and sustainability to the Vikings. William Stobart commented:

"We are delighted to have secured a position as main sponsor to Widnes Vikings and to reach agreement with Halton Borough Council for the stadium to be named after our company. We are already a leading employer in Halton and have major plans to develop our warehousing which could create in excess of 1,000 new jobs in Widnes.

While the country's most famous logistics company had made a substantial cash injection to Halton Borough Council, to secure the stadium naming rights, a separate deal was struck with the Vikings which saw the iconic haulier become the club's shirt sponsor. Recognising that "the Vikings are an important part of community life in Halton" Mr Stobart added: "After Steve O'Connor stepped in to guarantee the club's future, following its financial predicament, we felt that placing the Stobart brand alongside the Vikings will help bring the long-term stability that everyone is trying to achieve – and also underpins our commitment to the region."

To strike such a deal was really putting down a marker that the club, under the ownership of Steve O'Connor, was intent on rebuilding and regaining its former status within the game. While O'Connor's connection with Stobarts undoubtedly provided the club with an entrée it still ranks as something of a coup that the deal was pulled off. Not only was the sponsor a major player in their own field but they had demonstrated a strong bond with the area.

Global sports brand Nike came on board to supply the club's new-look kit, while other international brands Domino Pizza and Carlsberg both agreed two-year deals with options for a further three years. The pizza restaurant chain sponsored the new Family Enclosure at the Stobart Stadium while Carlsberg UK's Tetley's brand featured on the team's shorts. Further two-year deals were taken up by Lookers and Hattons Solicitors.

With the club now operating on a sound financial footing combined with its ability to attract such major companies, and on relatively long-term deals, the governing body could surely be in no doubt as to the long-term viability of the business. Or could they?

Possibly the most contentious criteria put forward by the RFL was the issue of stadia being fit for purpose. While there were several grounds in use by existing Super League clubs that could politely be described as 'tired', Ray French was on record as saying of the Stobart Stadium "This place is now a five star and probably the best stadium in rugby league".

As mentioned previously, the fact that the Vikings play in what Steve O'Connor described as a "sensational, genuine community stadium" is due to the Local Authority acting promptly on the recommendations of the *Framing the Future* policy document issued by the RFL in 1994.

Sited in among the houses Naughton Park made Widnes a true community club as it rubbed shoulders with its neighbours, many of whom were also its 'customers'. The modern Stobart Stadium still shares that close-knit sense of community but also provides a range of facilities for the benefit of that community.

The bid document underlined the fact that, in addition to an all-seated capacity of 13,500 on match-days, the stadium boasted a social club, a range of 30 executive boxes, and conference and banqueting facilities available for hire. Furthermore there is a fitness centre, café bar, sports injury clinic and table tennis centre for community use.

Although the stadium had been continually updated by the local authority – who assumed full ownership in 1999 – an improvement programme was commissioned by Steve O'Connor shortly after taking control of the club in November 2007. Completed within a period of 10 weeks the works concentrated on the areas and facilities utilised on a daily basis by players, coaches, administrative staff and the media. Significant among these were new office accommodation, and a physiotherapy treatment room under the North Stand, which also benefitted from an upgraded gym facility. The modernisation of the office accommodation for the 'admin' staff in the South Stand – which also had the added benefit of making the club a more open and accessible environment for supporters –went hand in hand with the provision of up-to-date media facilities.

At the Fans Forum in December 2007 Steve O'Connor had spoken of the use of technology in various areas of the club's operation. Apart from efficiency savings this would also allow the club to gather demographic data of its fan base, which in turn would allow the club to serve those fans better. One such area was ticketing.

The bid document highlighted that 'cash admission' on match-day was a thing of the past at the Stobart Stadium, and had been replaced by a Managed Ticketing Service in conjunction with Access Control software.

Entrance to the stadium was now by ticket only. Season ticket holders were catered for by the issue of a 'smart card' which replaced the book of vouchers, while 'walk up' supporters would need to purchase a ticket instead of paying at the turnstile. The new system allowed for three methods of purchasing that ticket:

- On-line sales through the club website
- Telephoning a dedicated ticket line
- In person at the stadium Ticket Office.

Access was controlled by a new network of data and voice communications which had been installed around the stadium. The key element of this was the installation, at each turnstile, of 'Ticket Reader' equipment which validated each card or barcoded paper ticket prior to granting entry.

In addition to making access into the stadium quicker, through automated turnstiles and removing the need for 'gate' operators to handle cash, the new system would help to provide the club with accurate data on attendance patterns, and other demographic information about its supporters. The latter would be of great value in marketing both the club and individual matches.

The move away from the conventional promotion and relegation to licensing had consigned success on the pitch to a bit part in the 2008 process, although this was later to be redeemed in the 2011 round.

However, having unashamedly made reference to the club's outstanding heritage, it was also acknowledged that the club had been beaten finalists in the Grand Finals of 2006 and 2007, thereby narrowly missing out on automatic promotion back to Super League. Evidence was also presented of the clear pathways that were established for talented, local young players from grass roots level through to professional status.

The key people heading up the 'playing' side of the club were seen to be Terry O'Connor (sporting director), Steve McCormack (head coach) and Stuart Wilkinson (head of youth performance). The role of sporting director was new to the club and Widnes-born Terry O'Connor's responsibilities ranged from working with the senior players to community initiatives. With regard to the senior squad his tasks included player recruitment and player welfare – offering practical support to the players leaving McCormack free to devote his energies to developing the team. Probably the most successful community initiative was the setting up of the partnership with Riverside College.

Working closely with Terry O'Connor was head coach Steve McCormack who had somewhat reluctantly moved on following the Administration saga, only to return once the club had been saved. Although having suffered the disappointment of those two Grand Final defeats – in addition to two previous occasions with Whitehaven – McCormack was the man who had guided the club to its first silverware for several years when they lifted the Northern Rail Cup in 2007. McCormack was also head coach of the Scottish national team that qualified for the 2008 World Cup Finals in Australia.

With a reputation as one of the most knowledgeable people in rugby league in relation to developing young talent the appointment of the vastly experienced Stuart Wilkinson was something of a coup for the club. His CV would show that as well as being assistant coach to the Leeds team that won the 2001 World Club Championship, he was the game's first player performance manager, again at Leeds, and went on to coach the England Academy team prior to being named head coach of the Welsh national side.

The document went on to demonstrate the structures in place to support the playing side of the club, by highlighting the other staff, full and part-time, who made great contributions to the successful running of the football operation.

Key among these was John Stankevitch who in addition to being assistant coach and conditioner to the first team was also head coach of the club's reserve team. Former player Stankevitch had returned to the club, where he had a previous spell as assistant coach, having left to take on the role of head coach at Doncaster.

Complementing the work of the full-time coaching staff was Dave Banks who, on a part-time basis, was head coach to the Junior Academy side. Banks had been recruited from Wigan Warriors where he combined the role of performance analyst with that of assistant coach to their Senior Academy side. Banks' experience also included membership of the RFL's World Class Performance Programme from 2000 to 2006.

In any sporting organisation there are the so-called 'backroom' roles which are necessary to its successful operation. The bid document again demonstrated that the Vikings were well served in this area with Sam Whiteson (physio), Karen Jones (assistant physio) and Kath Perten (first team doctor) with Paul Hansbury filling the role of equipment manager.

Specialising in sports physiotherapy Sam Whiteson, a graduate of Liverpool University, brought a wealth of experience to the role having worked in private practice and with both the Sale Sharks and North of England Under-18 rugby union teams. She was supported on a part-time basis by Karen Jones, a musculoskeletal physiotherapist with Warrington Primary Care Trust, who had worked within the Academy set up for seven years. The medical team was completed by Dr Kath Perten, recently appointed as first team doctor after a number of years covering academy games.

These are roles often taken for granted, but none more so perhaps, than that of the 'kit man' or equipment manager. Having worked for the club for over 20 years Paul Hansbury has the responsibility of ensuring that the appropriate kit and equipment is available for training sessions and matches alike. Not only that, his responsibilities also extend to the Reserve and Academy teams.

The bid document was also able to highlight a string of endorsements from a variety of high profile senior players demonstrating a clear desire among other clubs to see the Vikings return to Super League. Extracts of their comments are reproduced below:

> Not many sides can say they have been World Club Champions. With a great stadium and strong fan base they certainly merit a place in Super League. **– Danny Orr**

> Widnes Vikings and Salford are traditional heartlands of rugby league and both clubs would bring an added dimension to the Super League. **– Adrian Morley**

> Having Vikings back in Super League is vital. The name Widnes is famous in rugby league circles throughout the world and has produced some of the best rugby players we've seen. **– Jason Robinson MBE**

> Widnes have a fine stadium, strong supporter base, and very good overall facilities. Around the Widnes region there are many fine amateur clubs with a wealth of talent at grass roots level. **– Kevin Sinfield**

> I would much rather see Widnes Vikings in Super League than a Licence go to a region where there is no amateur structure in place. There are many amateur clubs in and around Widnes that are the lifeblood of rugby league. **– Lee Radford**

> A club steeped in such tremendous rugby league heritage as Widnes should be granted a Licence. They have a superb stadium with excellent facilities and a crop of exciting young players. **– Paul Cooke**

> Playing a local derby against Widnes is always a great occasion. They have a fantastic stadium and a great fan base and these both count for a great deal under the new set up. **– Paul Sculthorpe**

> I'm a Wigan lad and I know Wigan fans would love to see Widnes in Super League. The whole set up at Widnes is Super League standard and it would be great to see them back in the top league. **– Terry Newton**

> Super League would be at a loss if they did not include such a great club. The club has a lot of community spirit and they seem to bring in enough crowds to fulfil the requirements of a Super League club. **– Jamie Peacock**

Even to an impartial eye the quality and depth of this bid must have demonstrated the great strides made by the club under its new owner. At the time of Terry O'Connor's appointment Steve O'Connor's comments included the following:

"At the outset I made it clear we would transform this club by introducing experienced business professionals to work alongside talented and successful people from the world of rugby league. Terry O'Connor is ideally placed to help us achieve our goals of securing the long-term future of this club and mounting a successful campaign to win one of the coveted Super League Licences."

The chairman had clearly lived up to his promise and put in place a structure which would enable the club to move forward, both on and off the pitch. If there was one single message to come out of the bid document it was that Widnes Vikings circa 2008 was a well organised, well run, forward looking club with firm foundations. This together with its heritage would surely make it a valued member of the Super League competition.

With the club saved and the bid duly submitted Widnes fans breathed the rarified air of optimism and were surely entitled to 'Dare to Dream'.

The Outcome

Finally the day came that all Widnes fans had been anxiously waiting for – Tuesday 22nd July 2008. Arriving in Widnes that morning there was a sea of black and white as fans made their way to the stadium to hear the outcome of the inaugural award of Super League Licences.

I was fortunate enough to be invited to the club offices to hear the announcement made in the company of Steve O'Connor and his management team, Steve McCormack and his players, club staff and sponsors. As we gathered there was an excited air of anticipation in the general hubbub of confident conversations taking place around the room. Players were looking forward to pitting their wits against the so-called elite of their profession, Steve McCormack was looking for a second crack at coaching at the top level and Steve O'Connor dreamt of taking this giant of a club back to where he believed it belonged. While, no doubt, chief executive Alex Bonney and sponsors had half an eye on increased exposure and revenue streams there was one common desire – to see the Vikings readmitted to Super League on the back of the giant strides made in such a short time under Steve O'Connor's stewardship.

Eventually the room fell quiet as Sky TV's presentation of the live announcement began. After what seemed an eternity of pre-amble RFL executive chairman Richard Lewis got down to the business of the day and announced the names of the 14 clubs who had been awarded Licences for 2009-11.

By virtue of the fact that the clubs were announced alphabetically, Widnes officials, players and supporters who had 'Dared to Dream', gradually saw that dream fade and finally disappear.

There were no surprises as the names of Bradford Bulls, Castleford Tigers and Catalan Dragons tripped off Lewis' tongue. There was then an audible intake of breath as we waited for the next club to be named. This could well be a defining moment, and so it proved as the words 'Celtic Crusaders' were released from Lewis' mouth. Shoulders dropped and eyes rolled, accompanied by a collective groan as at this early stage the writing appeared to be on the wall.

There was still some hope as the next name to be announced was that of Harlequins which meant that both Featherstone and Halifax were unsuccessful. The fans of Huddersfield Giants, Hull FC, Hull KR and Leeds Rhinos were the next to be put out of their misery (as if there were any doubt). Near neighbours Leigh Centurions were overlooked which appeared to leave Widnes in a battle with two further clubs who were being touted as 'expansionist' – Salford and French outfit Toulouse.

As Lewis announced the name of Salford City Reds a disbelieving audience realised that the writing was finally on the wall, and that would be it for a further three years. There remained only the remote possibility that Wakefield Trinity would fall by the wayside, but that was not to be the case.

Disbelief gave way to silence closely followed by anger and, in some cases, tears as crestfallen staff, players and guests were numbed by the outcome.

Although she was not originally planning to go the club offices for the announcement Clare O'Connor stood shoulder to shoulder with husband Steve, "in support of all the work put in, by a lot of people", as the news came through. Looking back to that day she remembers being "confident" of success and the room having "an air of optimism. It was buzzing. It was exciting. I can clearly remember watching everybody as the names were read out and the silence was overwhelming when Wakefield's name was announced. It probably only lasted for three seconds but it seemed to go on forever. I cried and felt empty.

"Steve was upset but held his own counsel while he thought things through. He felt guilty. He had asked people to 'Dare to Dream'; had built their hopes up and felt that he had let them down." In fact so upset and disappointed was the Vikings' owner that Mrs O'Connor admitted to me that he had "made himself ill in the days that followed by working until the early hours in search of how to put things right".

With the benefit of hindsight it would appear that those fans who felt that Celtic Crusaders were a shoo-in from day one were right. For my part I was also nervous of the Salford bid, based solely on the number of occasions that their sudden re-location into Greater Manchester had been put forward in support of their bid!

But no one would have felt the disappointment more than Steve O'Connor who had put so much time, effort and no little money into getting the Vikings back to the top. Minutes after gathering his thoughts the chairman joined the army of 500-plus disappointed fans who had watched the announcement in the adjoining social club, to make an emotional declaration of his intent to carry on and see the Vikings in Super League in three years' time.

Shortly after the announcement had been made the RFL issued a statement via its website which included the following seemingly self-congratulatory comment:

'The RFL today announced that the 12 existing top flight clubs have been awarded three-year Licences together with Celtic Crusaders and Salford City Reds. It means, for the first time in the competition's 13 year history, that Wales will have its own Super League side, in the Bridgend based Crusaders, as well as a presence in England's second largest conurbation, the cities of Salford and Manchester, through the Salford City Reds.

'The decision to award Licences to Celtic and Salford also means that the engage Super League will have a greater geographical footprint than ever before from 2009. Games will be played in England, France, Scotland – following confirmation last week that the Magic Weekend will be held in Murrayfield next May – and Wales.'

In my view this was yet another indication that the outcome had been a foregone conclusion with the governing body hell-bent on so-called expansion of the game into Wales and the mythical move into Greater Manchester. It is also fair to say that those with far greater experience of the politics of the game than me were apparently proved right when they had said that there was no possibility of the governing body jettisoning a current Super League club. Despite a handful of clubs apparently failing to meet some of the most basic criteria they were welcomed back into the Super League family at the expense of ambitious and successful clubs who had 'put their house in order.'

To grant a Super League Licence to Celtic Crusaders, a club that had only been playing professional rugby league for two years at the time, seemed to me to be inviting a repeat of the doomed Paris experiment. This was ultimately shown to be true when after three turbulent years they withdrew their 2011 application at the eleventh hour, folded and were reinvented in 2012 back in Championship One as North Wales Crusaders. Even without the benefit of hindsight this appeared to be yet another example of the RFL indulging in revolution rather than evolution.

I also found it surprising that while the RFL's criteria included attendances and financial turnover they had engineered a position whereby existing clubs would effectively see their average attendances and match-day income reduced. The 14 team league now included three clubs with, at best, modest home 'gates' and next to no travelling support which would obviously impact on other clubs' finances. In turn the away support travelling to London, Perpignan and Bridgend would add very little value to the matchday experience, or turnover, of those clubs.

Richard Lewis commented at the time that the RFL were "once again being innovative and leading the way in British sport by implementing a licensing system that will improve standards both on and off the field in the elite competition," adding that "Licensing has already served to galvanise the sport, stimulating clubs into addressing the issues of facility improvements, spectator comfort and the production of more players.

"Licensing will undoubtedly help us to create great clubs whose athletes produce terrific contests, played out in modern facilities in front of large crowds.

"A three-year Licence provides an environment whereby clubs will be able to look long term, giving them a sounder base to invest off the field as well as on it. This will lead to improvements in stadiums, training facilities and club management as well as the production of junior players who will be given greater opportunity to play first team rugby."

While conceding that licensing offers, through its three-year term, the opportunity for clubs to rid themselves of short-term, boom or bust planning in favour of longer term development and stability, I personally think it was far too early to make such grand claims. There was still a high proportion of overseas players operating in Super League and, as the RFL admitted in their bid assessments (see Appendix III), several clubs who were still operating in sub-standard stadia.

When the dust had settled it became apparent that the Widnes' financial record under the previous ownership had been their downfall, with the RFL's executive chairman Richard Lewis conceding that it was a "fundamental problem" that counted against them in the Licensing process. He further admitted that the decision of the previous owners to put the club into Administration was a "significant" fact that affected the RFL's decision, adding that "it was a hugely difficult scenario".

Looking forward to the next round of licensing Lewis added "The clubs with sub-standard stadia do need to do something about their facilities. The goalposts will change, and standards next time will be higher. The clubs need to have much more solid plans and proposals than they have now. The battle for Licences in 2012 will be much tougher than it was this year".

Unfortunately these proved to be largely empty words as Super League kicked off in 2012 with two clubs still awaiting the go-ahead on new stadia, and others struggling to update existing grounds.

As the announcement was dissected by an eager media corps it became known that Steve O'Connor had offered to lodge £500,000 in a bond with the RFL to underwrite the Vikings financial future if a Licence was awarded.

O'Connor revealed that "To reassure the RFL I offered to put half a million pounds of my own money, in cash, into a bond to guarantee that we could see out the three years. The only stipulation was that I was able to have the interest.

"We were led to believe that 'solvency' referred to the future and not the past, and the £500,000 should have given them comfort. We seem to be paying for the sins of our fathers.

"We feel our bid was one of the strongest so we are bitterly disappointed. In our bid we outlined our intention to spend to the full salary cap limit, and I'm not sure that goes for all of the other clubs that have got in. We feel that we would have contributed an awful lot to the competition, and there is a real sense of loss here."

Five days after the announcement he addressed the fans at half-time in the match against Dewsbury. Following a rousing reception he offered this reassurance to the fans:

"Over the next three years I'm determined to stay. I'm determined to make something happen. Furthermore, it is our intention, whether or not we're the only club in the National League, to be operating as a full-time club. By the time we make it to Super League we will have learnt how to be successful, and how to understand the quality of our success. I'd be really pleased if you'll all come along with me."

Having opted, unlike some of his counterparts, for the dignified and conciliatory approach to the club's rejection, the Vikings' chairman had set up an early meeting with the RFL "to meet the decision makers with a view to developing a new relationship". O'Connor, along with Alex Bonney, Terry O'Connor and Pat Cluskey, duly met with Richard Lewis, RFL chief executive Nigel Wood, and RFL lawyer Rod Findlay.

Steve O'Connor continued: "It was essential to get around the table with the RFL as quickly as possible to discover the reasoning behind our failure to secure a Super League Licence this time around.

"The RFL has recognised that, in the period since my management team and I took over the operation, our organisational performance rates among the best in the league.

"It would appear that the Licence process came just too early for our new set-up. Unfortunately our impressive track record is only eight months old and this was not an appropriate length of time for the RFL to be satisfied of our long-term stability, despite the financial guarantees I gave to underwrite our bid.

"If we want Super League here, then there has to be a meeting of minds. By the time we left the Rugby League I genuinely believe, and so do the people with me, that the Rugby League had a different perception of Widnes on Friday afternoon than they did on Friday morning."

The Widnes chairman added that he thought the RFL were taken aback by the backlash to its decision, and the "fantastic" support the Vikings had received from the media and other rugby league clubs. It seemed as though the majority of the rugby league media were genuinely shocked at the club's exclusion, while many high profile players, and members of the wider rugby league community, were happy to indicate their surprise in interviews or column inches.

The *Viking Storm* for that Dewsbury match naturally devoted several pages to the reaction and repercussions of the news that the Vikings had again been denied a place in the top flight. The chairman took the opportunity to fully explain his thoughts about the issue in his programme notes, which merit repeating here in full:

"Tuesday July 22nd 2008 ranks as one of the most disappointing days of my life. I truly believed we had put together an irresistible case to the Rugby League for one of the coveted 14 Super League Licences. I felt our application carried far more weight than several of the existing Super League teams, let alone those of fellow applicants from Co-Operative National League One.

We had been told by the 'powers-that-be' at the RFL that we would be notified by e-mail shortly before the formal announcement was broadcast 'live' on Sky Sports News. I deliberately refrained from opening that e-mail, preferring to listen to the news as it was delivered by the RFL – at exactly the same time as our fans learned of the decision.

Players, officials, directors, staff, local media representatives and Sky Sports packed into Vikings' club room to watch the drama unfold on TV. A large number of our fans gathered together to hear the news from the Social Club at Stobart Stadium Halton.

As Castleford Tigers, closely followed by Celtic Crusaders, was announced my heart began to sink. When Salford's name was read out by RFL chairman Richard Lewis, the writing was well and truly on the wall for Widnes Vikings. The game was finally up when Wakefield Wildcats secured their slot in Super League next season.

Mr Lewis's announcement was greeted with a stunned and eerie silence in the room. My emotions were a mixture of shock, surprise and disbelief. I sincerely felt we had put a compelling case for our inclusion in Super League and honestly thought our application would be among the top ten – let alone the top 14!

As we all know, we live in a world of 24/7 instant news. Before being able to really take in the enormity of the decision, I was thrust into a whirlwind of TV, radio, and newspaper interviews after quickly addressing those devastated supporters in the Social Club.

Although we are still analysing why we failed in our bid and assessing how we move forward, it was vitally important for me to reassure all our fans and everyone connected to the club that, devastatingly disappointing as this is, I am determined to remain at the helm and continue to lead the campaign to secure Widnes Vikings' rightful place in Super League.

I came here in November last year with a mission to transform this great club and lead it into Super League. I intend to complete the job that I've started. It is important that our fans are reassured that I am fully committed to Widnes Vikings.

When I took over the club last November I told supporters I was in for the long haul – and I meant that. I believe we put together a very strong application, despite the fact we were working against the backdrop of a club that had gone into Administration under previous ownership. That was a fact of life, a big negative for us that at the end of the day may have been the deciding factor in our application being rejected.

My management team has made sterling efforts over the past eight months to re-organise this club and turn it into an organisation we felt would complement, and indeed would be an asset to Super League. We now need to take stock of the situation and discover why our application was rejected and where we go from here.

I do support the logic behind the new licensing system and hope that the new look Super League flourishes. I don't wish to comment on the rights and wrongs of the decision process but hope that all those candidates that were successful fully deliver on the promises contained in their application documents. I'm in absolutely no doubt that Widnes Vikings would have fully delivered on the aspirations contained in our application.

Should any Super League team fail to meet the criteria set down by the RFL at any stage over the next three years, rest assured Widnes Vikings will be ready, willing and able to replace them!

I do know how much our fans are hurting right now. I made no secret when I took over last year that my first love is football but I have quickly developed an affection for rugby league and most importantly a deep affection and respect for Widnes Vikings. It's a club with a great heritage and an exciting future at the very top level of the game.

My aspirations today are exactly the same as when I addressed the first fans' forum on December 6th last year. I promised to put Vikings on a secure financial footing with the business run by experienced professionals and with highly skilled and knowledgeable rugby people taking care of the playing side. We've done precisely that.

To achieve the ultimate goal of Super League, we still need to demonstrate to the RFL that we can generate support in large numbers here at Widnes Vikings. That is still very much a critical element. Our record National League One attendance against Salford earlier this season proved that we can fill this stadium. Next season it will be as important as ever to turn out and support your team in National League One.

On Tuesday disappointed fans were singing: 'We're Widnes 'til we die, We're Widnes 'til we die'! Is that just a song or do you mean it? Are you with us for the next three years? I'm in for the long haul…I hope you are all with me. Let's prove to the RFL that Super League without Widnes Vikings will be a poorer place."

Further reaction from within the club included the following from a "gutted" Terry O'Connor. "To say I'm disappointed is a massive understatement. I was so confident beforehand and I'm very surprised we are not in there. My 'phone has been ringing off the hook ever since from the likes of Wigan, Saints, Bradford and Leeds, saying they couldn't believe the outcome."

An indication of how far the club had come, and how confident they had been, was demonstrated when O'Connor confirmed that "we were in talks with Brett Kimmorley and Michael Crocker – two Test players – and they showed a big interest in coming to Widnes".

Referring to previous disappointments the former Salford, Wigan and Widnes prop forward added "It has happened before in 1996 and again in 2005 when I was still playing we got relegated despite finishing 11th. Tuesday's news is quite hard to take but we have to pull together and try to move forward."

Meanwhile skipper Mark Smith, on behalf of the players, offered this balanced view: "We are devastated about the decision but we have to stay together as a group and move forward. We have a quality coach in Steve McCormack, and an excellent chairman who has backed the club and made it what it is now, so we do have a lot to shout about.

"That doesn't mean that the players aren't upset over what has happened, as we are, but the situation isn't as bad as last year. We were in a worse place last season."

While conceding that "Licensing is the new way forward" Gary McGrath – 'the voice of the Vikings' – added, in that same edition of the *Viking Storm* that "in all honesty I would have to say that this is the lowest of lows that I've experienced in my time at the club, and surely it must rank as one of the club's darkest days too."

Like many observers McGrath felt that this licensing process seemed to be all about expansion, suggesting that Celtic Crusaders provided the RFL with "an opportunity too good to miss" for expansion into Wales. Similarly Salford provided the "chance to get the Manchester 'market' to embrace the game". Sharing the hurt felt by all connected with the club McGrath concluded that "It's important that, as fans, we all keep our heads up and even though it won't be against the likes of St Helens or Leeds Rhinos next year, you will see some extremely exciting games between Widnes and whoever their opponents are on any given day, in National League One."

While the focus of head coach Steve McCormack had to turn almost immediately to playing matters he admitted that Super League rejection was a "nail through the heart", adding "we were all convinced we'd get a Licence. There are not 14 better applications than ours so when we heard the news everyone was devastated."

"We are all going through a lot of mixed emotions at the moment; anger, disappointment, frustration and just a feeling of where did we go wrong? That will be with us for a few days but we have to crack on and move forward. The way I see it now is that it's the beginning of a new era at Widnes Vikings."

Echoing the dignified reaction of his chairman McCormack continued: "We must take this situation and make it into a positive and build on it from there. A lot has been said about our application and I know it deserved Super League status. We have a fantastic club here with brilliant fans and they deserved to make it to the top flight. We are in National League for three years and we will prepare accordingly."

While some observers could just about understand the award of a Licence, in the name of expansion, to Celtic Crusaders there were others, including regular *Viking Storm* columnist Paul Cook, who failed to see the logic of granting a Licence to Salford City Reds. Cook seemingly shared my conviction that Salford had always been part of the mancunian sprawl when he offered this: "The RFL are taking plenty on trust in Salford's aim to build support across the wider Manchester sub-region which hasn't exactly embraced rugby league in vast numbers before.

"The RFL has opted for a 'jam tomorrow' bid in choosing the City Reds because they can't possibly expect anything to change in the short term. We'll have to wait until Salford's three-year Super League Licence is up until they can demonstrate the facilities at their proposed new stadium and, once it's built, it's unlikely they will fail to get readmitted.

As it turned out this really was some leap of faith by the RFL as Salford's new stadium did not receive planning approval from the City Council until 19th August 2010 – more than two years after being granted their Licence – and even then it was a scaled down version of the original application and was subject to referral to the Secretary of State for final approval.

Adding a somewhat external view, Councillor Tony McDermott MBE speaking on behalf of the club's major partner Halton Borough Council, was quick to point out that he felt that not only the club, but also the community and the borough, had been let down by the RFL's decision. He explained "This is an extremely disappointing decision for the people of Halton, Widnes and all true rugby league fans. Widnes Vikings are at the heart of much of the council's community activities.

"The issue of Administration was there but in my opinion it's what Steve O'Connor, his team and the council have done since then [that should count].

"I find it hard to understand how the Rugby Football League has arrived at this decision. We now need to take a little time to digest this and will be in close dialogue with the Vikings over the next few days as we look to the future."

It was not only the 'Vikings' of today that were feeling the hurt. That feeling was also shared by several former 'greats' from the era of the 'Chemics'. When asked his opinion of the situation Jim Mills had this to say:

"I felt Widnes should have been in this time. I, like many people in the rugby league world, could not believe the decision, I feel the club is very well run and the ground is as good as any. It's very hard to think how the Rugby League came to that decision, especially when you look at some of the grounds in Super League. If you're going to call it Super League let's have some super grounds for a start. I think it is a good step to give the new clubs three years to get established, that's one of the problems Widnes have had in past years."

Speaking about the licensing system in general Eric Hughes struck a chord with many traditionalists when he added "I don't like it at all. It's fine for the ones who are in, but what of the ambitious clubs like Widnes and Leigh who have great stadia and ambition? British supporters believe in promotion and relegation!"

While Stuart Wright restricted himself to describing the decision as "a disgrace" and Mick George called it "unbelievable", another former 'black and white' hero, Keith Elwell, had this to say:

"The franchise system is fine for the game, but god help it if Sky ever withdraw their money. I, like every true Widnesian, was incensed that Widnes did not get a place in Super League, especially when it emerges that Wakefield and Salford now can't build their new stadia, and Celtic have a fan base of about 250. Who made the choices? Who next? Toulouse?"

There was also support for the Vikings' cause from further afield, when in January 2009, the recently retired Paul Sculthorpe looked back at the licensing issue. He told the *Widnes Weekly News*: "There have been numerous Widnes fans at my testimonial 'dos' who've come along to shake my hand and have a chat – probably more than from any other club apart from Saints.

"There's obviously a great rugby league following in the town and it's a shame they won't have a Super League team to shout for this season. I couldn't believe it when Widnes were left out, to be honest. I was genuinely shocked then, and it's still difficult to get your head round now. They've got a good fan base, an excellent ground and seem to be on a solid financial footing.

"I've been to Widnes and had a look at the set-up and it's obviously one of the best in the game. If you add in all the history and tradition, you can't ask for much more."

However, typical of the resilient approach of the Vikings, chairman Steve O'Connor said "You learn more about your organisation when you share difficult moments, and we're keen that what doesn't kill us will make us stronger."

He told Gareth Walker of *Rugby League World* "We're pleased for the clubs that have made it because we know how we would have felt if that would have been us. It's in our interest that the game's new system works because it allows for more robust business plans. We always had a Plan B and at the moment we're still unravelling and reflecting, but at the same time we wish the clubs that have got in all the best."

As Steve O'Connor had observed, the RFL seemed to be genuinely surprised by the amount of condemnation, from all quarters, of their decision to omit the Vikings. Not only did members of the media express their surprise but the 'Letters' pages of the trade papers were full of fans from a variety of clubs offering criticism of the decision and praise of Widnes' cause in equal measure.

However, there was one dissenting voice, that of Martyn Sadler of the *League Express*. Even then Sadler's argument was based more on 'moral' grounds than anything to do with rugby league or the published criteria. In his editorial comment he justified his stance by stating 'I can't think of any sporting organisation in the world that would reward a club for defaulting on its debts', and cites the cases of Leeds United and Luton Town to support his argument.

I would have to challenge the emotional language of 'rewarding a club for defaulting'. In Widnes' case they had been given a nine point deduction, to take effect for the 2008 season, in line with existing RFL operational rules for entering Administration. One offence, one penalty. Nowhere within those rules did it ever say that if such a club overcame the points deduction, qualified for the play-offs and won the Grand Final that they could not be promoted (or awarded a Super League Licence). In Widnes' case they committed one offence and received two punishments – hardly justice.

The analogies with Leeds United and Luton Town are similarly flawed. The Football League handed down 'points deductions' to both clubs which ultimately led to them both being relegated. However, the footballing authorities did not seek to prevent the rehabilitation of those clubs by excluding them from promotion for three seasons.

Take the situation away from the emotion of professional sport for a moment and it is easier to see the flaw in Sadler's argument. Take the case of your debt-ridden local garage going into Administration. You would not expect the new owners to be prevented from trading as they see fit, or be indignant if they flourished. Neither would they be penalised for the mis-management of the previous owners. In the case of the garage the service provided is the maintenance and repair of vehicles; for Widnes it is the provision of entertainment through rugby matches. Surely the liability is with the defaulting owners not the service or product that they provide!

On the positive side Sadler did however, state that "since Steve O'Connor became the owner of the Vikings at the end of 2007 they have probably become a stronger club than some clubs that have been awarded Super League Licences." He also paid tribute to the "superb stadium" and "junior talent" before identifying another reason why the club had failed. He pointed out that as the "new company has existed for just less than nine months it hasn't yet posted any audited accounts." However, limited research has shown that at least one longer-established club failed to submit the required accounts, but had still secured a Super League Licence!

Interestingly Richard de la Riviere, editor of the sister publication *Rugby League World*, put forward this more balanced observation:

"As for Widnes, the decision to exclude them on the basis that they went into administration last year wasn't right for me. It's fair enough for the licensing process to suggest that a club recently in administration should be at a disadvantage, but each case should be judged on its own merits.

"Under its present regime, and putting geography to one side, Widnes looked to be by far and away the strongest applicant with the best chance of building a strong Super League club from those currently outside the elite 12."

The reaction of fans to such disappointment is by definition more emotive than that of scribes and commentators, but there was a strong consensus among those fans who took the trouble to put their concerns in writing to the trade press. That consensus was that the RFL had got it wrong.

Such was the level of dissatisfaction and, dare I say, distrust of the governing body caused by the outcome of the licensing process, that there were even calls from some quarters for the National Leagues to form a breakaway organisation.

One correspondent highlighted the fact that Richard Lewis had admitted that "a lot of momentum has built up [in Wales]. It felt like the right time [for a Super League Club in Wales]". He then posed the question "which area of the criteria does this fall under?" The somewhat surprising answer came via the columns of *League Weekly*.

We were led to believe that there were set criteria that clubs would be assessed against, but in the debrief that followed it became apparent that that was not necessarily the case. One alarming comment came from Nigel Wood when he told Danny Lockwood of *League Weekly* that "one danger was to be too scientific, too analytical and too objective, and you almost lose control of the process because everything has a score. We tried to plot a path between a sound analytical assessment while retaining an overall feel and flavour."

He received support from Richard Lewis who added that "It was certainly analysed and looked at in great detail. It was also backed up by strategy that dates back to 2005, so it was based on those discussions. In the end it had to come down to a matter of opinion." He continued "there were more good applications than there were spots. So in the end it came down to a matter of opinion, but the RFL board was unanimous in its decision."

Not for the first time comment from the governing body posed more questions than it answered as talk of the 'number of spots' was plainly at odds with Lewis' statement, earlier in the process, that "although it is anticipated that Super League in 2009 will have 14 teams there is no upper limit on membership."

If a decision is not objective it surely becomes subjective. I personally feel that if you are deciding the fate of multi-million pound businesses on "a matter of opinion" you are in grave danger of doing a great disservice to that business and its customers.

At no point in the long build up to the whole process was it ever mentioned that 'we will use our scoring system to rank the clubs and then decide who the best 14 are based on a matter of opinion!' As John Lawless in that *Viking Storm* article, and other writers, had pointed out there was great scope for 'draws' within a scoring system that was black or white with no shades of grey. Worryingly there was never a mention of how that highly likely situation would be resolved. The comments above from messrs Lewis and Wood may have explained that void, but they certainly did give birth to a host of conspiracy theories.

While trying hard to dismiss bias and the various conspiracy theories I find it difficult to understand some of the reasoning, and anomalies, in the governing body's decision. Was it, after all, a waste of time and money? I think for all clubs, especially those that were unsuccessful, Lewis's comment that "In the end it had to come down to a matter of opinion" suggests that talk of criteria was only so much smoke and mirrors.

It is my understanding that Widnes met more of the criteria than some of the successful clubs but seemed to be excluded, at least in part, because of the administration issue. Here again the RFL seem to want it both ways. They used the misdemeanours of the previous owners to penalise the Widnes bid, yet the club were not allowed to claim credit for the production of young players such as Richie Myler and Adam Sidlow – because they came through under the previous regime!

Several letters in the trade press had resonance with the RFL's self-confessed talk of 'strategy' in the decision making process. While most criticised the RFL for 'propping up' clubs like Harlequins, Catalan Dragons and Celtic Crusaders and turning its back on the heartland clubs, cases were made for clubs like Leigh, Halifax and Widnes as having 'first class grounds' yet they were overlooked in favour of clubs who were now 'planning' new grounds. While conceding that Licences should not be awarded on the issue of stadia alone Leigh and Widnes would surely have matched, or surpassed some of the successful clubs across several of the criteria. One correspondent went on to point out that in the case of Widnes they had also shown the way to the rest of the rugby league world in terms of innovation – 'swipe card season tickets, state of the art IT suite, a great museum and a matchday programme (the *Viking Storm*) that is second to none'.

Recognising the apparent futility of the whole saga another who put pen to paper was moved to make the following eminently sensible suggestion: "If Red Hall's gambit is to expand the game in the provinces, especially rugby union provinces, then put a separate pot of money forward to facilitate that, and let a genuine fan-base grow with the game of rugby league. Then and only then can we consider amalgamating one or some of these clubs into our highest level of competition."

The exemplary logic of this argument is at complete odds with my contention that the RFL's expansionist policy is one of revolution rather than evolution. Over time the governing body has inserted Fulham (London Broncos/Harlequins RL/London Broncos), Paris St Germain, Catalan Dragons and Celtic Crusaders into the elite competition.

Of these only Catalan Dragons can be said to have been a success, and even then it took them three years to establish themselves. But at least the club had the benefit of having been operating in the French league, as Union Treiziste Catalane, for some time.

The London club – under any guise – despite financial assistance from the RFL and relaxed 'quota' regulations still struggles to establish itself as a meaningful member of the top division, and continues to attract attendances that are frequently bettered by some clubs in the second tier.

While the Parisian outfit folded after just one season the 'Welsh experiment' did manage to survive in Super League for three troubled seasons before folding – again with the benefit of a dramatically inflated quota of overseas players. After a good turnout for their opening fixture in 2009 attendances fell away alarmingly, and after many false dawns the club opted to withdraw, at the last minute, its application to renew its Licence for 2012-14. Again this was a club that had received a level of assistance from the governing body not made available to struggling clubs in the heartlands.

I would venture to suggest that if the Paris, London, and Bridgend clubs had had the benefit of growing in a sustained development programme, rather than being rushed into the top tier, they would have been a lot better for it. What grows gradually by putting down strong roots is far more likely to survive. And in that vein I believe that Hemel Stags – admitted to Championship One for 2013 after 30 years in the amateur ranks – will prove that point convincingly.

The general mood of dissatisfaction and frustration among fans was, I think, summed up by the following question posed in a letter from Blackpool. "Why set a series of criteria that they are not going to follow?"

Shortly after the fuss had died down there was another announcement, indirectly linked to the licensing debate, when the RFL confirmed that Toulouse Olympique had accepted an invitation to join National League One from 2009 while being handed an exemption from relegation for the first three seasons. The fact that this would see them safely through to the next round of Licence applications was seized upon by many as an indication of awarding 'preferred bidder' status to the French club for the next round of Licence applications in 2011.

According to the RFL's website the French club had accepted an invitation from their National Federation, on behalf of the British governing body, to be a part of the RFL's 'strategy to develop and enhance the Co-operative National League competition'.

RFL chief executive Nigel Wood said at the time "We believe their presence in the league will have significant benefits for the competition and its member clubs as well as Toulouse themselves. Offering a place to a French club will also support the continued development and progress of the French national side and of rugby league in the country".

Wood's comments did little to placate rugby league followers in this country who were finding it hard to comprehend the RFL's role in developing the sport in a foreign land. This had caused much debate, particularly among Widnes supporters, when the Catalan Dragons were admitted to Super League in 2006, but the logic of applying this philosophy at National League level was totally lost on the vast majority of the paying public. In support of this expansion programme the governing body had repeatedly pointed out that this area of France (Perpignan and Toulouse) was a hot-bed of rugby. This begged the question then as to why those clubs needed to join our competition. This was a question that was, in my opinion, never satisfactorily answered.

One thing for sure was that this development would ensure yet more debate, controversy, claim and counterclaim among fans and the clubs seeking admission to Super League for 2012-14.

However, in fairness to the Toulouse club, I can say that in my experience they were welcoming, professional and well organised. Sadly three years down the line they withdrew to their domestic league. Despite reports in the trade press that this was because the RFL baulked at the continued cost of travel subsidies, paid both to Toulouse and the English clubs, a representative of the Toulouse club told me that it was in fact due to pressure from the French Rugby League for them to return to the French Elite competition. With Toulouse being a big city the return of such an important club to its domestic competition was seen as a big boost for that competition. Looking back on their time in the Co-operative Championship it is true that while they struggled in their final year, despite reaching the quarter-finals of the Northern Rail Cup, it should be remembered that they only narrowly missed out on the play-offs in 2009 and 2010, when their average attendance of over 2,500 was higher than most clubs in that league.

In the meantime, with the full support of the French Rugby League and its President, Nicolas Larrat, the Toulouse club is working towards its goal of entering Super League in 2015, while keeping a reserve team in the French Championship.

CHAPTER SIX
Development and Disappointment

While 22nd July 2008 would rank among the lowest points in the club's modern history there had remained in the months before, and the weeks after, a group of players trying to win rugby matches, to claim the ultimate on-field prize of a place in, and winning, the Grand Final.

That group of players was hastily put together by head coach Steve McCormack upon his surprise return to the club following Steve O'Connor's takeover. Starting with just the 'Famous Five' McCormack embarked on a recruitment drive in an attempt to give the Vikings a squad capable of challenging the best and to achieve some level of success.

However, the flip-side of the loyalty of the 'Famous Five' meant that McCormack had to deal with the departure of 25 players who had seen first team duty in 2007 – several weeks after most clubs had completed their squad building. The fact that he did so, and produced a team that played some fine attacking rugby for large parts of the campaign, is testament to his ability.

While the inconsistent early-season performances may have in part been due to assembling virtually a completely new squad there was a certain unity within the ranks as the season wore on. This may have had its roots in a siege mentality to overcome recent events but a pre-season camp may also have proved its worth. While athletes and footballers typically go away to glamorous 'warm weather' training camps the Vikings of 2008 had to make do with a few days secreted away at the Whinfell Forest Centre Parcs resort near Penrith!

Cajoled, encouraged and, no doubt, barked at by the coaching staff, the players had, as McCormack put it, had the joint benefits of "using a local all-weather surface for skills and tactical sessions, and experiencing a number of team building activities including paintballing, obstacle courses and high-rope climbing exercises".

"The facilities were first-class and the players certainly worked extremely hard. It was really important for me to bring the squad together and build the team spirit which is such a vital ingredient of any successful sports team. It was also useful to work on a superb all-weather surface at a time when pitches are completely sodden with all the rain."

While the influx of players grabbed the headlines an equally important addition was made to the coaching structure as Stuart Wilkinson became the club's first head of youth performance.

On his appointment Wilkinson offered the following: "My knowledge of Rugby League Services locally, regionally and nationally is very strong and I believe I can make a valuable contribution to this new role of head of youth performance.

"There is no doubt Widnes Vikings face some big challenges in the future as they strive to secure a place in Super League. However, we can build on the strengths of the past while developing to meet new challenges of the future to ensure that our players and coaches can achieve their best and continue to grow."

Vikings' sporting director Terry O'Connor added: "Stuart's appointment is excellent news for the club. He introduced a fantastic youth development model at Leeds where 19 of their current championship squad are home-grown players. This is something for us to aspire to. He is a highly qualified and respected coach who can help strengthen our entire youth operation while also providing invaluable support to our existing coaching staff."

Speaking to the *Viking Storm* in February 2009 Wilkinson explained: "Ultimately the aim of the development team here is to provide the head coach with home-grown players from Widnes and the Borough of Halton. That is the aim, and already there are players who have broken through."

Demonstrating the success of the set-up Wilkinson added: "We are pipping the likes of Saints, Wigan, Warrington and Salford for the best players. They are coming here because the people involved in youth performance simply care about these young men, and the club. We haven't got the Super League badge or the money to get players in but they are choosing us because of the things we have in place."

In the build up to the season the club also launched its new lottery – the Vikings Dream Ticket. Recognising that successful lotteries are an important income stream for clubs, Widnes introduced their new scheme no doubt hoping to emulate the success of the likes of Leeds and St Helens whose schemes have thousands of members.

In return for supporting the club in its efforts to reach Super League, fans had the opportunity to win fantastic prizes. Those prizes included a £100 winner each week-day with an additional monthly £1,000 prize, and an annual draw for a £10,000 prize. The club also made available special prizes including VIP match packages and the opportunity to 'name' a Stobart truck.

With their pre-season work out of the way, and with little thought of what might happen some six months later, the squad assembled by Steve McCormack kicked off a season that was to see massive changes, both on and off the field, with a visit to a very windy Blackpool on 3rd February 2008 in the Northern Rail Cup.

Amid the Widnes faithful – who formed a large majority of the crowd of just 905 – on the terraces at Fylde RUFC that day was a new face, as new owner Steve O'Connor mingled with the fans for the first competitive match under his stewardship. With O'Connor having now, some four years later, achieved his goal, and promise, of returning the club to Super League it is appropriate to look back at that historic match, the first of the new era, where it all began, in some detail:

A convincing scoreline belied the hard-fought battle which was had with the Panthers as Widnes began their defence of the Northern Rail Cup, which had been secured with a one-sided 56-4 victory over Whitehaven in July 2007. Playing against a strong wind, and a truly determined Blackpool outfit, the Vikings took time to settle before Gavin Dodd, played in by Danny Speakman, broke the deadlock in the 13th minute, scoring the first try of the new era. Five minutes later Jim Gannon used his strength to convert a short pass from Mark Smith and Tim Hartley's conversion gave the Vikings a 10 point lead. The match was effectively over by the half-hour mark when first Danny Hill powered his way to the line and then Dean Gaskell did well to gather a deflected kick from Bob Beswick to touch down. As the half came to a close Rob Draper's outstretched arm claimed another try for the visitors who went into the break leading 26-0.

With the wind at their backs it was expected that the Vikings would run up the proverbial cricket score in the second period but, thanks to some dogged defence from the hosts, they had to settle for just two further tries. Midway through the half Hill notched his second while Hartley crossed just two minutes from time, separated by a consolation effort for Blackpool from Casey Mayberry.

Several of the team that ran out at Blackpool went on to make major contributions to the Vikings cause before moving on to pastures new, but one young man who made his debut in that match remains at the club – Ben Kavanagh. In the intervening years Kavanagh built a burgeoning reputation that eventually saw him become a key member of the Vikings' Super League team in 2012, before his season was cruelly cut short by a ruptured achilles tendon just three matches into the season.

The men who did duty at Blackpool were: Hardman; Gaskell (1t), Grady, Speakman, Dodd (1t); Hartley (1t, 5g), Roper; Morrison, Smith, Gannon (1t), Hill (2t), Noone, Beswick. Subs: Bowman, Gallagher, Draper (1t), Kavanagh.

On a lighter note fans arriving at the ground had been able to purchase an unusual memento of the game as the Blackpool club had produced 900 bars of rock with 'Widnes Vikings' running through it.

At the end of the afternoon O'Connor must have felt a mixture of relief and satisfaction as his new charges completed a workmanlike victory by 38 points to 4 over the Panthers.

Although McCormack had identified a successful defence of the Northern Rail Cup as one of the season's targets this was ultimately to prove to be beyond his squad. Three wins and three defeats – two at the hands of local rivals Leigh Centurions – did see the Vikings through to the knockout stages, behind group winners Leigh, where they took on Sheffield Eagles in front of a disappointing crowd of only 2,262 at the Stobart Stadium. On a day of persistent snow showers the Vikings turned up the heat on their opponents to cruise into the next round despite only scoring twice in the first half. With Mark Smith totally dominant, with excellent support from John Duffy and Lee Paterson, the Eagles were no match for their hosts as the Vikings ran in five further tries in the second half. The visitors did manage two late efforts before Gavin Dodd scored the try of the match. Fielding a loose kick from Dominic Brambani the winger gathered the ball just eight metres from his own line to outpace the Sheffield cover and sprint the length of the field to complete his hat-trick.

By the time they had dispatched Sheffield by a convincing score of 44-8 Widnes had overcome their early season inconsistency to strike a rich vein of form which saw them lose just once in 10 outings. Included in that run were their first three league fixtures of the campaign – a visit to Batley and home games against Leigh and Whitehaven. Victory in all three matches meant that Widnes had wiped out the 9 point penalty, imposed by the RFL for entering Administration, at the earliest opportunity.

The Batley match finally saw the fans' off-field anticipation transferred to match-day as the Vikings clinched an unlikely victory at a very cold Mount Pleasant. Trailing to an early strike from the hosts Widnes briefly achieved parity before going into the break trailing by 18 points to 6. Playing down the hill in the second half the Vikings managed to even matters at 22-22 before the Bulldogs seemed to have clinched the points with a drop goal. However, as the hooter sounded Widnes had possession inside their opponents' 10 metre line, with their fans screaming for somebody to 'go for the one', to level matters again. But in a bold – or reckless – move they retained possession in search of victory with a sweeping move which went from one wing to the other before Tim Hartley crashed over to snatch victory.

The painful memories of the early-season defeats against Leigh in the NRC were then erased from the mind as the Centurions were sent packing on the back of a 30-12 scoreline just three days after the Batley match. Despite scoring in the second minute Widnes were unable to establish any real dominance in an even first half as they traded tries to go into the break with the score 12-8 in Widnes' favour. Widnes eased away with three further tries to secure victory before Leigh notched a late consolation effort.

The final piece in the '9-point jigsaw' came with a hard-fought victory over Whitehaven in which the Vikings got home by the narrow margin of 32-28. Scoring first, Widnes conceded three unanswered tries in a spell which saw the visitors assume control before the Vikings closed the gap to 16-24 at the break. In the second half Dean Gaskell took his tally to four tries in the match before Mark Smith collected a kick from Gavin Dodd to see his team home.

Rarely can a team have been so pleased to be bottom of the table with zero points!

The next league match saw the team move into positive territory in the league table when they secured a point in a 16-16 draw against Salford City Reds at the Willows. From that point on performances and results became inconsistent and they were not to string two victories together again until mid-August.

Despite their inconsistency the Vikings managed to finish the league campaign in sixth position and qualify for the play-offs, and travelled to The Shay to take on Halifax. Although Ben Black gave the home side a fourth minute advantage Widnes fought back to take the lead through a converted Gavin Dodd try in the 27th minute – a lead that was to last just six minutes. From that point on Widnes were always chasing the game as Halifax eased into the next round. In what became an emotional farewell for several players the hopes of progressing through the play-offs dissipated into the Yorkshire evening air, following a 32-16 defeat, along with the flames of the half-time fire-eaters.

While there was a great deal of dis-satisfaction with the outcome of the Super League licensing process – and not just around Widnes – it is undeniable that over the 2008 season the two successful clubs had delivered on the pitch and also contested the Grand Final. Under the old system of promotion and relegation Salford, as Grand Final winners, would have been promoted to Super League, and with very little complaint.

The fact remained that in five matches against Salford and the Crusaders Widnes had only achieved one win, a draw and three losses. The three defeats all came against the Crusaders who became something of a bogey team in addition to being the club that most people feared would leap-frog the Vikings in the race for admission to Super League. The team from South Wales had already completed a league double over Widnes, in addition to knocking the holders out of the Northern Rail Cup, when they were awarded that coveted Licence.

The matches against Salford however, had been much tighter affairs. After that early-season draw the return, on a June evening in front of the Sky cameras and a record National League crowd of 8,189 inside the Stobart Stadium, Widnes took on the City Reds and put together one of their best 40 minutes of rugby of the season. However, the visitors were out of the blocks much quicker than the Vikings and their fast incisive rugby saw them establish an 18 point lead at the interval.

After the break Widnes showed their own brand of attacking rugby as the deficit was reduced with Matty Smith setting up two tries for Steve Tyrer. An unlikely victory was sealed just eight minutes from time when Chris Dean broke at pace, from his own '20' to the Salford 40 metre line, before handing over to Jason Crookes to sprint home for a 20-18 victory.

Widnes had worked hard off the field as well to make this a match-day experience to remember. A record-breaking crowd for a National League fixture and a stunning victory over the league leaders would surely offer a timely reminder to the RFL just a month before the Super League Licences were to be announced.

Chairman Steve O'Connor said: "Of course we are delighted to take the points and it was important for the team to get back on track after some disappointing results in recent weeks.

However, tonight was really about demonstrating to the RFL that Widnes Vikings can attract the sort of crowds demanded by Super League and that we can put on match-day experiences that are equal if not better than many Super League clubs. Our commercial and community departments have worked amazingly hard."

Year 7 girls' teams from Wade Deacon and Saints Peter and Paul schools had provided a curtain-raiser before the big match, and youngsters from Liverpool Stagecoach Theatre School provided half-time entertainment to highlight the work of the club's community department. In addition there was a spectacular parachute display by the Army's famous Red Devils who literally dropped into the stadium at half-time.

While during the course of 2008 the thoughts of the fans naturally swung between the team and the build up to the Super League announcement, the players continued to go about their business on the pitch, with several achieving personal milestones along the way.

Most noteworthy was skipper Mark Smith reaching 100 appearances for the club in the home victory over Leigh Centurions – an achievement which was marked with a special presentation by the Widnes Rugby League Museum. In addition three players – Gavin Dodd, Tim Hartley and Steve Tyrer – each contributed over 100 points to the Vikings cause, with Tyrer's coming in a 10 match loan spell from St Helens. Dodds' 116 points also saw him through the 300 point barrier in Widnes colours and topping 550 career points, while Hartley and Tyrer both moved beyond 250 career points. In addition Dean Gaskell and Lee Paterson both reached the 200 point career mark.

Shortly after the season had finished the departures of 12 players, led by Bob Beswick – who had chalked up his 100th career game during the season – ironically to join Halifax, and Paul Noone, were announced. In addition the return of loanees Matty Smith, Steve Tyrer and Chris Dean to their parent clubs meant that nine players who featured in the final match of the season would not be at the Stobart Stadium in 2009.

At the time head coach Steve McCormack commented: "It's always a sad time of the year when players have to be released and this time we had to make some really tough decisions to ensure we comply with the Salary Cap in 2009.

"None of the players have let us down throughout the 2008 campaign and I, along with all the staff at the Vikings, would like to thank them for their efforts and wish them well for the future."

In stark contrast to the events of late 2007 McCormack had already been able to start building his squad for 2009 before the curtain came down on what had been, both on and off the pitch, a truly disappointing 2008.

With Gavin Dodd and Jim Gannon already contracted until the end of 2009, the next building block towards 'qualifying' to make a Super League application for 2012-14 was laid when Dean Gaskell, top try scorer in 2008, put pen to paper. Along with Dodd Gaskell he was a member of the 'Famous Five' from 2007 and underlined his commitment to the club when he commented: "I really enjoy everything about Widnes, I'm not just a player but a fan as well, as is my girlfriend. Everyone at the club has been good to me and I'm very happy to commit my future to the club for the next two seasons. The future is certainly bright at the Stobart Stadium Halton."

Gaskell was closely followed by skipper Mark Smith, and the Supporters' Club Player of the Year Iain Morrison, who both penned deals that would keep them at Widnes for the next two seasons. Smith, another who had stuck by the club in its darkest days, and who had lifted the Northern Rail Cup in 2007, became the third member of the 'Famous Five' to extend his stay with the club adding: "Widnes is like a second home to both me and my family and we are well treated by the fans and respect them for it. That respect played a big part in my decision to sign a two year contract for the club. Super League is still my ambition but I want to play there with Widnes Vikings."

Scottish International Morrison was already contracted for 2009 but agreed a 12 month extension saying: "Widnes has been good to me and I've really enjoyed my time here. The Super League Licence decision was very disappointing but this is a great club to be at and by signing until 2010 it takes me closer to the next Licence decision. The extra 12 months also allows me to show my commitment to the club and the fans who have been so good to me this year."

While they were to be joined by further key players from 2008, including John Duffy, Richard Fletcher, Lee Paterson and Tim Hartley, the squad was also augmented by the signings of Anthony Thackeray, Danny Mills, and the returning Toa Kohe Love. Speaking on his arrival from Castleford Thackeray said: "Widnes will be one of the top teams in Division 1 so when the opportunity arose to sign for them it wasn't a hard decision to make. When I came over I couldn't believe the set-up, it was so professional."

"Widnes is a top club with a great tradition in the game and I can't wait to get across there" was the comment of fellow Yorkshireman Mills having put pen to paper on his Vikings deal. Joining the Vikings from Sheffield Eagles he added: "Obviously I've got to secure my place in the team first but I've normally been there or thereabouts in the try-scoring charts at every club and that will certainly be my goal at Widnes." Unfortunately Mills picked up an injury in pre-season and by the time he was fit he found himself behind Paddy Flynn, Dean Gaskell, Gavin Dodd and Kevin Penny in the fight for the two wing berths. After just two appearances as a substitute in 2009 Mills returned to the Eagles.

Kohe-Love, a try scorer in the 2007 Northern Rail Cup Final success over Whitehaven, commented on his return to the club: "I'm delighted to be coming back to Widnes. In truth I never wanted to leave but events off the pitch forced my hand. For the majority of the time it was really enjoyable and I'm glad to be given the opportunity to return because as far as I'm concerned it's a case of unfinished business."

As Steve McCormack continued to put the finishing touches to his squad for 2009 Richard Varkulis and James Webster moved to the Stobart Stadium on one and two-year deals respectively, while the club backed their judgement to secure Ben Kavanagh for a further three years.

Described by McCormack as one of the outstanding players in the National Leagues Varkulis confessed to being "surprised when they [Widnes] weren't given a Super League Licence. They've certainly got the best set-up outside Super League and I'm sure in 2012 they will be there. I want another shot at Super League and playing at Widnes should give me that opportunity."

Regular fundraisers for the club Vikings Quids In – VIQI – stepped forward to help the club secure the signing of Webster despite competition from some Super League clubs. Maintaining his base in Hull Webster said: "All the clubs I have spoken to had some good points to offer but Widnes was the best. I'm really excited about the move. I met Steve McCormack and Steve O'Connor yesterday and was really impressed with their plans for the future"

Announcing Webster's signing sporting director Terry O'Connor forgave the scrum-half for "ruining my last competitive match", as Hull KR defeated Widnes in the 2006 Grand

Final. "A stand-out player for Hull KR over the years, and also the best player in the National League in 2006," O'Connor was hopeful that Webster could "bring that form and professionalism to Widnes while showing our juniors what it takes to become a top player both on and off the pitch."

O'Connor was equally pleased with the extended deal signed by Kavanagh, adding: "I'm pleased that Ben has agreed to commit his future to the Vikings until the end of the 2011 season. He is a talented rugby league player and has the potential to play at the highest level"

Kavanagh added, "I'm really pleased to be at Widnes for the next three years. It's going to be an exciting time at the club and I'm looking forward to being part of it."

Indeed after Widnes' return to the top flight was confirmed in March 2011 Kavanagh's progress was rewarded when he became the first player to sign a Super League contract with the club.

Having tied down the senior members of the squad for 2009 the club moved swiftly to secure the signatures of seven of their highly promising youngsters. Anthony Mullally, Josh Simm and Shane Grady put their signatures to three-year deals while Matt Strong, Scott Yates and Paddy Flynn were retained for the next two seasons and Michael Ostick would remain a Viking until the end of the 2009 season.

Underlining the club's commitment to a strong youth policy sporting director Terry O'Connor said "Youth development is an important part of all clubs and the elevation of some of these players to the first team squad plus the extension of contracts for others shows that Widnes Vikings are keen to give home grown talent a chance at the Stobart Stadium, Halton.

"The coaching staff have identified these players as potential regular first team players and will also be members of the JETS (Junior Elite Training Squad) under the guidance of John Stankevitch and Stuart Wilkinson.

"These players have been given the opportunity to play first team rugby league and it is now up to them to step up to the mark and make a name for themselves in the world of rugby league."

O'Connor's words were indeed prophetic as all seven players did indeed play in the first team during 2009 with Ostick and Flynn only missing a handful of matches, and Flynn finishing as top try scorer with 20 in his first full season.

Headlines had naturally centred on the twin issues of playing and the Super League application but there was much work going on elsewhere as Steve O'Connor rebuilt this famous club. With an eye to future generations of players and fans the highly successful 'Vikings in the Community' team had been busy throughout the year delivering sessions in the core skills of rugby league. Having 'cut their teeth' at schools local to the stadium Martin Davidson, who led the community team, was particularly pleased with the response from schools further afield.

"The fruits of our labour are really starting to show" Davidson told the *Viking Storm* in March 2008. "We are working tirelessly in all the schools but we have put some special emphasis on the schools outside the catchment area of the stadium.

"We are already in Liverpool but we have tapped into Knowsley as well and our coaching team of John Foran and Tim Holmes are doing a brilliant job."

The irony is that the much-changed demography of this 'hot-bed' of rugby league meant that Davidson's team found themselves having to 'sell' the game in many 'football orientated' schools. This was a significant factor as the club attempted to establish a sizeable hard-core of fans in order to re-establish itself as a force in the game. The fact that rugby league is now played in the majority of local schools is testament to the work of Vikings in the Community. As Davidson confirmed: "Rugby League is being well received and youngsters are being taught some great skills by two ex-professionals, as well as picking up messages on diet and lifestyle."

Further broadening of Widnes' Community programme came with the introduction of 'Vikings against Bullying'. The project, pioneered by sporting director Terry O'Connor and delivered in Halton's Schools by Foran, Holmes and Davidson, was very well received by Head Teachers and pupils alike.

Former Vikings full-back Holmes said at the time: "We are working really hard in the schools to educate youngsters in how to respect each other and give support to their friends around them.

"We are doing sessions in the classroom which involve first-team players and Steve McCormack passing on our experience of how sticking together and respecting each other is pivotal to life in general."

As well as listening to the players' experiences the project also delivers academic sessions with the involvement of the teaching staff. Holmes added "we hope that by doing our bit it will bring the bullying figures down in the schools, and with a bit of luck eliminate it completely".

By this time the popular 'Sherlock' had been a member of the Vikings in the Community team for a couple of years following his enforced retirement as a player, and his experiences, good and bad, had helped to make him a fine ambassador for the club and the sport.

His rugby career had started as a member of the St Helens Academy setup at the age of 16 and continued until he went to Loughborough University. He then followed his coach, John Myler, to Widnes just a month after beginning his studies, "fell in love with the club" and played for the Vikings' Academy team throughout his time at Loughborough. Just a week after graduating he made his first team debut in a Super League match against Salford at the Willows in August 2004. playing in the remaining six fixtures of that campaign.

Further first team action followed in 2005 – the year that saw Widnes relegated from Super League – and Holmes was one of a group of players who felt "we have got the club into this mess, we'll help to get them out of it". Unfortunately he was denied that opportunity as he suffered a neck injury in the Mike Gregory Testimonial match which was to ultimately end his playing career. After a six month lay-off, and determined to play again, he returned to action in an under-21 match at Halifax only to be carried off again after 20 minutes suffering a recurrence of the injury.

It was at this stage that Steve McCormack invited Holmes to assist Andy Haigh with conditioning, which enabled him to put his Sports Science degree to good use, and put him on the path to a continuing career within the game. He also had a brief but successful spell coaching the under-21s to a Grand Final appearance, ironically at Halifax, before taking up his role in the community department which he finds "really rewarding" but "definitely no replacement for actually playing the game by any stretch of the imagination".

2008 also saw the launch of the club's new match-day magazine – the *Viking Storm* – so-named by editor Ian Cheveau after he had written in the *Liverpool Daily Post* about Steve O'Connor's acquisition of the club whipping up a storm of interest among the rugby league community. Moving away from the format of the traditional 'programme' the new all-colour glossy A4 publication proved such an immediate hit with the fans that a second print run was commissioned after the first issue sold out. This was indeed the first time for many years that the 'sold out' sign went up on a Widnes matchday programme.

Published by local company IMC Communications the new publication benefitted from contributions from some of the best rugby league columnists, both locally and nationally. While the local perspective was covered by the respected Paul Cook, John Lawless and Mark Naughton, the broader take on rugby league issues was provided by seasoned writers Andy Wilson, Gareth Walker and Andrew Kirchin.

Delighted editor Cheveau said: "IMC Communications is proud to be associated with Widnes Vikings in these exciting times. I have never known such excitement in the town since Steve O'Connor took over. Widnes is a Super League club in everything but name, and now we feel that we have given the club a Super League product which we think is among the best magazines in rugby league."

Vowing to make the Vikings programme the best in the British game, Cheveau set about producing a publication where "the content and design is in keeping with the times, and is a key tool to communicate with the club's fans and stakeholders. It is a crucial and effective way of doing that."

Not only was it considered by rugby league journalists to be the best programme in the National Leagues, but Batley Bulldogs chairman offered the opinion to club officials that it was 'better than Rugby League World magazine and more like a soccer Premiership product'.

On the club's return to the top flight in 2012 it was, in the view of journalists, the 'best in Super League', which is an excellent tribute to the very small team that put it together, often within very tight deadlines. Over the years it has proved to be a popular addition to the matchday experience while Cheveau believes that the "unique relationship" with the club is a vital component to its ongoing success, stating: "I might add that we wouldn't be here without the help and belief of people like Alex Bonney, Steve O'Connor and Julie Gaskell. They believe in us. They believe in the product."

While there had been many positives during 2008 the year was naturally defined by the massive disappointment of the realisation on 22nd July that Widnes Vikings were to face a further three years, at least, in the National League competition.

The Widnes faithful had, by and large, been swept along on a wave of optimism since Steve O'Connor assumed control of the club. Perhaps that optimism should have been reined in, but having seen their club narrowly escape extinction it was natural that the fans rode the wave of optimism until it finally ran out of energy and gave way again to utter despair.

There had of course been those who were suspicious all along that the RFL would 'stitch us up again' as they had done in two separate announcements in April 1995 and again to a lesser degree in 2005.

It is readily apparent that the sport of rugby league in general provides the most fertile soil for the conspiracy theorist to plant his seed. The depth of suspicion with which the RFL is held by a large number of those who follow the fortunes of the Vikings is equally obvious. However, in recent years it has become increasingly apparent, from supporters and columnists alike, that there seems to be an endless list of questions about how the game is managed. The process, and outcome, of the inaugural round of Licence applications in 2008 has only served to fan the flames of discontent, with supporters of many clubs expressing their concern.

While there may be ideological merit in the scheme the system by which it was to be implemented was sadly lacking. Having begun discussions about Licensing with the clubs some three years earlier I would have expected the process to be nailed down before the bids were received, and to be made public. But as discussed in the previous chapter the process did appear to be less than transparent with amendments seemingly being made on the hoof by those in power. The scenario painted by John Lawless is the clearest indication that the process had not been thought through properly, with no thought having been given to the highly likely need for a 'tie-breaker'.

To my mind the comments made by Nigel Wood and Richard Lewis, in that interview with Danny Lockwood of *League Weekly* just days after the announcement, gave cause for concern in terms of there having been a clear, transparent and unambiguous process used. Wood spoke of the danger of being "too scientific, too analytical and too objective," and of "retaining an overall feel and flavour". These worrying words were followed up by Lewis conceding that "In the end it had to come down to a matter of opinion," and there "being more good applications than there were spots". These comments gave far too much room for manoeuvre in the view of many fans while the comment about numbers was a direct contradiction of Lewis' previous statement that there was "no upper limit on membership" of Super League.

Such utterances gave no comfort at all to the supporters of Featherstone, Halifax, Leigh, Toulouse, and Widnes as they tried to understand why their club had not been successful. Indeed I believe that they gave cause for further mistrust of the governing body, as evidenced by comments from officials of some clubs and a succession of letters from disaffected fans to the trade press.

In the case of Widnes, as we have already seen, chairman Steve O'Connor swallowed his anger and disappointment to allow the club to move forward in a positive and progressive manner, not allowing the bitterest of disappointments to fester. His calm, confident and determined approach as he addressed fans, in the immediate aftermath, and again during the Dewsbury match five days later, set the tone for round two in 2011.

That Dewsbury match was the first of the five remaining fixtures in the league campaign since the announcement, and the players, perhaps fuelled by their disappointment, came out and blew away the hapless Rams. Despite this success, and wins against Featherstone and Sheffield, it was crucial defeats against Leigh and Whitehaven which saw the Vikings lose all hope of a home play-off tie as they limped into the play-offs, where the final disappointment of the season saw them bow out to Halifax in that match at The Shay.

So the curtain came down on a year that had begun with great optimism, for both playing success and a positive outcome in the bid for Super League status, only for inconsistency and doubt to lead to disappointment in both areas.

Not only had 2008 been a roller-coaster year it had been a real contradiction, being both a massive year and a 'nothing' year. Massive because the club had risen from the ashes of Administration, and yet a nothing year in the sense that the team had failed to make its mark in league or cups while the club had also suffered the ultimate setback of Super League rejection.

On the plus side the club had a new dynamic owner with clear ideas on where the club should be going and how to get there. Perversely the refusal to award the club a Super League Licence gave Steve O'Connor the platform to show his true mettle as he forged a new relationship with the RFL and put in place the infrastructure that would ultimately see the club achieve its goal of Super League status.

On the debit side were the twin disappointments of the RFL rejection and the lack of playing success. The arguments and counter-arguments relating to the licensing decision have been debated ad nauseam here and elsewhere. On the playing side the lack of success seemed to be caused, in the main, by inconsistency. Highs and lows came in equal measure with rampaging victories often followed by an inexplicably poor performance.

All would have been forgiven, however, if the 'right' club had been announced by Richard Lewis in July. As Councillor McDermott said at the time: "This is an extremely disappointing decision … for all true rugby league fans."

Picking up on that, and lamenting the potential consequences for the British game, Terry O'Connor made perhaps the most poignant observation while reiterating the club's intention to focus on British talent. He commented: "It's daft to say we won't have Aussies, or any overseas player for that matter, but what I am saying is that we are committed to bringing on our home-grown players. There will be a time when Widnes will need the top Aussies in our team but it won't be at the expense of players we have blooded. The Aussie lads we will bring over here are the ones who will give added value to the likes of Shane Grady, Ben Kavanagh and Scott Yates."

The Vikings sporting director continued: "We didn't want players coming to the club from Australia to be a squad number. We wanted quality and the players we had in mind could have given our young players the benefit of their experience."

To underline his concern he pointed out that at that time that "110 of the 238 players turning out each week in Super League were overseas players."

CHAPTER SEVEN
The In-Between Years

2009

Once the overwhelming sense of disappointment, caused by Widnes' rejection by the governing body for a Super League Licence had eased, the prospect of three years in a new 'wilderness' had to be addressed and plans formulated to prevent a repeat in 2011.

The whole purpose of licensing was to persuade clubs, both within and outside the new elite group, to adopt long-term planning principles to both their business and team building. That was great if you were in that elite group, but frustrating and demanding if your club was 'on the outside looking in'.

The major issue was how to deal with that frustration. As I see it there are three basic elements involved with any club: the Board of Directors and their staff; the coaches and players; and the fans. For any professional sports outfit to prosper all three of these groups must do their bit. In the Vikings' case the chairman had moved quickly to reiterate to the Widnes faithful that he was in it "for the long haul", even before the media had finished picking over the bones of the announcement. And very soon further news of changes and refinements to the organisation began to filter out of the Stobart Stadium. It was clear this was going to be no three-year sabbatical for the club staff. In some ways it could be described as business as usual.

It was a slightly different matter however, for Steve McCormack, his coaching staff and the players as the 2009 squad were facing up to a season that had been stripped of its natural conclusion. While the same could be said of 2008 there was then at least still the hope of 'promotion' via the Licensing process. The closest the 'class of 2009' could come was to put Widnes on the road back to Super League as there was now an on-field criterion to be met for entry to the top division in 2011. Winning the Northern Rail Cup, or claiming a place in the Grand Final, would see the club meet the minimum criteria required to submit a Licence application.

It was, in my view, the final but vital group that in some ways had the more difficult role to play over the next three years – the fans. Steve O'Connor and his board were tasking themselves and the staff to achieve certain goals. Steve McCormack was working towards Grand Final success and regaining the Northern Rail Cup, while the players at least had tough challenges to meet each time they ran out onto a pitch.

But what could the fans actually 'do'? The simple answer was nothing – apart from continuing to support their club in as large numbers as possible. Their role was obvious yet ill-defined with no targets or milestones with which to judge their success. This was no easy commitment for many as they felt cheated by the move to licensing at the expense of the traditional promotion and relegation system. In the days of promotion and relegation fans would rightly claim a contribution to their team's success as their bond with the players saw the '18th man' straddle the touchline. In this new situation 'all' – and I say that respectfully as one of them – they could do was roll up on match-day, pay their money and cheer on their team, knowing that no amount of silverware would alter their status for the next season. Increasing the cash flow and viability of their club, and demonstrating to the powers that be that the club has a strong fan base, is not why fans get up in the morning. There was an air of impotence and a feeling of being disenfranchised as a result of the brave new world of franchises, or Licences!

To some extent this new wilderness played into the hands of those 'spectators' who had, and continued to vow that they would not return until the club was in Super League. But thankfully the majority of the hard-core 'supporters' reacted positively to this latest slap in the face from the governing body, and helped to rebuild their club.

However, just doing 'what comes naturally' to the 'Widnes 'til I die' brigade – remaining loyal through thick and thin – was every bit as important to the club as the work carried out by Steve O'Connor and Steve McCormack. It enabled the club to tick another box when we next gathered at the Stobart Stadium to await an announcement from the RFL, as one of the licensing criteria was to achieve an average home gate in excess of 2,500 during 2009 or 2010. This they did with some ease as in 2009 the average attendance for the 10 home league matches was an impressive 3,808, although it fell to 2,980 in 2010.

There had, however, been much debate and concern among fans when it was announced that for 2009 the club would be testing the water with a variety of match-days and kick-off times, with a view to finding the optimum combination taking into account the range of counter-attractions. Three o'clock on a Sunday afternoon was, in the eyes of many, 'rugby league time' and the club came in for a considerable amount of criticism. Yet despite this criticism, and the fact that there was not a single match played on a Sunday at the Stobart Stadium throughout 2009, the club achieved that average attendance in excess of 3,800, with impressive turnouts in excess of 5,000 for the matches against Toulouse and Gateshead. Ironically with a return to Sunday matches halfway through 2010 the average fell by over 800.

As mentioned previously it had been announced that the licensing criteria for 2011 had been amended to include an on-field element. The RFL had decided that for a club from the National Leagues to be eligible to submit an application for a Super League Licence it must have either won the Northern Rail Cup or appeared in a Grand Final in 2009 or 2010. The first opportunity to 'tick the box', and thereby relieve the pressure on the club, would come with a successful Northern Rail Cup campaign.

The significance of this was underlined in an interview with Steve O'Connor in February 2009 when he told me that: "It's highly likely that if we meet our objectives in year one we would probably go part-time in year two, unless we see a marked improvement in attendances. We'd have to work on the fact that the fans voted with their feet. However, if we don't meet our goals in year one we will have to stay full-time in year two because we are at a desperate stage then to meet the minimum criteria for Super League."

It was perhaps as a result of this pressure that following a disappointing pre-season and a surprise defeat at home to Oldham in the opening Northern Rail Cup fixture that O'Connor acted decisively to relieve Steve McCormack of his duties as head coach. As O'Connor said in his programme notes: "Potentially we could have been struggling to qualify for the next stage of the Northern Rail Cup and then that puts us on the back foot for the start of the Co-operative Championship season."

In the same edition of the *Viking Storm* McCormack commented that "It was a disappointing day when Steve and I came to the decision about me leaving Widnes Vikings, but it was one which was made amicably."

Having enjoyed nearly four years at Widnes he pointed out that he had taken the club to two Grand Finals and won the Northern Rail Cup, while working for four chairmen, as the club lurched towards Administration before being rescued by O'Connor.

McCormack added: "I honestly feel my effort during this time has been decent, but the club has decided to move on without me. During the last 12 months the Widnes club has really progressed under Steve O'Connor and I particularly wish him well.

"As a coach you quickly realise this is a cut-throat profession. This time last week I was being presented with my World Cup medal. A week later I find myself out of a job. It just goes to show what can happen and how quickly fortunes can change."

The man who had coached Widnes to their first trophy for several years finished by saying: "I would like to say a thank you to the players, colleagues and fans who have supported me during my time here and I wish you all well."

Having coached teams to four successive Grand Finals (the first two with Whitehaven) McCormack left the Vikings with the best wishes of everyone at the club and this glowing endorsement from chief executive Alex Bonney:

"Since joining the club 12 months ago I cannot fail to be impressed with the work undertaken by Steve who almost single-handedly built a team from scratch to reach the play-offs. Prior to this he led the club to two Grand Finals and a Northern Rail Cup victory, and this morning's decision was reached amicably."

With McCormack dismissed O'Connor was faced with the task of securing a replacement who could take the club forward and secure that place in Super League.

"We had 17 applications and it was pleasing to see that the name of Widnes is one that is still held in high regard within the rugby league world," said O'Connor. In fact such is the level of esteem in which the club is held that three of those applications were 'expressions of interest' from coaches currently employed elsewhere. The Vikings chairman admitted that "it is difficult when people are in employment because I don't see myself seducing people from jobs that they've got. That is not fair on the sport." At the other end of the spectrum the club had also received an application from a Tesco employee in Doncaster.

While that process took some time to come to a conclusion the team was placed in the capable hands of assistant coach John Stankevitch. During his 'caretaker' spell Stankevitch returned four wins from five matches which saw the team score 248 points while just 46 points were conceded. The final two matches of that spell were quite remarkable, for differing reasons. 'Stanky's' penultimate match in charge was a Challenge Cup tie against the amateurs of Saddleworth Rangers, in which the largest winning margin in the club's history was recorded – 88-0 – as they ran in 15 tries, including a hat-trick from Mark Smith. Tim Hartley also weighed in with 14 goals which equalled the club record for the number of goals in a match, which had been held by Mark Hewitt since he knocked over the same number against Oldham in July 1999.

By the time Stankevitch's last match came round five days later his successor had been announced, but he oversaw the match against Toulouse Olympique before handing over the reins. Covered by Sky Sports this was the French club's debut in the British competition, having sat out the Northern Rail Cup competition. Despite the television coverage over 5,000 fans turned up to witness the Vikings' 70-0 victory over what many people had considered to be a strong outfit. The 12 tries were shared among eight players – including Paddy Flynn's maiden hat-trick – while Academy product Scott Yates, in the middle of a rich vein of form, converted 11 of the tries.

Two days prior to the Toulouse match the result of the search for a new head coach had been announced, when it was confirmed that Paul Cullen had been appointed. It is true to say that the appointment did not meet with universal approval among Widnes fans, but this was almost exclusively based on an irrational reaction to his former employers rather than an assessment of his coaching credentials. The former Whitehaven and Warrington coach, who also led England to Federation Shield success in 2006, was welcomed to Widnes by Steve O'Connor who commented:

"I have met with three of the applicants and during my meeting with Paul I was impressed with his enthusiasm and vision for the future of the club, one which I share with him.

"Paul has coached at all levels of the sport and will bring with him a wealth of experience to the role. This, coupled with the exciting squad we have, should give us the platform to launch an assault on the Co-operative Championship while being just two games away from the Northern Rail Cup Final."

Cullen, who was looking forward to taking up his role at Widnes, added: "I'm really excited to be joining Widnes. The plan is simple, we need to get Widnes into Super League where we belong."

While confirming Cullen's appointment O'Connor added, "I would like to put on record my thanks to John Stankevitch for the work he has undertaken over the last few weeks and I am sure he will be a valuable member of our coaching team for the future."

However, Stankevitch, who had successfully steered the club through the group stage of the Northern Rail Cup following Steve McCormack's departure, was to leave the club himself just three months after handing over to Paul Cullen. 'Stanky' who had finished his playing career with Widnes was "gutted" to have to leave the club and told the *Widnes Weekly News* "I was under the impression that I was in with a chance of being the next Widnes Super League coach, and so the decision is a massive disappointment to me."

In thanking Stankevitch for his 18 months service to the club chief executive Alex Bonney explained that as a result of a recent reorganisation the position of assistant coach had been deemed to be a part-time role.

Stankevitch conceded that "The club told me that they could no longer afford to pay me full-time wages, but I still wanted to stay." However, he felt that as "there was no sort of negotiation it feels as though I'm being made some sort of scapegoat".

A vastly popular man with the fans, 'Stanky' added: "But I'm still a huge Widnes fan and I'll be there on Saturday cheering for them, and then I'll be looking to get back into the game at the earliest possible point." In fact after a brief spell with rugby union side Rotherham Titans Stankevitch returned to the rugby league fold as head coach at Rochdale Hornets in November 2009.

Paul Cullen's arrival at the Stobart Stadium came after he had parted company, for the second time, with his home town club Warrington. No stranger to making the tough decision he had, as he explained to me, originally left Warrington "on a matter of principle because I wasn't happy with the way the club was operating. I left without any job to go to. I then sat down and thought what am I going to do now and where do I go. You have to consider what jobs are available in a very narrow market. I chose to break a so-called comfort zone of living, playing for, being captain of, being coach of 'my club' which was Warrington at the time. I couldn't find anywhere further than Whitehaven and that's why I ended up there as they had a vacancy."

While living away from home in a Cumbrian village for two years was a significant change in the life of Paul Cullen he admits that "When I left Warrington for the second time I couldn't have found a bigger challenge than coming to Widnes."

Although the former Warrington man didn't apply for the job he was approached to see if he would be interested. As he recalls "Terry O'Connor didn't need to sell the club or himself to me and I met Steve O'Connor at a hotel in Warrington. At that point, during that discussion, I decided that's the job I want. That's the biggest challenge that I'm going to get, it was the ideal opportunity. The fact it was the mortal enemy made it even better for me – it was a massive challenge to win over the Widnes fans. It was never a case of coming to Widnes because of the drama and battles between the Warrington and Widnes fans. It was the challenge to earn the respect of the Widnes fans that I couldn't have given anything else during my playing career to get the better of."

Looking back over old rivalries, as a Warrington fan and then player, Paul Cullen will tell you that his "fire for Warrington against Widnes didn't come through any nastiness or bitterness or parochialism, it came out of respect. My fight against Widnes was always because they put outstanding international players in front of me every time I came here. Widnes were the lead club over Warrington then and I did everything I possibly could as a player to upset that balance."

Since leaving his position as head coach at Warrington Cullen had taken up a more permanent role with Sky Sports, having previously worked with the broadcaster on a regular basis alongside his coaching responsibilities with both Whitehaven and Warrington. "It seemed a natural progression to continue with that work when I was no longer head coach at Warrington and then they offered me the regular gig on *Boots 'N' All*. It broke the week up and very few people have the chance to watch all seven games every single week."

In addition to his television work Cullen took steps to broaden his experience during his sabbatical from his beloved rugby league career. Naturally it was not realistic to expect clubs like Wigan and Bradford to invite him in to observe their training methods and facilities so Cullen turned to another game he enjoys – rugby union. "Part of my coaching philosophy is not to be narrow minded – I enjoy rugby union and watching how they work and operate."

So he set about his own personal development as a coach by spending time at 'union' clubs Munster, Saracens and Ospreys, concluding that "their off-field infrastructure is far better than anything I have seen in Super League" and that they are "miles ahead of us in terms of facilities and player preparation."

Having, in his own words, "used the media as a busman's holiday" allowed Cullen to "observe what is happening at other clubs and how they are playing". Basing his opinions as a Sky pundit on a playing career of 350 games and six years as a head coach with a Super League team, he concedes that he "may look at it [a game] with different eyes to most people – I'm looking for shape, structure, repetition. I tend to look at the games how I would look at them as an opposition coach. I'm looking for the strengths and weaknesses of the teams."

By the time Cullen had taken over the reins at the Stobart Stadium, Widnes had scraped into the knockout stages of the Northern Rail Cup, by finishing fourth in their group, and he still had both routes open to meet the minimum criteria for a Super League application. With the quarter-final tie some three months away the immediate task was to build on the opening victory in the league campaign, but the team suffered a reverse in Cullen's first match when they went down against old rivals Halifax at The Shay – a result that was repeated two weeks later in the Challenge Cup.

Individual and collective inconsistency had plagued the team for the first half of the season, but a convincing win over York City Knights in the NRC quarter-final set the team on a run of five consecutive victories. Included in that run was yet another visit to Halifax in which the Vikings saw off their hosts in the NRC semi-final, to claim their place in the Final against Barrow Raiders at Blackpool. Fifteen coach loads of fans – 12 of which were provided, free of charge, by the club for season ticket holders – travelled to The Shay in addition to the vast number of cars as Vikings supporters made up a high proportion of the attendance of just under 4,000.

The match was for a large part a typical hard fought semi-final, but was interspersed with some fine play from both sides. Having fallen behind in the 6th minute the Vikings fought back to take a 14-6 lead into the break courtesy of tries from Anthony Thackeray and Gavin Dodd, both converted by Craig Hall. The lead was extended to a comfortable 20-6 early in the second half when Hall converted another Thackeray try before Halifax, inspired by former Widnes player Bob Beswick, fought back with three tries in eight minutes to turn the match on its head and take a two point lead. Shortly after this came the incident for which this match is most remembered. With only 10 minutes remaining 'Fax scrum-half Ben Black, a regular thorn in Widnes' side, broke clear of the Vikings' defence and, with no one between him and the try line, inexplicably lost control of the ball. Instead of being eight points adrift Widnes regained the initiative to equalise just two minutes later through a Hall penalty before the on-loan winger edged the Vikings ahead with a towering drop-goal. The victory was ultimately assured when Thackeray completed his hat-trick two minutes from time.

The Final, on what was to become a 'red letter' day for the club, got off to a fiery start which resulted in both Jim Gannon and Barrow's Brett McDermott being sin-binned after just seven minutes, with Barrow taking the lead from the resultant penalty, converted by Darren Holt. However, Widnes eventually broke through to take the lead just seven minutes later when they capitalised on a penalty to re-start on the Barrow 40 metre line. The ball was driven down the middle then moved out to the left wing before, centre-field, Mark Smith and Anthony Thackeray created the space for Richard Fletcher to charge in from 10 metres out. Craig Hall's goal gave the Vikings a cushion of four points. Although Widnes had the better of the attacking play in the first half they could not manage to cross the Raiders line again, and were made to pay when Barrow regained the lead through Zeb Luisi's try which was converted by Holt with 14 minutes of the half left.

Paul Cullen immediately sent John Duffy on and within minutes the tide had turned for the final time. Taking a pass from Duffy, Anthony Thackeray was held up just a metre from the line. From the play-the-ball Duffy threw an outrageous dummy and dived over the line from dummy half. Duffy was making a record fourth Northern Rail Cup Final appearance – with his third different club – and his try signalled a purple patch for the Vikings as the interval approached.

Widnes then turned up the heat on their opponents with two tries from Kevin Penny within three minutes just before the break. The winger's first effort came from a James Webster kick to the corner from 25 metres out when the speedster just beat his wing partner Craig Hall to touch down, and followed up with a short range effort when Hall slipped a 'flat' pass to him just three metres out. Hall's third goal made it 22-8 at the break.

Widnes had dominated the early stages of the second half, again failing to reap the rewards of their possession, when on their first venture deep into Vikings territory a try from James Nixon reduced Barrow's deficit to 10 points. Widnes reacted immediately to remove Barrow's toe-hold in the game when Toa Kohe Love crossed the line just 56 seconds after the re-start. Barrow had fumbled the kick-off to concede possession to Widnes with first Thackeray and Steve Pickersgill being stopped just short. The ball eventually came out to 'TKL' for him to notch another trademark try. Receiving the ball 10 metres out by the left hand post he sidestepped three defenders to score by the opposite upright. Craig Hall extended the lead to 16 points.

Throughout the second half Widnes again restricted their opponents to occasional forays into their half, but from one such break the Cumbrians scored a consolation try through Scott Kraighan – converted by Holt – with just seven minutes left on the clock. Widnes had the last say when, with only 90 seconds left to play, Richard Varkulis took a pass from Webster to power in from 12 metres out for Hall to add his fifth goal of the afternoon. The hooter sounded almost immediately to signal the start of the celebrations as the 34-18 win meant that the Vikings had 'ticked the box', at the first time of asking, to meet the on-field Licence criteria and taken a significant step towards reclaiming their Super League status.

After the match Man of the Match John Duffy put the success down to "a massive team effort, from the backroom staff as well," and paid tribute to the Widnes fans describing them as "an extra man today as they were at Halifax". While the day had begun badly for Jim Gannon with that sin-binning the elder statesman of the team had the last laugh commenting: "I've been playing since I was four and a half years of age and this is the first first grade thing that I've won." The prop forward conceded that "everyone was writing us off, we did go through bit of a bad patch but cream rises to the top and we are absolutely delighted with today."

A smiling Paul Cullen was equally proud of the team's achievement, and no doubt relieved that 'the box had been ticked'. Aware of exactly how Barrow would approach the game he recognised that the players "have done it really tough, that was a bit tasty early doors and we are very pleased to come away with the spoils. We had to be good behind the sticks and we held our nerve. The call for the team was to hold your nerve because the fitness levels, character and the class we've got will out in the end."

Interestingly the match report on the RFL website included the following: 'They [Widnes] lost out to Salford and Celtic Crusaders a year ago but, with a first-class facility at the Stobart Stadium and coach Paul Cullen gradually rebuilding a useful team, it is surely now only a matter of time before Widnes are back in the big time.'

To underline the season's inconsistency the Vikings returned to league action the following week only to be turned over by Steve McCormack's Gateshead, which heralded an erratic finale to the season although they did manage to finish in fourth spot to again qualify for the play-offs. Convincing victories at home to Halifax (42-16) and Whitehaven (58-10) were separated by disappointing reverses at Featherstone and Barrow as fourth spot was finally secured. Whitehaven were the visitors in the first round of the play-offs with Widnes this time restricted to a narrow victory of 26 points to 21. Featherstone were the next visitors to the Stobart Stadium and eliminated the Vikings with a 32-24 victory.

During the run-in Widnes had also travelled to Toulouse, in what for many was another highlight of the season, combining a break in the sun with taking in Widnes' first battle for league points on foreign soil. Just two weeks after invading Blackpool the Viking Army set up camp on the other side of the Channel as large numbers of Widnes fans swapped the Golden Mile for a long weekend in the South of France.

The club had invited CFW Travel of Warrington, in association with Catalan Sports Tours, to put together an 'official' package and the 55 places available were sold out within three weeks of its launch (50% within a week). Indeed I was informed by Andy Walsh of

CFW Travel that while this was the only trip organised for a Championship club Widnes took "an above average number of fans" when compared to the figures for Super League clubs travelling to Catalans Dragons. In addition these numbers were dramatically swollen by a horde of fans who made their own travel arrangements.

While those independent travellers arrived by a variety of ingenious routes those of us on the 'official' trip had the ease of a Thursday morning flight from Liverpool into the somewhat spartan airport at Carcassonne. On a very hot afternoon we then journeyed on to Toulouse to find the inviting De Danu Irish Bar conveniently only 50 metres from our hotel. Over the next three days this was to become a second home for many, while for others the sights of a surprisingly attractive city beckoned.

As Friday came and went the sight of Widnes fans steadily became a more frequent sight on the streets and squares of Toulouse, while the constant 30 degree heat made the regular intake of fluids a vital and satisfying challenge. The De Danu was particularly helpful in this respect as the owners gladly exchanged vast quantities of various liquids in exchange for Widnesian Euros!

Eventually Saturday evening arrived and it was time for the 'main event' after our driver had skillfully negotiated a series of narrow streets to reveal the pleasant, modern, two-sided stadium in the tree-lined suburb of Blagnac. As kick-off approached the steady flow of Vikings fans into the ground had seen the Widnes contingent swollen to a figure that appeared to be in excess of 400.

The hosts certainly provided a much sterner test for the Vikings than they had at the Stobart Stadium in March. The evening kick-off belied the hot and humid conditions in the Stade Ernest Argeles, bordered by a mixture of neatly trimmed hedges and tall trees, but Widnes took the game to their opponents from the kick-off, and virtually camped out in their opponents' half. However, after 11 minutes it was Toulouse who took the lead when Martin Mitchell forced his way over the line for a try converted by Damien Couturier.

Widnes immediately returned to the attack and scored just four minutes later. Gavin Dodd collected a goal line drop out to run deep into Toulouse territory before Mark Smith and James Webster set up the opportunity for Jon Grayshon to score wide on the left. Widnes took the lead on the back of a surging run from Michael Ostick when, with Smith and Webster again the architects, Ben Kavanagh powered over by the posts. Dodd's goal gave the Vikings a lead of 10-6, but this was to last just four minutes as Toulouse full-back Rory Bromley was first to pounce on grubber kick under the sticks and set up an easy conversion for Couturier.

Unbowed the Vikings again fought back to take the lead moments before the break. From a play-the-ball on their opponents '40' Richard Varkulis and Lee Doran moved the ball smartly to Kevin Penny who outstripped the home defence by racing 35 metres down the touchline to score by the corner flag. Dodd's goal saw Widnes into the break with a narrow advantage 16 points to 12.

Toulouse started the second half much brighter than Widnes and by the 49th minute they had taken an ominous looking 24-16 lead, through two close range tries from hooker Adrien Viala, both converted by Couturier. The large contingent of Widnes fans were lifted again when, after 68 minutes, Jim Gannon forced his way over the line to score under the posts having taken a sharp pass from Doran some eight metres out.

Dodd's goal reduced the deficit to two points but within five minutes the Vikings had again edged in front in this close fought contest, with 'Doddy' again instrumental. Receiving the ball from Dean Gaskell 15 metres out in centrefield, the full-back instantly kicked over his shoulder to his blind side where Penny collected the ball to score in the corner and give Dodd his fourth goal, and Widnes a four point advantage with six minutes left on the clock. With Toulouse pressing hard to at least get on terms Doran collected a loose ball a couple of metres inside his own half and surged inside the opposition '40' before off-loading to the supporting Varkulis. Forced wide by the defence the centre sprinted to score by the corner flag to crush the hopes of a home revival.

The day was rounded off nicely when those on the 'official' trip were invited to join the players and officials at an informal post-match gathering, hosted by the amiable Toulouse president Carlos Zalduendo, before returning to the city and the welcoming De Danu!

This match will live long in the memory of those who were there, but not only because the exciting see-saw affair finally went the way of the Vikings. The whole weekend experience was, I think it is safe to say, enjoyed by all, except maybe the Catalan Sports representative who accompanied the 'official' party. Sydney born 'Dave' – a former youth grade teammate of a certain Shane Millard – had dared to predict a Toulouse victory with his goatee beard as the stake. On our return to the De Danu, to the massed cheers of the Widnes faithful, it was ceremoniously removed by one of our number!

Thus the Vikings first league encounter on foreign soil ended in victory and in some way made up for the shock exit from the Challenge Cup, in the same city, in 2005.

Looking back at the end of the season I asked Paul Cullen how he felt his relationship with the Widnes fans had progressed, and whether he felt that they had been won over.

"I don't honestly know whether I have [won them over] at this point. When we were beaten by Featherstone I left the field to a chorus of abuse and boos. I've simply got to work harder to win those fans over. I might never achieve that. My Warrington connection might simply be too much for some, but I've got to keep working harder. My principles are very simple. I want to be honest, I want to give value and last year [2009] the best way I can describe it is that we were inefficient."

With regard to the team's performances he added: "I'm spending other people's money. I'm spending the chairman's money; I'm spending supporters' money and that was inefficiently spent last year. We had players who I could see instantly when I came in were indifferent and that's a crime, a sin. They were simply indifferent – always injured, always ill, always dull. It's a privilege to get paid to play this sport. We're taking money from people sat in the stands who literally are, without being melodramatic, giving you their last quid at the end of the week, and that means something. I simply cannot and will not work with indifference. I can work with good players, I can work with bad players but I refuse to work with indifference.

"That's not across the whole lot because I've lost some players that I didn't want to because they've been offered more money by other clubs. I've got no complaint about that because it's a cruel, nasty, brutal way to earn a living, and you've got to respect that. You cannot force anyone to play for you as a coach or the club. You've got to have players who are prepared to give you everything they've got; they've got to be high yield and low maintenance. If not the effort of the coach gets diluted. I don't think I've got every decision right on who we are bringing in or who we are letting go. It's never 100% but the basis behind it is that we have got to give value to those who pay money whether it's the Board of Directors working at that level or it's the guy stood on the terrace who's given you his last quid to come through the door."

Coming back to work with part-time players after several years in the full-time environment at Warrington must have been a challenge in itself for the head coach. As he admitted "I'd rather have everyone living within 15 miles of the club and training full-time as full-time professionals" but "there's no point in dragging James Webster, for example, all the way from Hull six times a week. I am going to do more damage than he or the club are going to get benefit. For example on 'non-specific' training nights there is no point in a player travelling all the way to Widnes for a swimming session when it can be done at home. As a coach you can't be a control freak because you're working with 26 individuals and the best way to get the best out of individuals is to treat them as individuals. There has to be a club process but you can't treat every player exactly the same."

Recognising the need to change the structures within the club Cullen pointed out that "we [the club] were trying to be something that we're not and we couldn't be. We will be at some point in the future but you can't have a full-time club, a full-time environment with the vast majority of players on part-time contracts because it allows players to say I've only got a part-time contract so I'm only going to come in one day and one night.

"If you want consistent performance you've got to have consistent preparation and that was a major part of what I found when I came here. You had some genuine players who were literally stuck on a motorway and couldn't get to training, stuck on a building yard somewhere and couldn't get there. And you had some others who were quite simply 'swinging the lead'.

"I think the season has shown who was genuine and who wasn't, but that's not to be negative about everyone who has left. There have been many different reasons why blokes who were at the club last year won't be with us next year. Twelve or 13 players, or whatever the number is, that have left is far too many people within an organisation who had issues and had problems. With roughly 26 senior players that's 50% of your workforce had problems last year. I'm not saying that the 13 that we get, or whatever the numbers are, are all going to be perfect without issues but a lot of things need to be addressed."

As a portent of what was to come three years later Cullen offered the following: "As a coach you simply can't have baggage, if you keep it too long you'll get weighed down with it and you'll drown. The best thing is to make your mind up, make some firm decisions, be polite, be professional, 'cut' and move on, and get some players in who are going to come and not moan about the motorway, personal issues or work related issues."

Referring back to the events of 2009 from the heady days of 2012 Cullen commented: "When Widnes were denied a place in Super League in 2008, one of the issues that was flagged was that we needed to develop our youth set up. When Steve O'Connor gave me the job there were two objectives. One, was to change what wasn't working, stabilise the squad I had inherited, and get the box ticked by better performances in the Northern Rail Cup that would lead us to winning the trophy in Blackpool. Two, was to enhance the youth system set up and develop it to the point that it would eventually become the back bone of the team for years to come.

"The 2009 Northern Rail Cup win is probably not the most glamorous trophy this proud club has ever won but it is arguably the most important. Once we did that, we decided that youth development would never be a reason again to refuse Widnes a place in Super League. We worked tirelessly in this area and players that we had developed from within were drafted into the first team with a view to seeing them in that environment and spotting that potential for growth.

"We were working hard too in ensuring the best young Widnes talent stayed in Widnes and here at the Stobart Stadium Halton. That was the target back then, after 2009 when we had ticked the box, and now in 2012 we are seeing the benefit of that."

Mindful that there had been a frustrating conclusion to a roller-coaster 2009 season, which saw Steve McCormack and John Stankevitch leave the club prior to the Northern Rail Cup success, chairman Steve O'Connor promised that "we won't be resting on our laurels next season".

The Vikings' owner added "winning the Northern Rail Cup and seeing the Stobart Stadium Halton packed for the Challenge Cup semi-final has really whet my appetite for success, and one day I hope that people will have to wait for over half an hour to get out of the car park for Widnes games!"

Looking back to the Northern Rail Cup victory O'Connor admitted that "The final was absolutely nerve wracking. It was all the more important because of the box to be ticked. It was a great day, with a sell-out crowd and on the day we were worth the result. We seem to have come good at the right end of the season, but the start of the season wasn't the best."

Ironically Cup Final opponents Barrow had played a significant role in the Vikings late-season resurgence, when they inflicted a 27-6 defeat on the Vikings at the Stobart Stadium at the beginning of May. This was Widnes' fourth defeat in five games, and plainly a cause for concern, but in the next home game, against Gateshead, a determined Widnes fought back from 24-0 down to finally get home by 46-30.

The Widnes chairman admitted "After the Barrow game we realised that something was clearly wrong and Paul Cullen decided to change the training regime to nights only from days and nights. Since then not one player has missed a training session. There are no excuses on training night and they're all desperate to play, which is testimony to the discipline Paul has instilled in the players. The performances have been great over the last six to eight weeks."

Underlining his determination to succeed O'Connor said "We want to earn the right to be in Super League by being the best club outside of it, on all levels from our rugby to our matchday experience. We want to add value to the community, develop a winning culture and if we don't have six or seven fine young Widnes athletes in our team by 2012 then our investment in youth development will have been a huge failure."

Meanwhile the club's off-field activities had received further recognition through their community arm, the Valhalla Foundation. The Foundation, under the guidance of its chief executive Pat Cluskey, had already introduced several new projects with schools in the region, ranging from literacy and numeracy to sport and French when, in partnership with Wade Deacon High School, it won the 2009 Business Language Champions Innovation Award. Business Language Champions awards are made to 'businesses who can demonstrate an innovative approach to working with schools to support language learning'.

Explaining why Widnes had been successful Nick Chambers – director, Employer Taskforce commented:

"We chose Widnes Vikings for this award because we thought it was the most creative and innovative entry that was replicable by many football and rugby clubs around the country. The programme at Widnes Vikings duly highlights the benefits of learning languages and we think that is extremely important and talks to the audience – the children – in their own language and engages them in a very exciting way. It's in a real life context which is exciting and fun and inspiring."

Speaking after the awards ceremony Cluskey said, "It's amazing that an idea to enhance the game day experience for the visit of Toulouse has captured the imagination of the National Centre for Languages and to be recognised as the 2009 BLC Innovation Award Winners is a great achievement for a Co-operative Championship Club."

He also paid tribute to the "hard work of the staff and pupils at Wade Deacon [which] was instrumental in the success of the project, with teachers Carine Whitfield and Joanne Gaul to the fore."

The project, which included classroom sessions with French referee Thierry Alibert and members of the Widnes first-team squad, was subsequently featured by Sky Sports in the build-up to the televised game against Toulouse. The climax came when two Wade Deacon pupils were selected to make live announcements, in French, over the public address system during the match.

As 2009 drew to a close there was, aside from the playing of the game, the restructuring of the club, and events elsewhere, but one overriding memory. As 2008 was written into history on the back of the devastating announcement made on 22nd July, 2009 was defined by the events of Sunday 12th July when Widnes defeated Barrow by 34 points to 18 to lift the Northern Rail Cup, and began their journey back to the top tier.

2010

Once the dust had settled on 2009, with the on-field criterion box 'ticked', attention immediately turned to preparations for 2010.

Early additions to the squad included Steve Pickersgill, who made a big impression during his loan spell in 2009 and James Ford who was brought in to give more firepower in the three-quarters. With Dave Houghton and Dean Thompson promoted to the first team squad Terry O'Connor was confident that more young players would get their chance in 2010. While not discounting further permanent signings he also pointed out that the club were aiming to maximise the opportunities that the dual registration system gave them.

As the squad was developed through the close season a familiar face returned to the Stobart Stadium when Irish International Dave Allen rejoined his home-town club after spells at Oldham and Barrow, collecting a Championship Grand Final winners' medal with the Raiders. Commenting on the signing Paul Cullen said "David is a rare commodity in today's game, an 80 minute footballer who has played at the top level domestically, has international experience and has the desire to return to Super League with his home-town club." Another to be pleased with the return of Allen was conditioning coach Mick Cassidy who added: "The best is yet to come from Dave Allen. He's still young and will grow some more but he played fantastically well last year for Barrow. He'll put a lot of pressure on our back row forwards."

Allen himself commented that: "To play for your home-town club is a big thing and with the changes taking place at Widnes it's certainly the place to be. I have ambitions of returning to Super League and I think that by rejoining the Vikings I have a great chance of fulfilling them in 2012."

As the pre-season training was stepped up O'Connor stated the season's targets were "to defend our trophy [Northern Rail Cup] and with a little more consistency I am sure we will be there or thereabouts come Co-operative Championship Grand Final time."

By the time the squad had assembled to prepare for the new season Cassidy had freshened up the club's fitness regime with some of his own training plans and explained that the first week "was mainly a re-group after the lads had all had six weeks off. Two of those weeks were complete rest and after that they all had individual training schemes to follow. Now it's my job to take a look at the lads, identify their early strengths and weaknesses and help them to improve, so that when we start up next year we are stronger overall as a team and can peak around play-off time next season.

"We've got all new training gear, such as wrestling mats, and the next four weeks will be massive for us. We've introduced a lot of high impact training, so that the body is hardened up to contact once we get going for good."

With the pre-season slog out of the way attention turned to the real thing as the group stages of the Northern Rail Cup got under way. Kicking off with a home fixture against Gateshead Thunder the Vikings included six new signings as they ran in 11 tries – four from debutant James Ford – in a comprehensive 50-6 win. Amazingly only three of those tries were converted as the club suffered from the close season exit of three experienced kickers in Gavin Dodd, Tim Hartley and Craig Hall.

In what was ultimately an inconsistent and disappointing season Widnes again managed to qualify for the knockout stages of the Northern Rail Cup, reaching the Final for the third time in four years, and the end of season play-offs. After a promising opening to the season which saw progress in both cup competitions, and a solid start in the league, the team's form took a sudden dip in mid-season as they lost seven out of nine league matches, including a run of five successive defeats.

However, one of the highlights of the season was the progress of Widnes-born Shane Grady who, having played bit parts in 2008 and 2009, established himself as a regular in 2010. He went on to finish the season with 254 points from his 26 appearances, having crossed the whitewash 13 times and, with 101 goals, solving the team's goal-kicking problem. Operating mainly in the centre Grady really caught the eye in the 72-10 annihilation of Keighley Cougars on the opening day of the league campaign when he plundered a personal total of 32 points from three tries and 10 conversions.

Widnes were certainly providing entertainment home and away at this stage of the season as they continued to rack up some impressive scores. The only problem was that the defence was proving as generous as the attack was creative. Another fine performance in this early part of the season came when the Vikings defeated old adversaries Whitehaven at the Stobart Stadium. With both teams hit by injuries Widnes, with only 17 fit players, simply tore 'Haven apart with Anthony Thackeray picking holes in the opposition defence almost at will. With Widnes leading 30-2 after 25 minutes the game was all but over and despite a brief rally from Whitehaven the Vikings, with nine different try scorers for the second time this season, ran out comfortable 48-18 winners. The final try of the afternoon brought Paddy Flynn's Widnes points total to 100.

Although the Vikings had done battle for league points with French club Toulouse Olympique in 2009, the 2010 fixture list now threw up the rare sight of two French clubs providing the opposition on successive weekends as Toulouse and Lezignan visited Widnes. Having won both fixtures against Toulouse in 2009 the French outfit arrived at the Stobart Stadium determined to exact revenge and a poor, error strewn first-half performance from Widnes allowed them to assume control to such an extent that they led 42-12 on the hour. Toulouse were so dominant that at one stage they notched five tries without reply from their hosts.

In the last quarter Toulouse became as ineffective as Widnes had been for much of the game as the hosts fought to get a foothold in the game. Anthony Thackeray, operating at scrum-half in the absence of James Webster, was at the centre of everything, as well as scoring a hat-trick of tries, as Widnes somehow rallied to almost register an unlikely win. Indeed 'Thacks' scored the try of the match when he sold an outrageous dummy on halfway to sprint through a bemused defence, as the Vikings ran in five tries but, crucially, only converted two of them into six points, to lose by 42 points to 38.

The match was not to be without controversy either as Shane Grady attempted a quick last minute conversion in an attempt to give the Vikings one last play in which to snatch victory. With the touch judges giving a 'split decision' there was confusion within the ground as to whether or not the goal had been awarded. The confusion was increased as the two points, initially added on the scoreboard, were removed. Widnes threw the ball around in a vain attempt to save the game, but the hooter ended their chances. Not only were many fans unsure of the final score but several internet and written media outlets carried an incorrect score as the referee's signal was far from clear. The situation was finally clarified on the Monday morning when the Vikings' Media Manager, Mark Naughton, e-mailed Stuart Cummings at the RFL for clarification and was informed that the 'goal' had in fact been awarded by referee Jamie Leahy.

The week after the Toulouse game the Vikings were due to entertain another French side, Lezignan, in the Challenge Cup, but events a thousand miles away caused the match to be postponed. The eruption of a volcano at Eyjafjoll in Iceland on 14th April caused large areas of the skies of northern Europe to be covered by a volcanic ash cloud, causing massive disruption to air travel as flights were grounded. Eventually the match was rescheduled for the following Thursday evening after Lezignan had made arrangements to travel by ferry and coach. By the time that the match was played Widnes were already aware that victory would secure a home tie in the next round against Super League leaders Wigan Warriors.

However, the club were in the midst of an injury crisis and head coach Paul Cullen commented, on the Tuesday before the Lezignan match, that while he had experienced injury crises at his previous clubs "none of them have been anywhere near as serious as the one we're facing now. We don't have 17 fit players to play against Lezignan, and we haven't been anywhere near full strength all season." So bad was the situation that Cullen admitted that he was "very uncomfortable with the fact that I'm playing a bloke with a broken hand and one with a dislocated finger. But we've got no other option."

So with several key players missing the Vikings took the field with Scott Yates playing on the left wing and a bench comprising Danny Hulme (aged 19), Dave Houghton (20) Jack Smith (18) and Tom Kelly (18). While Hulme and Houghton had made two and 14 substitute appearances respectively Smith and Kelly were making their debuts.

Demonstrating a liking for French opposition Anthony Thackeray was again the tormentor-in-chief as Widnes advanced into the next round after a hard fought encounter. Although Widnes had the benefit of a third minute try from James Coyle, Lezignan showed their mettle by breaking back to take a 14-6 lead inside the first 10 minutes, including a try from former Viking Adel Fellous. Midway through the half Widnes had recovered from the shock and ran in five tries in the space of 16 minutes to effectively seal the win. While Yates grabbed the headlines with a hat-trick of tries and Shane Grady took his season's tally to 64 goals Paul Cullen paid tribute to his team's effort, saying "To have seven or eight players under the age of 21 is superb. The boys and the club thoroughly deserve to host Wigan."

Before the Vikings could take on the might of their Super League opponents there was an important league encounter with Featherstone Rovers, in what proved to be an untypical match, compared to what had gone before. To this point Widnes' 13 competitive matches had yielded an average of 64 points per game. But when league leaders Rovers came to town defences were very much on top as Widnes fell by eight points to nine in the lowest scoring game of the season.

In a match of just four tries, none of which were converted, it was ironic that the boot should decide the outcome. Unfortunately that boot belonged to Liam Finn as he made the most of a somewhat harsh penalty awarded by Jamie Leahy just two minutes from time. With the scores level at 8-8 the official hastily penalised, without the usual warning, the Widnes loose forward for not binding in the scrum.

A scrappy match punctuated by errors from both sides, and the referee's whistle, saw Featherstone take the lead in the third minute through Jessie Joe Parker, before ex-Viking Andy Kain doubled their advantage just before the half hour mark. The evening's poor kicking was underlined when, on the stroke of half-time, Kyle Briggs scuffed a penalty wide.

Trailing 8-0 at the break Widnes came out showing a more positive and determined attitude to register their first try on 44 minutes. James Webster had made a superb interception and sprinted 60 metres before being tackled by Matty Dale who, laying on for too long, earned himself a spell in the sin bin. In the next set the ball was moved out to Matt Gardner who powered over from close range. With the impressive Lee Doran showing the way Widnes drew level with 20 minutes remaining when Toa Kohe Love – making his 300th career appearance – set up Paddy Flynn. Try as they might the Vikings couldn't force the decisive score and fell to that harsh penalty decision.

So on the back of their third home defeat of the season Widnes went into their 2,000th competitive home match when they entertained Wigan in the Challenge Cup. With 16 members of the first team squad unavailable – including experienced campaigners such as Jim Gannon, Dean Gaskell, Gareth Haggerty and Mark Smith – Widnes took on the might of the Warriors with eight home-grown players in the side. It came as no surprise when Widnes were brushed aside by their opponents as Wigan ran in 12 tries at a canter to move into the next round with a 64-10 victory.

Playing at stand-off was the burgeoning talent of Sam Tomkins who shone throughout while helping himself to a hat-trick in the last 18 minutes. The best Widnes could offer in the first half was a couple of promising sets early on, while Shane Grady missed a penalty. By half-time Wigan had coasted to a 36-0 lead with two of the tries coming from former Widnes loanee Joel Tomkins who had made eight appearances for the Vikings in 2007.

Immediately after the break Karl Pryce completed his hat-trick and Sean O'Loughlin added another try to leave Widnes trailing by 48 points. However, the young Vikings refused to give in and, led by the in-form Lee Doran, finally got on the scoreboard, when Grady put Matt Gardner over in the corner, for the first of his brace of tries, with the young centre adding a superb conversion from the touchline. But this was only the cue for Sam Tomkins to step up and demonstrate the skill and athleticism that Widnes would be up against if they gained entry to Super League in two years' time.

Returning to Championship action it was to be nearly another two months before Widnes again tasted success in a league game. This was, however, offset to some degree by the almost customary successes in the Northern Rail Cup. A quarter-final victory over last year's Final opponents, Barrow, was followed by a comfortable 'Anthony Thackeray inspired' 48-18 victory at Keighley in the semi-final to take the Vikings back to Blackpool, for what would prove to be the last time.

Widnes fans had made two previous trips to Blackpool in recent years for Northern Rail Cup Finals and returned with the spoils on each occasion. However, 2010 was the year of the underdog as Batley Bulldogs snatched the trophy from Widnes' grasp just two minutes from time. Although the 5,000 plus fans who made the trip were crestfallen by the defeat they must surely have caused a stir among the games hierarchy as they demonstrated yet again how well the potential Super League new boys are supported.

As had been the case on several occasions during the season Widnes got off to a bad start as the Bulldogs established a 12 point lead, but the Vikings had fought back to lead 24-15 with 12 minutes left. It was only eight minutes into the match that Batley had established that 12 point lead through tries from Jason Walton and Sean Hesketh, both converted by Gareth Moore, to give Widnes an uphill battle to retain their trophy.

However, the Vikings got back into the game in the 14th minute when they were awarded a penalty by referee Robert Hicks. Following a quick tap Ben Davies, who had only been on the pitch for three minutes, barged over from close range for a try converted by Shane Grady. Widnes fans were breathing the damp sea air a lot easier just three minutes later when, following a Batley drop-out, Anthony Thackeray dummied his way through the defence to score under the posts. Grady's goal levelled the scores. But in the 34th minute Batley edged in front with a Moore drop-goal, after a failed attempt by Thomas Coyle seemed to prompt the Bulldogs' scrum-half into action. A penalty from the same player gave Batley a 15-12 lead at half-time.

Five minutes into the second half normal service seemed to be resumed when a converted Paddy Flynn try swung the advantage narrowly to Widnes before a Chris Gerrard try and another Grady conversion gave the Vikings a nine point cushion as the game entered its closing stages. Batley continued to take the fight to Widnes and just three minutes later winger Alex Brown cut inside to score a converted try to set up a tense finish. Brown then leapt high to cleanly collect a high ball from Moore to score his second from close range and clinch the trophy for Batley.

A tough local derby against Leigh Centurions provided the ideal opportunity to bounce back but Widnes' losing run in the league continued as Leigh ran out convincing winners by 38 points to 18 at the Stobart Stadium. After yet another defeat at Halifax the Vikings finally got back to winning ways in another high-scoring match against Toulouse.

In what turned out to be a close affair in southern France Widnes collected the three points to give their flagging play-off hopes a boost. Trailing to a converted Carlos Mendes fifth minute try the Vikings fought back to take the lead in the 11th minute. A Danny Craven try, converted by himself, levelled matters before a revitalised Mark Smith raced in from 20 metres. Further tries followed from Stefan Marsh and Paddy Flynn before Anthony Thackeray intercepted a Toulouse pass on his own '40' to sprint clear and score under the posts. Dean Gaskell's touchdown in the corner and Craven's four goals gave Widnes a commanding lead at the interval. Toulouse's only response had been a Nathan Wynn penalty as the Vikings had surged to a 32-8 lead at half-time.

This became a typical game of two halves as Toulouse hit back strongly after Marsh had extended Widnes' lead. The centre, on loan from Wigan, collected the ball inside his own '40' to sprint into opposition territory before exchanging passes with Flynn 15 metres out, side-stepping five defenders and cutting inside to score under the posts. The hosts took control almost immediately and ran in four unanswered tries in the space of 11 minutes as Mendes added his second followed by a brace from Maria, separated by a clever effort from Eric Anselme. Wynn added three conversions to reduce the Vikings' lead to just eight points, and set Widnes nerves jangling with 15 minutes left on the clock. It wasn't until Matt Gardner took a short pass from Smith to crash over two minutes from time that the Widnes faithful could again breathe easily.

Further wins followed, against Sheffield Eagles at the Stobart Stadium, and trips to Barrow Raiders and Keighley Cougars, to secure their place in the play-offs. With the comfortable win at Barrow being notable for Richard Varkulis' first senior hat-trick, the limelight at Keighley was stolen by two Vikings Academy products. Danny Craven had an excellent afternoon, scoring three tries and notching four goals, but the lasting memory for most Widnes fans was the length-of-the-field try scored by Alex Brown, which later won him the Supporters' Club Try of the Season accolade. Collecting a loose ball out wide on his own 10 metre line the young winger showed agility and electric pace to outrun the entire Keighley side to touch down under the posts.

But although Widnes had secured that spot on the back of another mini revival they were to limp out of the play-offs at the first hurdle on their return to Barrow, losing by 38 points to nil. But typical of an injury ravaged season – 40 players had pulled on the first team shirt – the Vikings lost Danny Craven and Scott Yates during the early stages of the game and played the entire second half with just one fit substitute.

One bright element of the year had been the emergence, in the latter part of the season, of Craven as a genuine first team player. Making his debut off the bench, in front of the Sky cameras on a wet and wild evening at Whitehaven, the 18-year-old Academy product turned in an encouraging performance at full-back which included two goals. He returned to the starting line-up for the final seven matches and enhanced his growing reputation with a total haul of five tries and 23 goals from his eight appearances.

At the end of the season there was naturally a cull of the first team squad as plans were made for 2011 and beyond, but the defeat at Barrow was a particularly unsatisfactory way to publicly bid farewell to players who had been loyal servants to the club.

James Webster and Toa Kohe Love, who had been valuable members of the team that 'ticked the box' in July 2009, had already left the club in mid-season, but for differing reasons. Webster had been released from his contract in May to return to Hull FC to begin a coaching career alongside Richard Agar. In the relatively short spell that Webster had with Widnes he had come closest to surviving the poisoned chalice of the No. 7 shirt by displaying a high level of consistency in the 43 games he played for the Vikings. Kohe Love, a firm fans' favourite, had sustained a knee injury in the Vikings Northern Rail Cup semi-final at Keighley in June, and following reconstructive surgery, was forced to announce his retirement. In his two spells with Widnes the classy centre scored 32 tries in his 54 games.

While home-grown products Scott Yates, Matt Strong, and Dean Thompson were all to move on to Rochdale Hornets, there were three experienced, and very popular, players who also brought down the curtain on their Widnes careers on that miserable night in Barrow.

Stalwart pack members Lee Doran and Jim Gannon had consistently given their all in a Vikings shirt, seeing both highs and lows in their Widnes careers, which had seen them clock up 90 and 87 matches respectively. While Doran took on a player-coach role with Whitehaven, Gannon returned to his first English club, Halifax, having made his 300th appearance in the English game in that Northern Rail Cup Final defeat to Batley Bulldogs.

However, the most surprising name on the list of players leaving the Stobart Stadium was that of former skipper Mark Smith, arguably the most popular player to pull on a Widnes shirt for many years. A true leader Smith, a Challenge Cup winner with Wigan in 2002, always led from the front no matter what the circumstances, and became one of the 'famous five' when the club sank into Administration. When 'Smithy' moved on he had made 167 appearances in a Widnes shirt, scoring 60 tries and two drop-goals, in a career of 290 senior appearances and 72 tries. Many felt that his loyalty to the club in its darkest hour deserved at least another year, but it wasn't to be, and he linked up again with former coach Steve McCormack at Swinton.

There remained a significant number who felt, that despite losing the captaincy to Dave Allen in mid-season, the talismanic hooker was the ideal man to lead the club back into the top flight – a desire which Smith, at the time the club's longest serving player, had expressed earlier in the season. Having sampled life at the top with home town club Wigan, after signing for them at 14 years of age – including a winning Challenge Cup Final appearance and a Super League Grand Final – Smith was looking forward to returning to that level with Widnes. No doubt the appeal of running out at the DW (JJB) Stadium was high on his agenda as he admits that after 123 games for the Warriors he "left Wigan under a bit of a black cloud really. I'd signed a contract and two weeks later I was at Widnes."

From his first day at Widnes Smith had enjoyed life at the club, even though they suffered relegation at the end of his first year. "It was the best year I'd had because I enjoyed turning up every day. I enjoyed training; I enjoyed my life and I enjoyed playing because it was something I wasn't doing at Wigan – I was getting five or six minutes. When I came here I was getting 50 or 60 minutes."

At the age of 28 'Smithy' still felt that he had something to offer at the highest level and admitted that he hoped to "carry on playing for Widnes, hopefully in Super League. I want to stay at Widnes and lead the club into Super League, but I know I have to play well to be offered a contract for that to happen."

Indeed so strong was his desire to see out his career at Widnes that he offered to take a pay cut in order to stay at the club when he was informed of the "hugely disappointing" decision to release him. However, Terry O'Connor informed Smith that the decision wasn't about money, but the fact that Paul Cullen didn't see him in his plans for 2011. Accepting the decision, and bearing no grudges, Smith commented that "rugby league coaches are there to make tough decisions, and I respect the decision not to keep me. I've seen players moved on before and its part and parcel of the game."

Looking back over his six years at Widnes Smith added "I would like to say a big thank you to the club and the fans at Widnes. They have been phenomenal. It will be very emotional for me and my family when we say goodbye."

Speaking before the full list was announced Sporting Director Terry O'Connor said "Mark Smith has given us six years of outstanding service and has been a stand-out performer throughout. Mark, Lee, Scott and Matt have all worn the Widnes shirt with pride and never given less than their best."

Ironically had Widnes beaten Barrow in that play-off fixture they would have then had a home tie against Sheffield, the chance to progress further, and the opportunity for players and fans to show their mutual respect and thanks. The players had earned the right to say goodbye in front of their own fans.

2010 had begun with Terry O'Connor, Phil Finney, Head of Youth Performance, and Reserve team coach Dave Banks taking a young squad to France to take on Carcassonne as part of the 70th anniversary celebrations of France's most successful club. The young Vikings had a brief taste of celebrity, enjoying the trappings of visiting the historic town, an official reception and post match festivities in addition to taking on their host's first team. In front of a crowd of 800 fans the Vikings second string did themselves proud with an excellent performance in the 32-14 defeat.

Trailed in promotional material as 'Super League candidates', the invitation was another feather in the cap of the club as they continued to build towards the next licensing application process.

However, as the intensity of the application process picked up, there was a significant change in the off-field team, with the appointment of Julie Gaskell as the club's new chief executive, in succession to Alex Bonney.

Having fulfilled his remit of "controlling costs without interfering with playing budgets" Bonney identified Ms Gaskell's differing skill set as key to establishing the club as a "real contender" in Super League. Introducing his successor in his final programme notes he added that "Julie has worked in a number of senior management roles at both United Utilities and the Stobart Group, and more recently has run her own consultancy business.

"She has significant professional experience in the management and delivery of large scale sponsorship programmes that have included the [2002] Commonwealth Games, World Firefighter games and Liverpool's European Capital of Culture Year in 2008."

An interesting, but little-known, fact about the Vikings' new chief executive is that having left United Utilities she very nearly gained employment at Buckingham Palace. While an application for the post of Assistant Private Secretary to the Queen resulted in Ms Gaskell being short-listed for the post, it subsequently became a case of 'The Palace's loss is Widnes' gain.'

Although recovering from a broken back when the call came from Steve O'Connor, Ms Gaskell came down to the club for a few weeks to "try it out" and subsequently agreed to take the post. In her early days with the Vikings Ms Gaskell described the club as "being like a toddler – just about standing up but still dribbling and biting on the furniture and needing to stand on its own two feet and look after itself".

While paying tribute to the great support received from Paul Cullen and Terry O'Connor, she conceded that she was immediately struck by the dedication of all the staff who, as fans themselves, were "very supportive and not motivated by rewards".

Although he was later to return as Financial Controller on the club's return to the top flight, Bonney's parting message in August 2010 was "I would like to thank all the staff here at the Stobart Stadium Halton. It has been a pleasure working with them all. Your club is in safe hands."

Alex Bonney had stood down after a hectic and demanding three year stint that helped to put the club back on its feet after Administration. Among the initial targets Bonney identified changing the public perception of the club as paramount. "A lot of people disliked the club and disliked the lottery. It was a case of starting from scratch and getting people on side quickly."

It really was 'backs to the wall stuff' as the former chief executive explained: "We had to get in a new coach; build a new team, and we had no contacts at all within rugby, and no kit or kit suppliers. We arrived so late in the day that we had no time to organise kit and bought the Nike kit off-the-shelf and sent it away to be embroidered."

Top: *Champagne corks pop as the journey back to Super League starts.* (Photo 1)

Middle: *…and the fans sang… "Cullen is a Viking".* (Photo 2)

Bottom: *Red Letter Day.* (Photo 3)

Adam Blinston and Anthony Thackeray deliver the 2011 Super League Licence Bid in an Eddie Stobart truck. (Photo 4)

Super League here we come! Clare and Steve O'Connor lead the celebrations. (Photo 5)

David Parr, Julie Gaskell, Steve O'Connor and Cllr Phil Harris prepare to turf out the old pitch. (Photo 6)

The new i-Pitch under construction. (Photo 7)

Dean Gaskell. The last of the 'Famous Five' to move on. (Photo 8)

Ben Kavanagh. The sole survivor from the first match of the O'Connor era. (Photo 9)

Danny Craven. Scorer of the club's first Super League try of 2012. (Photo 10)

Lloyd White scoring the drop goal that beat Wigan Warriors. (Photo 11)

Denis Betts and Mick Cassidy celebrate the win over Wigan. (Photo 12)

Patrick Ah Van. Top scorer in 2012 with 16 tries and 34 goals. (Photo 13)

Above: In his 125th game Ben Cross finally claims the first try of his career. (Photo 14)

Left: Hep Cahill – aka the 'Masked Man'. (Photo 15)

A more recognisable Hep Cahill receiving his Player of the Year Award from Denis Betts. (Photo 16)

Helen Baxter and her original 'Kemik'.
(Photo 17)

Stuart Wright presents his 1977 World Cup suit to Deb Townsend, Curator of Widnes Rugby League Museum. (Photo 18)

Mark Smith presents Gavid Dodd with the Widnes Rugby League Museum Award to mark his 100th game for the club. (Photo 19)

Situated among several Super League clubs, who were a better option for sponsors, Bonney pointed out that "the only sponsors that the club had at this stage were the Stobart Group and Halton Borough Council, and commercially the business wasn't viable at that without a benefactor".

Looking back to those early days Bonney told me that a major success was "the fact that the club kept going and survived. People don't appreciate how much money you lose when you are spending the salary cap and running a youth development programme – it's not a sustainable business without a substantial benefactor. When the costs of running a Super League Academy structure, coaching staff, physios, and back office staff are added to the £400k salary cap the true cost is nearly 1 million."

This is emphasised by the disparity in central funding between the leagues, as the Championship clubs only receive £100,000 per year as opposed to their top flight counterparts receiving that amount per month.

Steve O'Connor acknowledged the work done by the outgoing Chief Excecutive saying "Alex has done an excellent job since he came on board and I am very sad to see him leave. He has put in a lot of hard work behind the scenes, and that hard work will hopefully pay off next year – I am sure it will."

Charged by chairman Steve O'Connor to deliver a successful Super League Licence application Ms Gaskell said on her appointment "It's not fair that people think Widnes are definitely in. I think it's disrespectful to other clubs, if that's what people are saying."

Ms Gaskell added: "I have already been working alongside Alex and the rest of the management team and I have been impressed by what I have seen. I see my role as continuing the club's progress, ensuring a successful Super League application and making sure that we are in the best possible shape to fulfil our ambitious long-term targets."

Admitting that the application was a large part of her role, the self-confessed target-driven Ms Gaskell immediately began work on setting a variety of objectives to enable the club to deliver an "irresistible application". "We have to put a solid and attractive application in, and we will ensure we have met all the criteria set by the RFL" added the Vikings' chief executive.

"Widnes is a great club and has a tremendous and decorated past of which we are all very proud. But we can't live in the past, we have to be a forward thinking club, and up there with the best in Super League.

"The first priority is to re-engage with the fans and keep the people of Widnes working alongside us over the next few years. The club has been run very well but I think that I can bring in some new ideas that will help take Widnes to the next level."

A massive step in the right direction came when the club was able to announce a staggering £1 million profit from the financial year ending November 2009. These excellent results came just three years after Steve O'Connor had saved the club from extinction, and just 12 months after posting losses of £986,381.

The figures for 2008 necessarily included, in the words of O'Connor, "much needed investment in infrastructure, personnel and processes" while "outstanding payroll, commissions and Rugby League debts from the previous club had to be settled in order to receive a playing Licence". In addition "significant professional consultancy and marketing costs" were incurred in the abortive 2008 bid for a Super League Licence.

Nevertheless the turnaround in 12 months was remarkable, as it included a turnover figure of £2.5 million, far in excess of the £1 million required to meet the licensing criteria.

In addition the Widnes owner was able to inform Vikings fans, and the wider rugby league community that he was "very proud indeed to report that our club is free of debt and is in robust good health and underpinned by a sustainable business plan". Another timely boost came at the annual Co-operative Championship Dinner, just weeks before the Super League Licence application had to be submitted, when the club received the Club of the Year Award. This award recognised not only the excellent off-field achievements but also the impressive successes of the club's youth set-up.

That youth set-up, under the guidance of Phil Finney, had indeed earned a glowing reputation in the sport, the culmination of which was an announcement that the club had secured the signatures of no fewer than 13 juniors. Twelve of those players had come from the Vikings' all-conquering under-16 team. Head of Youth Performance Finney commented: "To sign players of this calibre is fantastic for us as a club. What is even more pleasing is that each of these players only wanted to sign for Widnes Vikings, despite offers from elsewhere, which gives us great hope for now and the future." Indeed at the time of writing two of these young hopefuls, Tom Gilmore and Jack Owens, had made their Super League debuts for the Vikings.

As the year drew to a close Finney and the club were given further cause for celebration with the announcement of four young Vikings in the England Academy Squad. Alex Brown, Tom Gilmore, Declan Hulme and Jack Owens had all been selected as members of the squad to face Wales and France after the turn of the year – a marvellous achievement for a Championship club. Acknowledging the "well deserved recognition for each of the players' efforts" Finney went on to add "I am appreciative of the club's policy to invest in its youth which has provided our town's local players with a platform to achieve accolades such as this," before paying tribute to the work of Martin Cunningham, Paul Hulme, Dom Smith and Dave Rolt.

Demonstrating the long-term planning of the club Paul Cullen commented: "We are not promising to commit to youth development if we get to Super League, we are well and truly up and running, and have been for a number of years.

"In fact we were the most successful under-18s team in last season's Super League under-18s competition which was a remarkable achievement on a Championship budget. We are delighted that these young players can achieve international recognition at a Championship club."

The major event, however, of the 2010 close season was the restructuring of the coaching department with Paul Cullen 'moving upstairs' to become Director of Rugby and the appointment of Denis Betts as head coach. As a result of the new structure Stuart Wilkinson, who had contributed much to the youth set-up, and was latterly Assistant Coach to Cullen, left the club. In announcing the new structure chairman Steve O'Connor commented that "The board and I are delighted that Paul has agreed to become our first Director of Rugby and we are equally delighted that Denis Betts has agreed to join us as our head coach.

"The role of Director of Rugby is to ensure that we work hard in a strategic fashion in every aspect of our rugby operations, and have a consistent coaching policy across all our teams. I am confident that Paul Cullen has the experience to make a success of this new role and that he will play an important part in the future of our club."

When Cullen hung up his boots in 1996 he began a coaching career that, beginning with Warrington Under-21s, took in head coach roles with Whitehaven and Warrington, as well as coaching England to success in the 2006 Federation Shield. Now some 14 years, and 300 games later, and having completed two years as head coach with the Vikings he was to take on a new role.

Commenting on his new role Cullen told the *Widnes Weekly News*: "It's a little bit strange to be fair, a little bit bizarre. I've been coaching for a long time now. I've got to put the tracksuit down and allow Denis [Betts] to get on with what he's good at. My role is simply to support him in anything and in any way that he wants. I'm not here to coach Denis or to coach the players, I'm here to provide support if necessary, and work on all other aspects of what's required. Not only to get the club up to Super League standard but to be self-sustainable and to succeed."

Confirming that he was "without a shadow of doubt" looking forward to a Super League return in 2012 Cullen added: "I've got some long-term plans and long-term ambitions and they're all built around the soundbite of getting Widnes back to the position that we deserve to be in.

"I am really looking forward to working with the board and senior management to build our club into one of the most successful in rugby league. This is a great club with a great future and I am privileged to be a part of it."

Referring to his successor as head coach Cullen added: "Denis has accepted the challenge and we are really pleased that we're able to bring back an English coach of Denis' ability and also potential, so it's very exciting times."

Commenting on the appointment of ex-Great Britain second row forward and ex-Wigan head coach Betts, Steve O'Connor pointed out that "Denis Betts has considerable experience of coaching at a senior level with both Wigan Warriors and Gloucester RUFC, and his decision to join the Vikings is a symbol of our determination to return to Super League and build a team of the highest quality."

Betts himself said: "I know from my conversations with Steve O'Connor and Paul Cullen that the Vikings have very exciting plans for the development of the club. My role is to coach the first team squad and achieve a consistent level of success on the field.

"It is a challenge that I relish, and I look forward to working with Paul and the rest of the rugby operation to give the Vikings' fans a team they can be proud to support, and a team equipped with the skills and ability required to play to the highest levels in the Championship and, eventually, in the Super League."

Betts had begun his coaching career with the Wigan Academy before being appointed assistant to Mike Gregory in 2003, subsequently taking over the reins when Gregory was taken ill. Twelve months later Ian Millward's experience was preferred by the Wigan hierarchy and Betts worked with the former St Helens head coach until the end of the 2005 season.

While some observers had felt that Betts was not ready for the 'top job' the man himself said significantly that "I was ready to be head coach. I knew as much about the game then as I know now. What I've learned since has been man-management".

Betts' escape from an unhappy alliance at Wigan came about when he was invited by Bryan Redpath, formerly of Sale Sharks, to help out at Gloucester rugby union club. Betts explained: "I knew Bryan Redpath really well and he asked me to come down to Gloucester on a part-time basis. I went down a couple of times to help put some systems in place. When I decided to leave Wigan and resigned Gloucester offered me a role and I signed an initial six month contract to see if I would like it. I ended up moving down there full-time and stayed for five years."

Betts' new role at Gloucester saw him assume responsibility for skills and development, working with both the forwards and backs. He describes it as "a varied role which covered every aspect of the game outside of the nuances of rugby union which I had very little knowledge of such as kick-off, lineout and scrum set pieces". In particular he worked on "movement patterns in defence and attack, and core skills such as tackling techniques, carrying the ball, and catch and pass."

The Widnes vacancy coincided with Betts' desire to return to rugby league. "I had been in rugby union for five years and got to the stage where I felt that if I was to get back into rugby league it had to be now. I'd spent five years coaching in rugby league – from the Wigan Academy side to 18 months as head coach – widened my coaching base through courses and working in a different environment and stretched myself, but rugby league was where I really wanted to be.

"I had a couple of enquiries and Wigan came back to me and offered me the assistant coach's job, but I was ready to head up an organisation and lead from the front."

Before securing the Widnes post Betts had been interviewed for the England head coach role which ultimately went to Steve McNamara. He explained: "The RFL approached me and asked if I'd like to apply for the job, which I did. I went for an interview and got through to the last two with Steve McNamara. That was one of the driving forces that pulled me back towards the game a little bit. It made me think where do I want to be in 10 years time? And this is where I want to be, back in rugby league."

So, after a couple of calls from Terry O'Connor, to see if he was interested in the Widnes job, Betts met O'Connor and Paul Cullen in a Manchester hotel where he outlined his thoughts and plans about where he saw his career going. Happily this coincided with the club's aims and ambitions and the ex-Wigan man subsequently became Widnes' new head coach, saying of his new club: "It's not a sleeping giant, it's a giant, and we're ready to move forward now and under some very good people we're trying to build some momentum. I want to be a career coach and finding the right club, with the right values and the right people took time. As soon as I met Terry and Paul, I felt excited. "

Speaking to the *Widnes Weekly News* a week after his appointment Betts, recognising the stature of the club, identified his ambition: "To win – This is Widnes", adding that "this club needs to start winning trophies again [and] be a successful organisation, building on what's happening behind the scenes." He also considered it a "massive help to be around people who have been successful, who you can disagree with and know nothing bad will come of it", adding "I don't think I've ever agreed with Terry O'Connor, because he's always wrong!"

But with a club of Widnes' stature comes a particular type of pressure, which the phlegmatic Betts readily accepted with: "That's just the nature of the beast. There's no hiding from it. That's the way it's always been. Professional sport is like that. Hopefully, when you meet the people, you find out what the organisation is all about. Is it a flash in the pan? Does it want something it can't achieve? And the answer is no and that's why I'm here."

While he would no doubt be recruiting his own squad for 2011 Betts also had the benefit of inheriting the pool of talent coming through the club's youth structure, as a result of Steve O'Connor's decision to commit investment into producing their own player pathway. Identifying Widnes as the only club in the Championship with a youth structure that develops its own players Betts added: "this area produces world class rugby league players who don't want to play for anybody else. They want to play for Widnes Vikings. It's one of the driving forces behind the club, it's about a sustainable future for the club and the two criteria when you're looking at a club. One is development and one is recruitment."

Also, during the course of 2010 one of the club's most successful supporters' organisations had achieved a marvellous landmark when its fundraising passed the £100,000 mark. Formed on the 10th anniversary of Widnes becoming the first official World Club Champions in 1989, Vikings Quids In (VIQI) had at the time of writing raised in excess of £128,000, of which £115,000 has already been handed over to the club to assist in the signing of several key players. Although Widnes had been able, with VIQI's assistance, to complete the signings of players such as Martin Crompton, David Peachey, Damien Blanch and Anthony Thackeray the successful 2009 Northern Rail Cup Final team clearly demonstrated the value of the organisation to the parent club. No fewer than six players in that team – John Duffy, Richard Fletcher, James Webster, Thackeray, Steve Pickersgill and Kevin Penny – had joined the Vikings due, at least in part, to VIQI's contribution of £17,500.

Spurred by the fact that Crompton was about to join Leigh, as they had offered him £50 per game more than Widnes, Jason Shaw and a group of like-minded fans resolved to do something about it. So at an inaugural meeting at Appleton Village Social Club VIQI was founded with an initial membership of 25, which has since grown to a figure in excess of two hundred. In return for donating the equivalent of £1 per week fans can, and plainly have, contributed in a tangible manner to the recruitment and retention of players.

The funds raised by that initial group were sufficient to ensure that Crompton spent his final season as a player at Widnes, leading them to Grand Final success and entry into Super League, before joining the club's coaching staff. VIQI's contribution to that deal was an impressive £5,300 which was made up of a signing on fee, weekly payments and shirt sponsorship.

Another landmark for VIQI came in 2006 when they handed over a total of £28,000 to the club, with the single largest contribution of £20,000 making the signing of Australian international full-back David Peachey possible. Peachey, having agreed to join Widnes if they gained promotion to Super League, honoured that agreement despite the Vikings' Grand Final defeat against Hull KR, with VIQI's contribution enabling the club to seal the deal. Peachey's early return to Australia allowed the 'unspent' £10,000 to be re-allocated to help fund the club's under-18 team and the retention of Damien Blanch, while a further £8,000 was used to recruit John Kirkpatrick from London Broncos and to support the under-15 and under-16 squads.

During its 12 years VIQI has assisted the club to sign or retain more than 30 players, ranging from senior professionals to products of its highly successful Academy structure. While the trustees of the scheme are regularly in talks with the club to see how the funds can best be used to help bring in the highest calibre of players available, the signing of James Webster allowed VIQI to break the mould. By providing the former Hull KR and Hull FC player with a personally sponsored car, VIQI enabled the club to clinch a deal despite the Hull-based player being chased by several Super League clubs.

Further demonstration of VIQI's value to the club came at the end of 2010 when it appeared that Anthony Thackeray was about to move on to pastures new. Having already aided the initial signing of Thackeray in 2009, and in the face of interest from other clubs, VIQI launched a recruitment drive which saw 100 new members sign up in 10 days and enabled the Vikings to retain the half-back. The extra funds generated were sufficient to allow the club to offer Thackeray a contract as a Community Development Officer, in addition to his playing contract.

As Shaw, who runs the scheme with his wife Joanne, and has been a Widnes fan for 37 years, said at the time: "Anthony clearly showed his desire to remain a Widnes player and he was overwhelmed by the generosity of the Widnes fans. It's at times like this when I remember why we started this scheme. It's about making a difference and for me it's a way of trying to bring back the glory days when I watched us regularly picking up silverware."

Speaking in May 2010 both chief executive Alex Bonney and chairman Steve O'Connor applauded the scheme. Bonney commented that "VIQI has specifically helped this season with the recruitment of Chris Gerrard and Shaun Ainscough, and together with the 'Dream Ticket' is the ideal vehicle to support the Vikings."

Looking back to 2009 VIQI can rightly claim to have played its part in Widnes meeting the on-field criteria for a return to Super League, a sentiment echoed by O'Connor. The Vikings chairman commented: "The fact that fans are able to raise such significant amounts of money from such a simple idea is really impressive. The quality of last year's loan players was a factor in winning the Northern Rail Cup, and VIQI's contribution was influential in ticking that box."

Being one of the clubs to 'tick the box' Widnes were an interested party when in August the RFL put some flesh on the bones of the process for admission to Super League as they published the minimum criteria for Championship clubs wishing to apply for a Super League Licence for 2012-14. At the same time the governing body confirmed that at least one Championship club will be admitted to the top tier, provided that they meet those criteria.

In order to clear the first hurdle any aspiring club must:
i) have appeared in a Championship Grand Final, or won the Northern Rail Cup in 2009 or 2010.
ii) have a stadium with an 'operational' capacity of 10,000
iii) have achieved an average attendance of at least 2,500 in 2009 or 2010
iv) have not suffered an act of insolvency during 2008-2010
v) have achieved a turnover of at least £1,000,000 in the financial accounting periods ending in 2009 or 2010.

Any Championship club which met these criteria would then be assessed in the following areas along with the existing Super League clubs:
a) Commercial, Marketing, Media and Community
b) Facilities
c) Finance
d) Governance & Business Management
e) Playing strength & Player performance Strategy

With these announcements large numbers of Widnes fans, notwithstanding their customary suspicion of the RFL, began to share chairman Steve O'Connor's firm belief that the club would gain one of the coveted Licences and be elevated to the top tier in 2012.

This belief was underlined by experienced rugby league journalist Andy Wilson who, in his column in The Guardian, suggested that of the likely candidates Widnes were the only club in a position to meet all the criteria.

By the time the 2010 season had ended there were five clubs who had met the on-field criterion – Barrow Raiders, Batley Bulldogs, Halifax, Featherstone Rovers and Widnes. But as most of us were aware, and Wilson pointed out, Barrow and Featherstone would fall foul of the stadium and attendance criteria, while Halifax's gates were also below par. However, thanks to a reported attendance of 4,795 for their last home match of 2010, Halifax did manage to boost their existing average from 2,255 to 2,509 for their 10 home league matches.

With Batley and Featherstone electing not to submit an application it eventually became a three horse race between Barrow, Halifax and Widnes. With Widnes also meeting the solvency and financial criteria they were the media favourites and all seemed well, but that in-bred suspicion of the governing body that is part of the DNA of Vikings fans made it an anxious wait until the announcement on 31st March 2011.

Widnes had run a competition to find a young supporter to accompany Anthony Thackeray and the management team to hand in the Bid document to the RFL headquarters at Red Hall. That honour fell to 12-year-old Adam Blinston who travelled to Leeds with 'Thacks', on a cold and snowy December day, in an iconic Stobart truck to deliver the document that was to seal Widnes' fate for 2012. In contrast Barrow had e-mailed their submission while Halifax director Ian Croad travelled the 16 miles by helicopter to hand in their application, dressed as Father Christmas.

This is how an excited Adam described his day to the *Widnes Weekly News*:

"I was really excited when I woke up this morning. That beats being nervous, like I was when the TV cameras came in. That was nerve-racking!

"When I got to the stadium I met Paul Cullen, Terry O'Connor, Denis Betts, Chaz I'Anson and Anthony Thackeray and all of the staff. I was speechless! Widnes did a buffet but I was now too nervous to eat."

Leaving his Widnes shirt with Terry O'Connor to be signed by the first team squad, Adam donned his Back the Bid T-shirt and took centre stage for the photo-call before setting off for Leeds.

Adam continued: "I got into the Eddie Stobart truck and it felt really strange. I had never been so high in my life! The newspapers were there taking photos and I had to sit inside the cabin while leaning out of the truck, and a pile of snow slid off the cab roof and landed on me. I almost dropped the bid but fortunately nobody saw me.

"We set off for Leeds and an hour-and-a-half later I was told we would be on Sky Sports News. I got out of the truck while the cameras filmed me handing the bid over. I then got interviewed again. When we got home we turned the TV on and there I was on Sky Sports News. I have now seen myself on YouTube, television twice, in the *Widnes Weekly News*, the *Liverpool Echo* and I've even heard myself on the radio.

"It has been weird seeing myself everywhere and I now feel like a celebrity… but please don't get me out of here!

"It has been the best day ever and I would like to thank everyone who has made it possible."

With the Bid finally submitted chief executive Julie Gaskell commented: "I'm really pleased with the submission, it's been a real team effort. I just think we've got a really concise and robust bid, so I'm really pleased."

Reflecting on the process Ms Gaskell told me that she had become "passionate about the organisation and the club and want us to succeed" adding that "it's like sitting an exam – we've done everything that we can".

In the meantime while clubs were completing and submitting their applications the subject of 'Facilities' was causing a deal of concern among some of the established Super League clubs. This was particularly true of Wakefield, Castleford, Salford and St Helens who were at varying stages of moving to new stadia, while others such as Hull KR and Bradford had recognised that some updating of their grounds was required. Their peace of mind was hardly helped by this caveat in the licensing guidelines issued by the RFL: "New stadiums or redevelopments of existing stadiums will only be taken into account if the RFL is satisfied that the stadium will be open or the redevelopment finished by the start of the 2012 season."

2011

It is fair to say that 2011 was a season that flattered to deceive as far as events on the field of play were concerned. There were many theories put forward, ranging from poor recruitment, through bad coaching to disinterest among players who felt that they wouldn't be accompanying the club into Super League. Without being privy to the day to day processes of the club none of us can really claim to know the reasons behind a poor season. Sometimes things just don't work out the way the fans expect. And the same goes for owners, coaches and players.

If we fast-forward briefly to 2012 we will get an understanding of how these things are far from straightforward. During a fans' forum the club gave an insight into the problems of recruitment for their Super League campaign, where some players had pledged their futures to the club only to subsequently sign elsewhere, either for more money or more medals. That is their right of course. It is quite feasible that similar problems were encountered in 2011, although the rewards would be much less. None of us really 'know' but rugby players like any other employee will choose where they want to work. Also, operating with a part-time playing staff, and investing heavily in their youth structure, I suspect that the club had at least one eye on 2012 and beyond.

The coaching issue is a very subjective one and I would venture to suggest that, in tandem with the recruitment and retention of players, is not aided by the limbo state of Championship clubs in-between licensing rounds. Under promotion and relegation a coach could build a team for promotion at his own pace, whether that be one year or five. With licensing you have the certainty of three years at least – once you are on the inside.

However, the ambitious Championship clubs who wish to move up to Super League are, in my view, forced into short-term recruitment in the hope that they are awarded a Licence, and therefore a coach is dealing with a regular turnover of players. Although never having coached a team sport I would imagine that this brings with it severe limitations. The irony is that licensing was intended to bring about long-term planning but that is not possible in this scenario.

With regard to the argument about 'disinterested' players Denis Betts conceded in his final programme notes of 2011 that: "There is no getting away from the fact those Super League contract talks have had an effect on our squad, and as you can expect, it's been a pretty anxious place to be at for all concerned. With so much uncertainty surrounding many of their futures it could also be argued that some of them may well have been trying too hard to impress in recent weeks." With regard to claims that some players were not trying you would need to be inside the players' minds to know what was going on, but I am firmly of the belief that no professional sportsman goes out to deliberately not try. With the very odd exception it is the nature of the beast to compete once they cross that white line, especially in a contact sport, as that is when injuries occur.

But back in February 2011 the season kicked off with a lot of promise as the Northern Rail Cup campaign got off to an encouraging start with Widnes winning all four matches to finish top of their group. Comfortable wins against London Skolars, Toulouse and

Rochdale Hornets were followed by a narrow win at Post Office Road against Featherstone to secure their place in the knockout stages. When this was followed by a win at The Shay over Siddal in the Challenge Cup, and a convincing 44-16 victory against Sheffield Eagles, in which Dave Allen scored a hat-trick, in the first league encounter of the season things were looking rosy for the Vikings.

But in somewhat typical Widnes fashion they immediately slumped to a home defeat to newly promoted Hunslet Hawks and a 54-16 thrashing at Leigh Centurions did little for good humour among the fans. Although it had no relevance to the licensing outcome the defeat at Leigh, in what was the 100th competitive match of the Steve O'Connor era, could not have come at a worse time – just four days before the big announcement.

With the Super League Licence safely in the bag Widnes bounced back, sporting a commemorative 'Green for Go' kit, to pulverise York City Knights, in front of over 4,000 fans at the Stobart Stadium. The celebrations of the award of that coveted Licence had continued unabated since Thursday's announcement and the match was played out in a party atmosphere as the Vikings ran in 13 tries to see off their hapless opponents 76-12.

There was no sign of the run-away win to come as the teams slugged it out in an even opening 15 minutes, but once Paddy Flynn had capitalised on work by Danny Craven, Simon Finnigan and Macgraff Leuluai the flood gates were opened. The opening try was followed by a brace from Tyrer, with Chaz I'Anson and Dean Gaskell doing the spadework on each occasion, before Craven's converted try gave Widnes a 22-0 lead after 25 minutes. Minutes later the young full-back picked up a serious shoulder injury, following a bad landing from a dangerous looking tackle, and left the field not returning until the last two games of the season. Although the visitors got on the scoreboard with a converted try from Matt Barron just before the break Tyrer gathered a loose ball 20 metres out to complete his hat-trick on the hooter.

During the half-time break chairman Steve O'Connor took to the pitch, amid a standing ovation, to make the first of two groundbreaking announcements that were to come during 2011. This was the public launch of the 'Viking Stronghold', a scheme to initially replace conventional season tickets with a membership scheme. The scheme would offer exclusive benefits to members, in addition to admission to matches, that would range from attending a training session to discounted meals in a local restaurant. In outlining the principles behind the scheme, which was designed to encourage fans to support their club all year round, O'Connor stressed the importance of the success of the scheme as it would have a direct bearing on the club's ability to spend to the full salary cap.

Seemingly inspired by their chairman the Vikings increased their lead early in the second half when Anthony Thackeray, coming off the bench, put Leuluai in for a try converted by Tyrer. As early as the 49th minute the points were secured when Richard Varkulis barged his way to the line, after breaks by Thackeray and Flynn, to make the score 40-6. As the second period became a procession to the York line the Vikings pulled further away as Chris Lunt, with his first senior try, and Thackeray crossed before John Davies pulled one back for York on the hour. Widnes eased to their biggest score of the season with two tries from Steve Pickersgill, one from Simon Finnigan, and a second from Thackeray with Tyrer bagging a personal return of 36 points for his afternoon's work. All in all it had been a very successful week for the Vikings.

However, a sterner test was to follow as Widnes travelled back to Leigh Sports Village for their quarter-final tie in the Northern Rail Cup, conceded 50 points against their arch rivals for the second time in 11 days, and bowed out of the competition. Another defeat followed at Batley as Widnes had plainly lost their early season promise, but the visit to Mount Pleasant did provide one of the highlights of the season as Danny Hulme scored the try that was later to be voted the Supporters' Club Try of the Year. Fielding a kick deep in his own half the 20-year-old full-back, taking the direct route to the line, showed pace and agility as he tore through the heart of the Batley defence to score under the posts.

As if to underline their inconsistency Widnes returned to the Stobart Stadium just four days later to defeat Halifax 47-36. This welcome return to winning ways came just 48 hours after the club had taken the first steps towards formalising the squad for 2012. James Ford, Chris Gerrard, Kirk Netherton and Anthony Thackeray were released from first team duties and told that they would not be part of the club's initial Super League squad. Citing the home defeat to Hunslet and the two heavy defeats to Leigh, head coach Denis Betts explained the early cull, less than three weeks after the Licence announcement by saying: "This has been forced upon us by performances on the field. That has caused us to refocus our thoughts as to where we are going to take this side, and what we are going to do with it. A lot of pressure has been created about the place and some people respond to it and others don't."

Ford and Thackeray were quickly snapped up by York for the remainder of the season while Netherton moved on to Featherstone and picked up a winner's medal in the Grand Final. In July Gerrard's contract was terminated following a conviction for Grievous Bodily Harm.

The remaining players, however, put on a performance to see off 2010 Grand Final winners, Halifax, despite conceding another 36 points. On the way to a half-time lead of 38-18 Danny Hulme helped himself to a hat-trick in the space of 10 minutes before Halifax clawed their way back into a game that seemed to pass them by through ex-Widnes Prop Michael Ostick, one of six former Vikings lining up for the visitors. Although Simon Finnigan restored the Vikings' advantage this was quickly nullified by a Lee Paterson try before Widnes again extended their lead through Logan Tomkins and Thomas Coyle.

Tomkins, on a dual registration deal from Wigan, grabbed his second as he wriggled through the Halifax defence, only for Dylan Nash to reply before Steve Tyrer's penalty from fully 60 metres gave the home side a 20 point buffer at the break.

A Widnes team that had failed to register a second-half point in three of their last four matches was immediately on the back foot as Paul White claimed a try within three minutes of the re-start, but this was cancelled out when Finnigan claimed his second try. Chaz I'Anson, who had a hand or foot in five of the Vikings' tries chipped in with a drop goal, but further tries by Sam Barlow and Nash had ensured a tense finish to the game.

In the middle of May Widnes brought an end to the speculation about the identity of the coach who would lead the club on their return to Super League. With rumours of a so-called big-name appointment bouncing around internet forums and social media sites the Vikings appointed a man much closer to home when Denis Betts' appointment was confirmed.

Although Paul Cullen's recommendation of Betts to the board was described by chief executive Julie Gaskell as a "no brainer" it seemed a large number of fans – or more likely a noisy minority – felt it showed a lack of ambition on the club's part. While many named specific targets that they felt the club should have gone for some went as far as saying that they wanted an Australian – any Australian! Fast forward to mid 2012 and this noisy minority had fallen virtually silent on the back of a string of impressive performances and improved results.

As Cullen told the *Widnes Weekly News* "Denis Betts has always been, from day one, part of the long-term plan and strategy. I am convinced Denis has all the attributes to handle the difficulties that are going to come, and takes us forward. We have to have somebody in charge of the club who can handle negativity and can handle difficult situations. I am confident that Denis will grow to be one of the best Super League coaches."

Confirming that the club had also looked at a number of other candidates Steve O'Connor added: "It was abundantly clear during this process that Denis was the best fit for our club. He has the right values, ambition and capabilities to take this club forward and we are absolutely 100% behind him."

Cullen continued: "Denis Betts will take full responsibility for the identification and selection of players for our entry into Super League. I will be supporting him with the recruitment of these players and already we have had a great deal of interest from both overseas and UK players, but it would not have been either appropriate or fair to enter into any negotiations prior to Denis's appointment. Now we will both be working hard to identify current squad members and new signings and we are determined to attract the best there is to come to Widnes and be part of our future. Youth development continues to be an intrinsic part of our longer-term strategy and Denis fully supports what we are doing as a club."

Identifying player retention and recruitment as "the toughest task ahead" Betts added: "I am extremely honoured that this great club has put its faith in me. I am looking forward to working alongside Paul and Julie and putting this club back where it belongs… at the top."

Although there had been no interview in the formal sense Betts stated that "the interview was an on-going appraisal of the year, and their appreciation of what I had done, by Paul, Terry, Steve and the other members of the Board. My job was to keep Steve in the loop with what was going on and how we were doing things. They seemed quite happy with what was going on and we talked about me working here under another coach as head coach.

"I outlined the fact that I would work under one of three coaches, and none of those coaches had ever coached in England. So if they wanted to bring in a [Head] coach it had to be one of three that I felt I could learn from. Other than that if they didn't want me to do the job then I wouldn't, but thankfully it didn't work out like that."

Now that the new coach had been identified it cleared the way for members of the current squad to stake their claim for a contract for 2012 and beyond.

Meanwhile the team's inconsistency continued until they entertained Barrow Raiders in late May, and the win signalled a run of seven consecutive wins, before the season fizzled out with another consistent run – of five straight defeats – which saw them bow out in the first round of the play-offs, going down 36-20 at Sheffield.

The Barrow match, arguably the best performance of the season, was also notable for the Championship debut, in front of the Sky television cameras, of 16-year-old Jack Owens at full-back, who had made his full debut in the Challenge Cup-tie against Siddal at The Shay in March.

Trailing to an early Jamie Rooney penalty Widnes hit back in the ninth minute when Chaz I'Anson exchanged passes with Simon Finnigan inside the Barrow '20' to score under the posts, allowing Steven Tyrer a simple conversion. The lead was to last just a few minutes before Barrow regained their two point advantage through Andy Ballard, but the early tit-for-tat ended there as Widnes crossed twice within three minutes midway through the half to establish a lead that was never relinquished. The first came as the ball passed quickly through the hands of I'Anson, Owens and Tangi Ropati to Paddy Flynn who, from 30 metres out, shrugged off the attentions of five Barrow players to force his way over the line. Then in the 23rd minute came one for the record books as Owens leapt to collect a chip over the Barrow defence by I'Anson to register his first senior try, with Tyrer's goal giving the Vikings a 16-8 lead. The final score of the half came when Kevin Penny took a pass from Tyrer on the halfway line to scorch along the touchline and outstrip the defence to score under the posts. Tyrer's goal made the half-time score 22-8 in the Vikings' favour.

After the break Widnes killed the game with early tries from Logan Tomkins and Tyrer, before Ballard gained a consolation effort for the visitors. In the 50th minute Flynn took a pass just inside the Barrow half to charge at the heart of the Barrow defence, only being halted on the 10 metre line. From his quick play-the-ball Tomkins scooted between four defenders to touch down. This was followed within minutes by Tyrer's try as Kevin Penny palmed a high ball from I'Anson back into the path of the centre. Despite the attention of three defenders Tyrer stretched out a 'telescopic' arm to place the ball on the line, to give the Vikings a lead of 32-8. Ballard's effort came midway through the half but Widnes had the final say with two more tries in the closing eight minutes. The first came when Steve Pickersgill, surrounded by defenders 12 metres from the Barrow line, managed to off-load the ball to Joe Mellor who fended off one challenge before twisting between three defenders on the line to score. The final try of the evening came when Mellor, in possession just inside the Barrow half as the hooter sounded, sprinted through the defence to play Thomas Coyle in 20 metres out for the hooker to score out wide.

At the end of the match Widnes-born Owens was selected as the 'Sky' Man of the Match after his assured league debut, but at 16 years of age was unable to receive the bottle of champagne that went with the accolade! He also earned this plaudit from head coach Denis Betts: "He has been training with the first team for most of the year and I was looking for an opportunity to give him a home debut in front of the fans. He played well at the weekend [for the Academy team] and I thought it would be a good chance to put him in and see how he went, and he didn't let me down."

Having shown a maturity beyond his years on the pitch Owens also displayed a sense of realism when he told the *Widnes Weekly News* "The coaching and support that I have received at the Vikings has been first class. Phil Finney has had a huge influence on my development. He has undoubtedly helped me to become a better player.

"I know that I am only young and need to improve but I am hungry for it, and in years to come I will hopefully be making regular appearances in the first team. Widnes is my home-town club and it is such an honour to play for them."

The accolades for young Jack didn't stop there as only eight days later, on his 17th birthday, he made his debut for the England Under-18 Academy side when they took on their French counterparts. Owens, who played from the start, was the only player in the England squad not attached to a Super League club as the English triumphed by 28-19 in Palau.

Commenting on his international call-up Owens said: "I was absolutely made up when I got called into the England squad. Obviously it was the first time I have had the opportunity to represent my country and it was a huge honour. Hopefully there will be many more caps to come."

Next up for Widnes were matches against York and Sheffield in which hard-fought wins were gained before the Vikings travelled to the South Leeds Stadium to seek revenge for the home defeat against the Hunslet Hawks. Trailing to an early strike from Hawks' Danny Grimshaw Widnes fought back through a converted Ben Kavanagh try to hold a short-lived lead of 6 points to 4, before the home side came back to establish a 16-6 lead at the end of a scrappy first half.

Despite the lack of any cohesive play the Vikings fought back again after the break to take a 20-16 lead just after the hour. Steve Tyrer forced his way over out wide to signal the comeback before determined play by Shane Grady enabled him to score on 56 minutes to bring the Vikings to within two points of their hosts. Paddy Flynn then scored, again through strength and determination, and with Tyrer's conversion they had a four point cushion. Again the lead was short-lived as Hunslet's Luke Haigh scored by the posts and the conversion put the home side two points to the good. A spurned penalty goal by Widnes seemed to have cost them the match as they failed to make any inroads to the opposition and the clock ran down. But with the final play of the game they snatched, what had seemed for most of the afternoon, an unlikely win. Following a break from defence by Tangi Ropati Paddy Flynn lobbed the ball infield to Danny Hulme, who from just inside his own half darted into opposition territory before passing to Kurt Haggerty 25 metres out. The Second Row raced towards the line and, with the defence expecting an off-load to the supporting Tyrer, he charged between the defenders to score the match-winning try.

Home wins against Dewsbury Rams and Batley Bulldogs were separated by another successful trip to southern France where the Vikings recorded their third win in three visits. Going on the attack straight from the kick-off Widnes were 12-0 up after 17 minutes as Steve Tyrer was on the end of two clever kicks by Joe Mellor. However, Toulouse dominated the second quarter to score three unanswered tries and go in to the half-time break leading 16-12. Although the hosts didn't register any points in the second half Widnes fans could not breathe easily until Simon Finnigan's 76th minute try from close in. Widnes had regained the lead in the 48th minute when Matt Gardner, receiving the ball from a scrum on his own '40' outwitted and outran the Toulouse defence as he sprinted to the corner, and with Tyrer's goal the Vikings led 18-16. This was improved to 24-16 in the 55th minute when Ben Kavanagh burst through the French defence 20 metres out and passed to the supporting Dave Allen who scored under the posts.

The two point victory over Batley was to be Widnes' last win of the season as they immediately went down 18-24 at home to Leigh before defeats on the road at Halifax and Featherstone set up a final home game of the season against the Rovers. In losing both matches against Featherstone by a combined score of 100-20, and going out of the play-offs to Sheffield, the curtain came down on the club's final year of Championship rugby as they limped back into Super League after an absence of six years.

A landmark which came and went, virtually unnoticed, earlier in the season was the 100th game since Steve O'Connor bought the club. This milestone came, ironically, in the defeat at Leigh just a few days before we learnt that the Vikings were to return to Super League. For the record a breakdown of the top-ranked players who wore the Vikings shirt during those 100 games appears in Appendix V.

When reviewing 2011 it must be remembered that it was another learning curve for Denis Betts who was not only working for a new club but also working in a part-time environment for the first time in his senior coaching career. "It was a shock to my system" he told me while conceding that "I was very demanding at first and had to back off a little bit as the majority of the lads had full-time jobs. The work they did at the night affected their work during the day and vice versa. I remember a couple of times picking Steve Pickersgill up from his factory floor in his work boots, and then wondering why he didn't play that well come game time, when he'd had to work all day on a shop floor and then play front row in a rugby league side! So yes, it was a very strange environment and something that again I had to adapt to; had to find a way round."

The man who was ultimately to lead the Vikings into Super League has no doubt that he improved as a coach during his sojourn in rugby union. Going into rugby union with no great knowledge of the game he had to gain the trust of the players. "They knew who I was and what I had done but obviously I'd never played or worked in rugby union." Completing a 'Director of Rugby' coaching qualification – the highest possible in rugby union – gave Betts a piece of paper to show what he knew, but the man himself believes his biggest gains in those five years were in "people management, skill management and my ability to develop certain areas of coaching."

Although team success had eluded the Vikings through 2011 there had been a crop of individual landmarks for several players. (See Appendix V for a full 2008-12 summary).

Simon Finnigan, who had returned for his second spell with the club took his Widnes points tally through the one hundred barrier to finish the year with 120 points. The same barrier was broken by Richard Varkulis who finished his Widnes career on 124 points, while Shane Grady's 2011 contribution saw him finish on 302 points for his home-town club.

Ben Kavanagh who, as already mentioned, had become the first player to sign a Super League contract with the club, moved on to 110 appearances for Widnes while (Finnigan (209), Dave Allen (116) and Matt Gardner (123) had also moved through career appearance milestones.

In the career points scoring stakes Thomas Coyle (117) had broken through the 100 mark, while Tangi Ropati's eight tries had seen him onto a total of 170 points, and Anthony Thackeray (274) and Richard Varkulis (268) had both broken the 250 point barrier. Pride of place must go, however, to Steven Tyrer whose 2011 total of 304 points took his Widnes total to 414 and his career mark to 630.

As preparations began for Super League the club had announced in August that 13 members of the first team squad would be released at the end of the season. Heading the list of departures was Dean Gaskell, the last remaining member of the 'Famous Five'. 'Deano' who made his Widnes debut in February 2007, against London Skolars in the Northern Rail Cup, went on to make 93 appearances for the Vikings, scoring 42 tries in the process. Irish International Gaskell, who was the club's top try scorer in 2008, picked up a Northern Rail Cup winners' medal in 2007 and was also a member of the team that 'ticked the box' with the 2009 victory in the same competition. Those two winners' medals, together with one from his time at Leigh, made him the first player to hold three Northern Rail Cup winners' medals.

While Mark Smith, Paul Noone, Gavin Dodd and Bob Beswick have continued their rugby careers since leaving Widnes, Gaskell opted to retire from the game despite receiving some good offers from other clubs. Despite believing that he "could have still done a job in Super League" the popular winger told me that he "felt that I had played for long enough and it was time to get a job and live a normal life." He is now working full-time as a Residential Care Worker – a career he began on a part-time basis during his Widnes days.

As a Widnes fan as well as a player he was "ecstatic" when the club was awarded the Super League Licence, and he identified "all of it" as the highlight of his Widnes career. Although he hasn't been to any matches he does watch them whenever they are on television and, praising the efforts of Steve O'Connor in saving and rebuilding the club, Gaskell is confident that Widnes have "smart people in key positions and by investing in youth and buying quality" will continue to progress.

Those fans with broader sporting interests may yet see 'Deano' in action again as, building on his wrestling experience as a teenager, he is currently training to be a cagefighter!

In many people's eyes Richard Varkulis was a surprise name on the list. Joining the club from Halifax as a centre 'Varks' really blossomed when he was moved into the forwards and was a consistent performer throughout his three years with Widnes. He finished with 31 tries from his 79 outings in a Widnes shirt. Another to leave the club was Gareth Haggerty, who having begun his career with Widnes in 2001, had seen service with Salford and Harlequins. Unfortunately Haggerty's return to Widnes was interrupted by injury and only 12 of his 175 career appearances were for the Vikings.

While it is always disappointing to see locally produced players leave the club hard decisions invariably have to be made when a club, in any sport, moves up a level. That was the case with Danny Hulme, Shane Grady, Chris Lunt, Greg Scott and Dave Houghton who were released as part of the build-up for Super League rugby.

Grady was another to make his debut at the beginning of the Steve O'Connor era and his 75 appearances for his home-town club had seen him gain considerable senior experience. Indeed during the 2010 season he solved the 'goal kicking' problem following the departure of recognised 'kickers' Gavin Dodd, Craig Hall, Tim Hartley and Scott Yates. Houghton, who had become a regular member of the first team in 2010, was another local product on the road to establishing himself, while Hulme, Lunt and Scott had just broken through to the senior squad.

Other senior players to be released at this stage were Chaz I'Anson, Matt Gardner, Daniel Heckenberg, Danny Sculthorpe and Tangi Ropati, while Anthony Thackeray, Steve Tyrer and James Coyle were later added to the list.

Fans' favourite Thackeray, who had moved to York on loan following his earlier release from first team duties, finally left the club after making 70 appearances which included 48 tries and 1 goal. Thackeray, who had finished 2010 as the club's top try scorer, was voted the *Rugby League World* 'Championship Player of the Year' for the same year, and was largely expected to be a key member of the 2012 squad. Another possible contender for a Super League contract Tyrer had spent three separate spells with Widnes, the first coming in 2008 when he returned 100 points in his 10 matches. A brief stint of three matches came in 2009 before a highly successful spell in 2011 saw him return 23 tries and 106 goals from 25 appearances to take his Vikings record to 414 points from just 38 matches. Following a successful career with Oldham and Barrow Raiders Coyle had joined his brother Thomas at Widnes in a bid to recapture his earlier promise, having represented the Vikings on 31 occasions in 2006.

One of the certainties about life as a professional sportsman is that at some point you will be released by your employers. It's the nature of the beast; the downside of a wonderful life. However, after releasing the group of 13 players head coach Denis Betts conceded that: "It has been a very tough week for everyone involved at the club. We had to look at what is best for the club and the players' development. The hardest thing is that they are all fantastic blokes but we can only have a 25-man first team squad next year.

"There was a lot of debate between myself and Paul Cullen and we decided the time was right to make these decisions so that these players can find new clubs and continue their careers."

Citing the release of Danny Hulme as the toughest decision he had to make, Betts commented that: "He has been great for us this year, but I have got Shaun Briscoe coming in, as well as Danny Craven and Jack Owens. There is no point in signing him to sit there and not progress."

Moving away from playing matters there had been one consistent area of growth and improvement throughout the 'intervening years' – Widnes Rugby League Museum. While some clubs are now in the process of setting up 'heritage centres' Widnes had launched, in August 2007, the first club-based rugby league 'museum' in the world, with its volunteer staff having undergone professional training from the MLA (Museum, Libraries and Archives) body.

Although there are plans to find a permanent home for the museum it currently remains under the East Stand at the Stobart Stadium, where it continues to attract high visitor numbers, despite Friday and Saturday being the only regular opening days. Deb Townsend, the driving force behind the project and Museum Curator, confirmed that tours on other days are available by appointment, adding: "In the past we've even opened on Boxing Day for a special visit."

Since the doors opened in 2007 nearly 6000 visitors have enjoyed the wide range of memorabilia on display, in addition to representatives of Sky TV, the RFL, 1 Mercian Regiment and sponsors, not forgetting the regular visits from local schools.

The museum's vast collection of memorabilia, much of which has been donated by past players, has now grown to such an extent that it has outgrown its home and has necessitated the regular rotation of the displays. In addition to the traditional static displays of medals, shirts and equipment the museum has in excess of 400 matches on DVD while a dedicated computer has a permanent slideshow of over 1,000 photographs from all eras. In a recent innovation it is also possible, subject to availability, to combine a visit to the museum with an extended behind the scenes tour which includes the changing rooms and the player's gym facilities.

Curator Deb Townsend concedes that while the current site "is a good starting block for us we have ambitions of relocating to a more suitable location. It's hard to get funding, but I think we've shown a lot of people what we're capable of. Both Nigel Wood and Richard Lewis, the former executive chairman of the RFL, made positive comments on our museum, and it's nice to have it in the stadium itself, so people who come to the games can have easy access."

In recent years the success of the museum has allowed it to sponsor an award to players who have made 100 appearances for Widnes in a single spell with the club. Recipients of that award so far are Mark Smith, Gavin Dodd, Ben Kavanagh and Paddy Flynn.

The key challenge for the museum and its partners, as they move into 2013, is to secure the funding that will support that permanent home, enabling its treasures to be displayed in the correct environment and to maximum benefit.

Returning to matters on the pitch, the overriding objective as 2011 began was to secure a return to Super League in 2012. Looking back at 2011 Denis Betts felt that: "We grew as an organisation and put some things in place but I was always judging these players on hopefully moving into a SL environment, and there had to come a point where big decisions had to be made and those were the tough things we had to do."

There had, however, been one season-long absentee from the battle for Super League contracts. Since the season got under away back in February the Widnes first team squad had been playing out the campaign while, on the other side of the world, one of their number had been experiencing the opportunity of a lifetime.

Following a visit to Australia and New Zealand for the Four Nations tournament in 2010 Paul Cullen came away with an idea to help young English players improve, and set in motion a pioneering exchange scheme. The first beneficiary of the scheme was 19-year-old Anthony Mullally who spent 2011 playing for the Brisbane Broncos in the Under-20 Toyota Cup competition. Before he left for Australia the young prop forward, who joined the Vikings at the age of 15, commented: "I can't believe it's actually happening. When the club first put the idea to me I had no hesitation in saying yes because opportunities such as this don't come around too often." At the time of his departure Mullally had played just one match for Widnes.

"Long-term we hope this scheme benefits us here at Widnes" said Paul Cullen, adding "If it proves a success we will send over more of the best young Vikings players and let them reap the rewards of spending a season in the company of the game's leading players in the Australian competition."

Former Australian International and Warrington Wolves player Allan Langer, now a coach with the Broncos, said: "I fully support the idea of players from Widnes Vikings coming to the Brisbane Broncos for their development. All of our football staff are looking forward to working with Anthony. It's our aim to send him home ready to play Super League for the Vikings if they are successful with their Licence application."

Mullally duly arrived in Brisbane having squeezed his 6 feet 5inches, 17 stone frame into an economy class seat on his flight to Australia. Having acclimatised to the conditions, he got down to training and commented via a 'blog' that the training sessions were very intense and were made all the more difficult by the heat – as his 4 kilogram weight loss testified. However, he certainly did enough in his first trial game to impress Paul Bunn, the development officer at Brisbane Broncos who informed Paul Cullen that "he carried the ball ok, used his footwork well and his defence was sound. One thing for sure, there is a stack of potential in him".

Despite missing the occasional match through injury 'Mull' played 22 competitive matches in what was a reasonably successful Toyota Cup campaign, regularly taking on the cream of young Australian players.

Academy product Mullally had already been in Australia for several weeks when he learnt of the Vikings' elevation to Super League. While Widnes fans were watching the announcement on television and celebrating 'Mull' was asleep thousands of miles away. It wasn't until he woke that he was able to log on to the club website to learn the good news, and sent the following message via his 'blog': "I'd like to pass on my congratulations to everyone at the Vikings. I know just how much the Super League decision meant to the club and its supporters, so it was great to hear the news. It means a great deal to me too, and part of me was obviously gutted that I wasn't there to join in the fun."

Looking back on his experience Mullally said: "The last eight months have been fantastic, both on and off the pitch and I'll always be grateful to both the Vikings and the Broncos for offering me the opportunity to spend a full season over here. From day one, everybody involved welcomed me with open arms and made me feel at home.

"The standard of the NYC (Toyota Cup) competition is very good and every single week was a tough test. Before a ball was kicked this year, hopes were high that we could really make an impression, but our inconsistency cost us dearly. I genuinely believe that I've matured as a player and I'm hoping to prove this when I'm back.

"I'm really excited about next season and with a bit of luck and a lot of hard work, hopefully I can play my part in the club's Super League plans in 2012."

While playing at major grounds such as The Suncorp Stadium, Sydney Football Stadium (Allianz Stadium) and the Toyota Stadium (Shark Park) were highlights of his antipodean adventure, Mullally was also thrilled when the Broncos Under-20 team was invited to provide training opposition for the Queensland State of Origin team. Asked if there was any particular lesson that he had learned while in Brisbane he replied: "It's a basic one, but to always run hard and tackle hard." The only down side that he can recall was, in part, due to his living arrangements. After a bad game he would want to switch off from rugby, but living with the Broncos Development Manager meant that he couldn't avoid the topic!

Back in England there was much for the Widnes faithful to look forward to as 2011 came to a close and 2012 beckoned. In April Ben Kavanagh had put pen to paper on a contract that would keep him at Widnes until the end of 2014. Having consistently proved himself at Championship level since joining the Vikings in 2008 the club tied 'Kav' down before other top-flight clubs could pounce. Halifax-born Kavanagh who had proved himself popular among the fans said at the time: "I'm really enjoying myself at Widnes and I have done since day one. That's why I've signed this extended deal with the club. I am ready to test myself against the best players in Super League, and hopefully there will be some big signings coming in – players that I can learn from.

"Performing in front of the Vikings' fans is a special experience for me and something I look forward to doing each and every week. Hopefully we can go on to big things together."

Kavanagh, who at one time enjoyed an unbroken run of 72 appearances for the Vikings received this tribute from director of rugby Paul Cullen: "One thing that strikes me is that he has played 72 consecutive games which shows real durability. He is doing the tough stuff every week and over a period of time has shown that he is the right man for us on and off the field."

But while there was a dearth of other concrete news on new signings there was nonetheless a lot happening behind the scenes. During June Paul Cullen and chief executive Julie Gaskell had been on a fact-finding and scouting mission to Australia, only to return with the knowledge that Widnes simply could not afford any marquee signings. Having previously been able to sign several top-ranking Australians for Warrington the Vikings' Director of Rugby brought fans expectations down to earth on his return.

"There's a reality check that we all need to pay attention to" admitted Cullen. Citing the vast change in the Australian Dollar exchange rate since his Warrington days Cullen pointed out that whereas the rate was once 3-to-1 the pound is now only worth one-and-a-half dollars. "So in real terms if I'm spending £100,000 previously I'm getting a $300,000 Australian player. You could also get 40% of your money off-shore and you can't do that these days."

On her return Julie Gaskell told the *Widnes Weekly News*: "The trip was extremely insightful, we learnt a lot. We covered just about every aspect of club management and were pleasantly surprised that a lot of our plans are heading in the right direction." Echoing the comments of Paul Cullen regarding expensive imports she added: "This trip was about building relationships so that we are at the top of people's lists when players become available."

There were also other factors which mitigated against antipodean players wanting to come to England. Under threat domestically from Aussie Rules and rugby union the NRL took action to prevent its loss of talent. Two additional clubs were added to its competition, while at the same time increasing their club squads from 25 to 30 players, and thereby creating more job opportunities for players in Australia. In addition to these measures Cullen pointed out that the NRL had raised their salary cap "to a figure that goes well and truly beyond Super League, with a minimum wage of around $60,000."

The combination of these factors, together with the understandable reluctance of some players to join the 'new kids on the block' would mean that the Vikings had to target a different type of player.

Earlier in this chapter we learned of Steve O'Connor's public launch of the Viking Stronghold days after the club's return to the top flight. Addressing an audience of over 4,000 fans he set a target membership of 7,000, urging supporters to get behind the team and match his ambition of being able to spend up to the full salary cap of £1.65 million. By supporting the club in this initiative – the first of its kind in rugby league – fans would play their full part in helping to make Widnes a force on their return to Super League.

O'Connor told the fans: "I'm often referred to as the club's backer, but the real backers are you the fans. I am not just here to fill the gap between revenue and expenditure. Whether or not we spend up to the salary cap depends on supporters being prepared to buy into what we are trying to achieve."

Pointing out that the club had already been approached by top class players wanting to come to Widnes, the chairman laid it on the line that: "Before we look at recruitment we need to look at ways of bringing in new fans. We realistically need a minium of 7,000 members to join us in order to commit to utilising the full salary cap.

"If everyone here today brings a friend with them next year I guarantee we will be able to build a very competitive team. We are determined to do well and I think this is an innovative way to give fans a direct influence on how successful we can be."

While the scheme would allow the club to manage its finances more efficiently through a regular monthly income it would also achieve the aim of making the game more affordable to fans by spreading the cost throughout the whole year.

As the official club website reported: 'The 'Viking Stronghold' is a genuine club membership aimed at delivering the Vikings' strategy and protecting and nurturing a lifelong bond with our supporters, old and new. The membership aims to make the sport affordable by spreading the cost and benefits throughout the whole year and delivering fabulous value for money. Membership will entitle fans to attend all home games in Super League. Membership benefits will also include a free exclusive Viking Stronghold retro shirt, team sheets by text, Board Member recognition as well as many, many other exclusive offers and opportunities. It also has no minimum period – you really can leave if you consider that the club is not delivering value.'

Within four weeks the club reported that '800 or so new people' had joined the scheme which placed alongside the existing season ticket numbers meant that they had already achieved 40% of their target. By the time the 'earlybird' offer – guaranteed for three years – had closed on 31st May new membership had risen to 1,300 while the take-up by existing season ticket holders took the overall total to 3,220.

While Steve O'Connor was "delighted" with the early response from fans he underlined the need for more to sign up. With Paul Cullen about to depart to Australia, in a bid to sign up players ear-marked by Denis Betts, O'Connor said: "This I'm sure will convince those people who are still unsure of our intentions to compete to sign up," adding that "Many of the Super League clubs have shown an interest in our Stronghold and we are sure that this is the most modern approach to supporter engagement."

Meanwhile director of marketing Brian O'Connor issued a rallying call for fans to sign up to the Stronghold when he said: "I would like to urge fans who are considering joining the Stronghold, but are perhaps delaying their decision until closer to the start of the Super League season, to contact the club and make their intentions known, to allow us the opportunity to plan our budget accordingly."

Innovative as it was the Viking Stronghold was soon to be upstaged by the next major announcement emanating from the Stobart Stadium. This was the staggering news that, for their return to Super League the RFL, who were already in the process of developing a standard for artificial grass pitches, had given Widnes permission to install a state of the art artificial playing surface.

However, this was not the first time that Widnes had been linked with installing an artificial pitch. When Doug Laughton returned to Widnes in 1986 Wigan were getting all the publicity and Laughton determined that he needed to get the name of Widnes in the papers. As he recalls in his book – *A Dream Come True* – he thought 'we'll have a plastic pitch' and travelled to London to see the artificial pitch installed by Queen's Park Rangers. He continued: "So, the next thing, I've got a piece of plastic outside the Widnes Social Club in the car park. The BBC came to film the story [and] I came out with all this stuff about how this new playing surface was going to revolutionise the game."

Laughton got John Fieldhouse and Kurt Sorensen to run and tackle on it and they were given their 'lines' for the press conference that followed. On the morning of the press conference the RFL contacted the club and informed them that they 'couldn't have a plastic pitch as it is against rugby league bye-laws'. Laughton's reaction was "Wahey, more fuel for the fire" and responded by saying "They can't tell us what we can and can't play on, who do they think they are?"

With the national press present Laughton had achieved his objective of prime column inches for the Chemics which put them back in the spotlight.

Laughton's plastic pitch may well have only been a publicity stunt but some 25 years on it became a reality when, with the benefit of Steve O'Connor's vision, Widnes were granted permission by the governing body to install the sports first artificial playing surface – another 'first' for the club.

Naturally the new pitch was the subject of much debate, and conjecture, throughout the game, but as Steve O'Connor said: "Technology has moved on. We are not talking about the football pitches of the '80s where the consistency of the performance was to be questioned. To all intents and purposes we now have 21st century grass. This is the surface that had it been around before grass, grass wouldn't have survived!

"We need to understand what the Rugby League see as the ideal, so that it's hard enough so that the game's performance is consistent, it's fast, it's not too soft underfoot, but at the same time it's still safe.

"There's a lot of empirical evidence that suggests that players are protected from injury on this type of pitch, more so than the inconsistency of a conventional pitch. I hope the other clubs embrace the idea. As long as the playing surface is consistent it's the same for both teams. I think it should be as good as the best grass pitch on the best day."

Head coach Denis Betts also spoke positively, from a position of experience, about the surface, having been on the coaching staff when England played on a similar surface in Moscow. "It was a great game, it was fast-flowing with no problems with anything that was going on with the ball."

There was also a good level of support for this latest Vikings initiative when *Boots 'N' All* devoted nearly 10 minutes to the subject. Perhaps most surprising of all were the positive comments from Mike 'Stevo' Stephenson. 'Stevo' told viewers "I think its great and I think that Steve O'Connor will bring a breath of fresh air to this Super League competition because, when all the chairmen and CEO's meet each month next season, he won't be quiet. He'll be coming up with different ideas. He's a very successful businessman and I'm pleased that he is within our game. I think it's a great idea, looking forward to it."

Shaun McRea was in broad agreement with 'Stevo' saying: "I applaud it. I think it's a great idea" but preferred to "wait to see how games go before I make any judgement. The biggest change will be the kicking game where the ball will tend to hit and run, and when it's wet it will get extremely slippery." While there was merit in McRea's more cautious approach I would suggest that, with the benefit of a season's experience, the ball didn't behave any differently than on grass, and similarly players have been known to slip on grass when it is wet! McRea's most telling comment however, was: "I don't see it as a great advantage for Widnes – I see it as a great advantage for the game of rugby league."

With news that both Saracens and Leeds Carnegie were considering installing a similar pitch it will be interesting to see how many clubs, league or union, follow the Vikings' lead in the next few years.

The new pitch was supplied by Desso Sports Systems, who have installed a range of artificial grass and hybrid grass pitches around the world, and installed by J. Mallinson Ltd of Ormskirk. Constructed with Desso's iDNA artificial grass the pitch is made to feel as natural as possible by adding sand and rubber granules, or 'crumbs'. These give the players the same feel and shock absorption as natural turf laid on soil.

Alex Stead of Desso Sports Systems explained to me that the Belgian company has been designing artificial sports surfaces for 25 years, concentrating initially on hockey pitches. In recent times however, they have manufactured and installed training surfaces at St George's Park, the new National Football Centre in Burton, as well as at several Premier League clubs including Everton, Stoke and Chelsea, before making the Widnes i-Pitch their first venture into rugby league.

Developed in accordance with the RFL's 'Performance and Construction Standards for Synthetic Pitches' the Widnes pitch had to initially undergo laboratory testing to ensure it met the performance specifications laid down by the RFL. Approval and certification was then dependent upon those tests, carried out by Labosport of Heanor, Derbyshire, being repeated successfully on-site once the pitch was installed. The final element of pitch ratification is an annual re-certification, following further testing, to ensure that the surface still meets the standards.

The laboratory tests concentrate on the assessment of 'player/surface and ball/surface interaction' with particular attention to 'Head Impact Criteria', 'Ball rebound' and 'Shock absorption'. In view of some of the scare stories that came out in early 2012 it should be noted that tests are also required for 'skin friction', 'skin abrasion', and the 'rotational resistance' of both studded, and dimpled rubber soled footwear. In all cases the required standards for these tests were set after analysis of data gathered from the same tests carried out on grass pitches.

It is interesting to note that while the RFL specification requires a firm surface to replicate the natural conditions of 'summer rugby', their rugby union counterparts opted for a softer surface. The IRB identified the greater height from which 'union' players can fall to the ground – i.e. in line-outs – as one of the key issues and their 'Head Impact Criteria' were adjusted accordingly.

Taken at face value it may seem natural that the Widnes pitch is the only one which the RFL requires to be certified – simply because it is different. However, it seems ironic to me that, while the standards specified by the RFL are based on research carried out on grass pitches, the apparent criterion for grass pitches is only that they are green! The logic seems to be that grass is grass and must by definition be safe, regardless of the properties of what it is laid on. The technology is there to measure the 'natural shockpad' and I think there might be a few surprises if pitches in the professional game were measured against the RFL's criteria.

The background to the 12-week installation process was explained by joint Project Manager John Lamoury of J. Mallinson Ltd.

Once the existing pitch had been removed the site was levelled and a full drainage system installed before the pitch could be built up, layer by layer. A woven fabric membrane was then laid over the new surface to act as a load-spreader and to prevent material mixing with the layers above. A base layer of broken and crushed stone was then put down and consolidated before a binding layer of grit was added to provide a level and true base for the 'shockpad' to be laid on.

Mr Lamoury added that: "We had nothing but co-operation and assistance from both the Local Authority and the staff of Widnes Vikings. All those involved with the project need to be congratulated and in particular Mr Steve O'Connor chairman and owner of the Vikings, who had the vision, tenacity and courage to pursue an idea that I assume did not meet with a great deal of enthusiasm from his counterparts in the Super League."

Once the new surface was laid and handed over to the club the reactions were very positive. Although admitting to being sceptical at first the club's first major signing for 2012, Shaun Briscoe, said: "I wasn't looking forward to it but once you start trying it out it goes out of your mind and it feels like a normal surface. When you land on it or slide on it reacts the same as grass."

His coach Denis Betts commented: "Twelve months ago we were running up huge 'phone bills trying to find a pitch to train on because our own stadium was unavailable. Twelve months on there's not a single puddle or muddy patch in sight and the i-Pitch will always look like that, regardless of the weather, which will only benefit our training schedule.

"We did an hour-and-a-half of full contact and afterwards it didn't look like we'd been on it. We don't believe injuries are any more likely to happen on this surface than they would on grass. It's a true surface, there are no divots, so in many ways it's better."

Unsurprisingly the i-Pitch became the subject of much debate in the game but it certainly provided various benefits for the club, the team and the community. While the new pitch provides the players with a consistent playing surface, for home matches anyway, and the ability to train on it in all weathers, this ground-breaking development was also to be of great benefit to the community.

Announcing the arrival of the new pitch chairman Steve O'Connor said: "This is a first, not just for the Vikings or rugby league but for sport as a whole. The i-Pitch at Stobart Stadium Halton will modernise the game and create a fantastic match day experience. Our members and visitors will be able to see more games, it will create a pathway for our young players and it will be utilised as a community resource. We are working with our partners at Halton Borough Council and have exciting plans to transform the i-Pitch into a seven-a-side football sports facility throughout the week. This will generate income for the club and the stadium.

"It is my vision for people to be able to *'keep on the grass'* after the game and enjoy community and family fun activities. It is absolute nonsense to have a stadium and not be able to access the pitch for 90% of the time.

"Denis Betts and the team have been training regularly on a similar surface over the last few weeks and we have received some great feedback. We need to dispel the myth of grass burns and safety issues, technology has vastly improved in recent years and this simply doesn't happen! It will also reduce the risks of cancellation through frozen pitches."

O'Connor was supported by the RFL's chief operating officer Ralph Rimmer, who commented: "Not only is it a ground breaking decision by Widnes Vikings, it is also a huge leap forward for the sport and another example of rugby league taking a first step in the history of sport in this country.

"The benefits that accompany artificial grass pitches are numerous. Not only do they provide clubs and teams with a consistent playing surface which will help reduce injury occurrence and improve player performance, [but] due to the longevity of the surface Widnes will be able to host Academy games on their main pitch prior to any Super League games without worrying about surface deterioration, which will encourage fans to watch the next generation of stars coming through the main ranks."

Having trained on the surface in differing weather conditions during pre-season head coach Denis Betts said that he had "no worries whatsoever" adding "If you ask a rugby player what he would like to run on then that's what we have done with this surface. It's true and quick and has plenty of give in it so that players don't hurt themselves."

When I spoke to Betts at the end of the 2012 season he commented that "The positives far outweigh the negatives. The positives from my perspective are that we train all the time on it. You can see our performances are so much better because of our understanding of the pitch. It generates revenue and it is a way of bringing the community closer to the team because they can get on the pitch, sample the pitch. It's only when you see people on the pitch after the games, or walking out at night or early evening that you can see a pitch full of people and appreciate how much it has given to this area. Only time will tell how we move forward with it and whether it affects us in any other way, but my initial thoughts are that it has been great for this club and great for this town."

The benefits to the community were identified by Councillor Phil Harris who stated that: "The introduction of the very latest artificial pitch technology at the Stobart Stadium Halton will allow the Council to significantly increase community use of the pitch, as well as providing Widnes Vikings with a new pitch to support their re-entry into Super League.

"The Stobart Stadium Halton is a community facility and we will use this opportunity to offer increased use of the pitch to the local sporting community and others such as schools. This re-engineered pitch will help make a positive contribution to improving the health and well-being of a wide range of people."

Although the installation costs of approximately £500k were initially borne by Vikings' chairman O'Connor the pitch will remain in the ownership of Halton Borough Council and will be jointly managed by the club and the local authority.

With an average life expectancy of 10–15 years this latest generation of artificial pitches represents a sound investment when combined with the much reduced maintenance costs. Whereas a traditional grass pitch would require the attention of a full-time groundsman the i-Pitch only requires approximately five hours of 'brushing' per week to keep it in top condition, and the major benefit comes in the amount and flexibility of the use of an i-Pitch. The Widnes pitch was almost immediately in regular use for seven-a-side football (it accommodates three pitches running at 90 degrees to the rugby pitch) while corporate events, children's parties and a wide range of others activities are planned.

In February 2012, just four days after the first senior professional match to take place on an artificial surface, the i-Pitch played host to a programme of 'Touch Rugby League' organised by Rugby League Development Officer Dave Rolt. This proved to be a great success as the local rugby league community came out in force to support the 10 week programme. With 12 teams taking part in the inaugural session Rolt commented: "It was great to see so many people enjoying themselves playing Touch Rugby League. From the outset, this was the main thing I was looking for and to receive such encouraging signs at our first event was fantastic."

Within the next seven days the pitch came to the rescue of two matches that would otherwise have fallen foul of the weather. Firstly the Valvoline Cup clash between Huddersfield Giants and the Vikings, originally due to be played at Huddersfield YMCA, was switched to the Stobart Stadium when the severe weather conditions left the YMCA pitch frozen and unplayable.

The pitch again earned its stripes when an eleventh hour request came from the RFL for the Vikings to host a semi-final of the North West Champion Schools Year 10 competition between Hope Academy of St Helens and St Peters of Wigan.

Dave Rolt, who played a major role in ensuring the game went ahead said; "Due to the recent adverse weather conditions, there was no facility available in the North West to host the game and I was determined to play my part in ensuring that the Champion Schools semi-final was played on time. That's the beauty of the i-Pitch of course, and once again it proves just how valuable a resource it actually is."

At senior level there was naturally much debate about whether the new pitch would lead to a greater injury risk than natural grass, and whether Widnes would have an unfair advantage in matches played at the Stobart Stadium.

Following the club's first home match of the 2012 season there was further discussion in the written media of the safety issue, exacerbated by some hysterical comments on social media sites, after some players picked up cuts and grazes. In fact these appeared no more serious than similar injuries picked up on hard, rutted grass pitches at various times of the season. Indeed there were more serious-looking cuts and grazes on show in the televised match at Salford the following evening which was played on a snow-covered pitch. The telling factor, overlooked by many observers, was that both matches were played in temperatures that fell to minus 7 degrees Celsius.

In the same way that a grass pitch would be affected by frost the i-Pitch is not immune to extreme weather conditions. As water can be held within the rubber crumb infill it is this part of the artificial pitch which can freeze. However, as such pitches are maintained to a high level by regular brushing and the use of specialist treatments to 'de-compact' the infill, this makes the management of frost far easier to temperatures as low as minus 3 degrees, while applications of air-dried salt can be used in harsher conditions.

After the initial, but short-lived, hysteria there was hardly a murmur about the surface for the remainder of the season.

Equally I believe that the 'unfair home advantage' theory espoused by those against the new surface is flawed. At a very simplistic level this theory was dispelled by Widnes' early season performances and results. 'Home advantage' is a phrase that has been common parlance at all levels of all sports for centuries. The fact that this particular surface encourages a faster, slicker passing game was possibly, for a team trying to establish itself in the top tier, actually a disadvantage.

If you consider professional football for a moment it is clear that the pioneers of Oldham Athletic, Preston North End, Luton Town and Queen's Park Rangers did not achieve any great level of success by playing on an artificial surface. In the end it comes down to the skill of the players. It is also worthy of mention that Widnes, like their predecessors with the round ball, had to adjust to a different surface every other week, not just once a season as is the case for their opponents.

Whatever the success rate of the Viking Stronghold and whatever the pros and cons of the i-Pitch, as 2011 drew to a close Widnes fans were anxiously awaiting the release of the 2012 Super League fixtures. The Vikings were returning to their rightful home!

CHAPTER EIGHT
Grounds for Concern

One of the most emotive issues around the licensing process was that of stadia, both in 2008 and 2011, with some clubs, it seemed, having barely lifted so much as a paint brush in the three intervening years. Indeed several grounds appear not to have changed significantly since the RFL had published its blueprint for the game's survival, *Framing the Future*, back in 1994.

With the Halton Stadium being bizarrely assessed as 'adequate' in 2008, despite being plainly superior to several existing Super League grounds, this was a subject of great interest and concern to Widnes fans throughout the 2011 process.

At the time of issuing the Licences for 2009-11 the Rugby Football League were reported to have told Castleford Tigers, Celtic Crusaders, Salford City Reds, St Helens and Wakefield Trinity that they needed to either move to new grounds or significantly improve their current facilities in order to safeguard their Super League Licences. With the RFL also promising to promote at least one Championship club in 2012 it was plain that the issue of grounds could well be a determining factor for the Super League survival of those five clubs. Although not under immediate threat from the RFL, Bradford Bulls' Odsal home was also in desperate need of updating.

Claiming in April 2008 that the licensing process had already had a beneficial effect as "clubs have undergone their own searching assessments" to identify areas they need to strengthen, Nigel Wood the RFL chief executive, also pointed out that successful applicants will be playing "in 21st century facilities for supporters".

However, by the time the Licences were awarded just three months later the following repetitive comments appeared in the RFL's official application assessments:

Bradford Bulls:
The Coral Stand offers good hospitality but the remainder of the stadium requires improvement.
Castleford Tigers:
While well maintained, the ground is limited and old-fashioned.
Celtic Crusaders:
While well maintained, the ground is limited and old-fashioned.
Salford City Reds:
While well maintained, the ground is limited and old-fashioned.
St Helens:
The ground is an old and tired stadium. However, a new stadium is planned.
Wakefield Trinity Wildcats:
While well maintained, the ground is limited and old-fashioned.

We were further informed that Bradford have 'some development plans'; Celtic Crusaders 'recognise the need to develop a new facility'; Castleford have 'relatively advanced plans'; Wakefield 'have plans for a new stadium'; Salford are 'on site'; and St Helens have 'recently secured planning permission'. With the exception of St Helens and to a lesser extent Salford, it came as no surprise to the average fan that by the next application round in 2011 none of the above had come to fruition.

The eventual success stories started when St Helens, who moved into Widnes' 'adequate' stadium for 2011, received full planning consent on 7th July 2008 although they had to wait until early 2010 for work to begin, and until 2012 to play their first match at Langtree Park. Originally planning to move into their new home during 2011 Saints were committed to leaving Knowsley Road, after 120 years, at the end of the 2010 season. However, what was described by chief executive Tony Colquitt as "an incredibly complex process, accentuated by the wider economic climate" had delayed the construction of the new stadium. The search for a temporary home "for a few games of the 2011 season" eventually saw the Saints take up residence at the Stobart Stadium, described by chairman Eamonn McManus as "very comfortable and atmospheric", for the entire 2011 season.

Similarly Salford moved into their new home for the 2012 season but had to suffer several false dawns in their quest for the new stadium. Full planning consent was not gained until 19th August 2010, some two years after the RFL had said that they were 'on site', and even then they had to await the outcome of a referral to the Secretary of State before work could commence.

While not expecting clubs to be jettisoned from Super League just because their ground was not up to scratch it did seem that the RFL, having made these observations, was again reduced to being a paper tiger. The governing body seemed to take assertions from clubs at face value, with no checking system in place, and this must cast some doubt on the administration of the licensing system. This was underlined again in 2012 when the parlous financial state of Bradford Bulls began to unravel despite their being 'assessed' by independent auditors as part of the 2011 licensing process.

This was underlined when at the time of writing – August 2012 – more than 12 months after the second round of licensing, Wakefield and Castleford have still to break ground on their new stadia. In fact, contrary to reports and 'artists impressions' in the press, I am informed by the Planning Department of Wakefield Council that neither club has yet got the final green light for their new ground.

Submitting an 'Outline Application' request in December 2006 for a 'mixed development comprising sports stadium with ancillary facilities, 2-10 storey offices and hotel', along with access and parking, Castleford had to wait until 8th April 2011 for 'full' planning permission to be granted. However, at the time of writing, it would seem that this project is stalling as no application has yet been received by Wakefield Council for the development of Castleford's current home, The Jungle, which I understand is necessary to fund the new stadium. It seems that until that is resolved Castleford will not be in a position to proceed with their new stadium and, with an estimated construction timescale of 12–18 months, it looks unlikely that the new ground will be built before Super League Licences are again reviewed in 2014. That would be an astonishing 20 years after the RFL published its *Framing the Future* document.

Wakefield submitted their Outline Application in February 2010 for 'permission for a mixed use development comprising a community stadium; multi-use games area, warehousing and distribution units, business units and hotel', along with infrastructure and landscaping. Despite claims to the contrary in an article on the Wildcats' official website I was informed in late August 2012, by a representative of Wakefield's Planning Department, that planning approval had not yet been granted by the Secretary of State. Although

Wakefield Council are 'minded to approve' the application the official status of the application is 'pending decision' until such time as the Secretary of State makes a final decision. It is not until the Secretary of State gives his approval to the application and the Section 106 legal agreement is in place that 'Reserved Matters' approval can then be sought and the project given the final green light. Again planning and construction timescales would suggest that the new stadium will not be built by 2014. With the Castleford and Wakefield clubs both coming under the jurisdiction of Wakefield Council one scenario which had been discussed on more than one occasion was that of ground-sharing. However, the intense rivalry between the two clubs seemed to prevent this eminently sensible solution getting off the ground as neither wished to be seen as a tenant in the other's stadium.

In the run up to the second round of licensing, in 2011, the combination of financial problems and the lack of progress on their new stadium had made Wakefield favourites to lose their Super League status following Widnes' admission to the elite competition. However, the even deeper crisis at Celtic Crusaders saw the Wildcats win a reprieve as the Welsh outfit withdrew their application.

There also seemed to be confusion over the exact status of Salford's application when back in July 2008 it was mentioned in the RFL's official bid assessment that they were 'on site'.

The RFL's comment is all the more worrying as Salford City Council's Planning Department only received the application for 'remediation work' – site clearance – on 17th November 2009, which was subsequently approved on 28th January 2010. Although there is some evidence of earlier, lapsed applications Salford City Council did not receive a new Outline Planning application until 29th October 2009, and this was also subsequently allowed to lapse. It was replaced by an application for full planning consent for the stadium, along with an Outline application for 21,831 square metres of 'non-food retail' outlets, received on 8th June 2010.

Thus at the time of the 2008 Licence application no permission for any works had been granted by the local authority. It would therefore seem that Paul Cook's observation that the RFL were accepting a 'jam tomorrow' bid from Salford is borne out by the facts. After an initial plan for a joint venture with Salford College foundered when the Learning and Skills Council declined funding the City Reds were forced to seek other funding avenues. Ironically while new partners were sought time progressed through 2009 and 2010 with a stream of announcements from the club repeatedly trumpeting the imminent 'commencement of building work'.

Even though full planning consent, scaled down from 20,000 seats to 12,000, for the stadium was finally granted on 19th August 2010, it was still not without controversy. Attending that meeting of the planning committee I heard concerns expressed by various councillors about the true 'community' nature of the stadium. Indeed one member of the planning committee was so incensed by the proposal that she left the room having told the meeting: "This is not a community stadium. It appears to be driven by Salford's desire to maintain their Super League Licence." As she, and other ward councillors, later told me outside the meeting the source of their anger was that "the stadium is costing the rate payers of Salford £22 million despite there being very limited community use".

During the meeting it was also confirmed that the move to the original capacity would be done in two stages and "would be dependent upon new business plans, and success on the field", with the developers later explaining to me that this would be achieved "by simply making the bike sheds bigger".

Two years down the line the Reds had taken up residence in their new home but the wisdom of the council's investment was questioned amid rumours of the club's financial difficulties. It had been expected that the completion and occupation of the retail development would cover the cost of building the stadium, but that part of the site remains untouched today. Faced with an annual rent for the stadium in the order of £600,000 an 'on-off' but ultimately 'on' arrangement with Sale Sharks for a ground-share agreement eventually cut that figure in half.

Bradford Bulls, like St Helens had achieved high levels of success on the pitch, but were also not immune from a blunt assessment of their facilities by the RFL. In fact proposals to develop Odsal had been discussed as far back as 2004 as the council-led Odsal Sporting Village project took shape, which was to include an 18,000 seat stadium for the Bulls, a community sports centre, a 120-bed hotel and retail outlets. But in March 2010 the Bulls' suffered a similar blow to Salford when their partner, Bradford College, was also refused funding by the Learning and Skills Council, which created a large shortfall in funding for the project, and placed it on hold while scaled-down alternatives were drawn up. Worse news was to come in 2011 when the local authority withdrew its £15 million commitment to the scheme in favour of other building projects, and Odsal remains the iconic, yet outdated, ground it has been for many years.

On the positive side of the argument it should be noted that, although not under threat from the RFL, Hull KR were another club to take steps to upgrade a less than ideal facility. Boosted by a significant investment by the Local Health Authority, the club was able to extend the East Stand, thereby increasing practical capacity and income. Club chairman Neil Hudgell had realistically admitted that a significant proportion of their capacity was in "very poor facilities, mainly uncovered, and that puts people off coming". Significantly in the run up to the 2011 licensing process the Robins also took heed of the apparently stricter ground criteria to be applied by the RFL, by announcing planning consent for a new 2,600 seat North Stand. While the East Stand was to contain a community 'health and lifestyle' centre the North Stand, due for completion in 2013, is to benefit from business and education facilities.

Ironically financial worries allowed Celtic Crusaders to side-step the issue of their ground, although they were to catch up with them later. Having failed to build any sort of sustainable fan base in South Wales the owners opted to sell the club to the owner of Wrexham Football Club, and make the highly controversial move to the Racecourse Ground some 160 miles from their existing base.

Meanwhile, while some clubs in Super League continued to ignore the state of their grounds, improvements were taking place outside the top tier as ambitious clubs took note of the Super League criteria. While Widnes were in the fortunate position of having had an excellent stadium – despite the 'adequate' tag – for many years others hoping to make the step up were not so fortunate.

Of the clubs needing to improve their facilities in order to challenge for a Super League spot Leigh Centurions led the way when they moved out of Hilton Park in 2009 in favour of the new 11,000 capacity stadium at Leigh Sports Village.

Another club to forge ahead with redevelopment was Halifax. Finally opening their new stand in early 2010 – some 10 years after construction began – Halifax chief executive Graham Clay confidently claimed that: "We know the stadium will exceed minimum standards. We will have a capacity of 15,000 with 5,000 seats." My own perception, based on my last visit to The Shay, is that those figures may be on the generous side with one terrace and part of the remaining 'old' stand unfit for use.

So it would seem that the intended hard line on stadia standards had some effect on some clubs, both in Super League and below. But the fact remains that there are still, in 2012, clubs operating in grounds which are far from the "21st century facilities for spectators" identified as a requirement by Nigel Wood in April 2008. While the lack of progress in some quarters can be put at the door of 'economic downturn' we should remember that clubs have had ample opportunity to literally 'put their house in order' since *Framing the Future* was published in 1994.

As it stands Castleford, Wakefield and Bradford (if they survive Administration) will be entering Super League XVIII without a redeveloped or new stadium, while the itinerant Harlequins seem to have the choice of remaining at The Stoop or sharing with Gillingham or Leyton Orient. They could even end up at the Olympic Stadium as Leyton Orient have yet to be ruled out of the running for the tenancy there. Either way there are no development costs or problems for them! Of the likely candidates for 2015-17 from the Championship only Leigh, in my opinion, can rest easy while Halifax would at least need to be able to re-open the terracing which is currently deemed unsafe. The remaining clubs, including any of the favoured Cumbrian cabal, would be facing a stiff task to convince Red Hall that they would have a stadium fit for purpose in that timescale.

As this book was about to go into print it was announced that another chapter had opened in the saga over Castleford's proposed new stadium. After promising to deliver a new stadium through two rounds of Licensing it now seems that the club is to remain at The Jungle. Due to the ongoing lack of funding it now appears, according to chief executive Steve Ferres, that the Tigers may opt to develop Wheldon Road instead. With the supermarket firm, who were to buy the Wheldon Road site for development, putting the project on hold Ferres admitted that "This club hasn't had a plan B for years and now we need to look at options to redevelop our ground." That being the case I would suggest that it will be another lengthy period before Castleford have a home that matches the requirements of the RFL.

CHAPTER NINE
Elsewhere in Rugby League

While Widnes were confidently moving forward to establish a firm foundation for their next Super League Licence application things were running far less smoothly elsewhere. Although many of these issues had no direct bearing on life at the Stobart Stadium they were naturally of interest to the Widnes club and its fans.

Away from the action, but of great interest to Widnes and their fans, the RFL brought in two significant changes for clubs in the two Co-operative Championship divisions. Both would come into force for the 2010 season, and were in their own way seen by many as controversial.

Firstly the salary cap for Co-operative Championship and Championship 1 clubs would be lowered for the 2010 season, following a debate by clubs, which led to the proposed changes being ratified by the RFL Board.

The current salary cap system operated by limiting a club's player costs to no more than 50% of the club's income with an absolute limit of £400,000 for the Championship clubs and £200,000 for clubs in the lower division. The revised scheme meant that players' salaries and other costs could be no more than 40% of the club's income with the financial limit revised down to £300,000 for Championship clubs and £150,000 for those in Championship 1.

This had an immediate effect on clubs' recruitment for 2010 and Widnes, although seen as the 'big boys' of the Championship in some quarters, were no exception. First team regulars such as Gavin Dodd, Richard Fletcher, John Duffy, Tim Hartley and Michael Ostick along with other senior professionals Danny Mills and Lee Paterson were casualties of the 25% reduction in the cap. As sporting director Terry O'Connor said at the time: "I know some of the players leaving would prefer to stay, and we would like to keep them, but with the reduction in the salary cap to £300,000 we have to spend accordingly."

While there was the facility to seek dispensation to spend up to £400,000 this was subject the to club demonstrating that the annual revenue would be £1 million or more. As this would require significant increases in season ticket sales, gate receipts, sponsorship and Dream Ticket sales it was naturally a step that the club declined.

The second initiative from the governing body brought in a variation to the existing loan transfer system. On the face of it the 'Dual Registration' scheme was a good deal for clubs in the Co-operative Championships, but it certainly had a mixed reception from fans and clubs alike.

In essence the Dual Registration scheme was an arrangement between clubs where a Super League player continued to be registered with his 'parent' Super League club while also being registered to play for a club in the Co-operative Championship or Championship 1.

The RFL's press release stated that "the purpose of the new dual registration system is to provide a flexible development pathway for young Super League players who might not be quite ready to make the step up to Super League first-team duties on a permanent basis.

"We were of the view that, for such players, there may be an opportunity for his Super League club to enter into a mutually beneficial arrangement with a Championship or Championship One club with a view to giving the player quality first-team experience in a manner that will hopefully prove cost-effective for the Championship club."

The scheme would only be open to players "under the age of 23, and who were outside the top 20 by value" (salary) at their parent club. It also allowed for dual registered players to be "eligible to play and train with both clubs in a format agreed between the clubs, subject to registration, salary cap and competition eligibility rules."

There were initially safeguards for the players in that they could only play in one game in any scheduled round of fixtures in any given week. For example this would prevent a player turning out for a Championship club on a Thursday and for his parent club over the same weekend. This stipulation was however, relaxed in June 2010.

Existing regulations that limited the number of 'loaned' players that a club may use to four were to stay in force. Thus a club could still only utilise a maximum of four players whether they be 'loaned', 'dual registered' or a combination of both. In addition a club could take no more than three such players from the same club.

The key difference between a traditional loan deal and dual registration was one of flexibility. With a loan deal there was no 'recall' within the first 28 days, but dual registration allowed flexibility week by week. Ironically it was this flexibility which gave rise to concerns among some fans about the viability of the system. While the advantages of the scheme were plain to see, from both sides, it soon became apparent that there was also a downside to any such arrangements. It was all well and good, for example, for Widnes to have the benefit of fringe Super League players in their squad but these players were subject to recall at short notice. The yo-yo effect of a player potentially moving between his two registered clubs during the course of the deal was naturally a disruptive one.

The success of these deals would, naturally, to a large extent depend on the form, fitness and depth of the 'parent' club's own squad. For example if they were to pick up a couple of injuries their dual registered players were likely to be recalled.

Widnes did indeed suffer from this scenario as Chris Dean, the club's first dual registration signing, made just one appearance for the club before returning to St Helens to play in 11 first team matches. Similarly Liam Farrell was recalled by Wigan, after making six impressive performances for the Vikings, and went on to make 23 appearances for the Warriors in 2010, scoring nine tries. In a more unusual scenario Shaun Ainscough was recalled by Wigan, to be 'loaned' to fellow Super League outfit Castleford who had been impressed with the winger's four tries in just three outings for the Vikings. A more successful deal was that for Ben Davies who, despite also being recalled to Wigan on occasions, clocked up 17 games for Widnes, scoring three tries in the process.

Widnes had mixed results from their dual registration signings, due to factors outside their control, but there were clubs who had almost unfettered access to their dual registered players. Those clubs and their fans would no doubt look upon the system in a different way to the Vikings and their followers.

In a further attempt to revitalise the game below Super League level the RFL launched a review of the lower leagues in late 2010, with its recommendations to be implemented in 2013. The aim of the governing body was to 'create the best, viable and competitive semi-professional competition possible', and in a scaled down licensing procedure the RFL would ensure that 'the clubs have strong management and their levels of investment reflect the level of return to the sport'.

However, outside influences determined that there was an interim restructuring in 2012 following events at Barrow Raiders, Celtic Crusaders and Toulouse Olympique during 2011. Barrow's salary cap breaches saw them demoted to Championship One for 2012 where they were joined by the former Celtic Crusaders after the North Wales club withdrew their Super League application at the eleventh hour, reformed as North Wales Crusaders and accepted a place in the bottom tier, where they would do battle with South Wales Scorpions who were based in the Crusaders old back yard of Neath! Toulouse's decision to withdraw to their domestic competition threw further confusion into the mix, and eventually York City Knights and Dewsbury Rams were reprieved from relegation at the end of 2011, with two divisions of 10 teams being formed for 2012.

When the review of the semi-professional game was eventually completed it was announced that the revised structure would see 14 teams in the Championship and 10 in Championship One. This was to be achieved by promoting the top four teams from the lower division to join the 10 clubs who competed in the Championship in 2012.

Hemel Stags, Gloucester All Golds, and Oxford were subsequently admitted to a nine team Championship One for the 2013 season. The original intention for a 10 team league was thwarted when Coventry Bears, a replacement for original choice Northampton Rebels, were found not to be ready for the step up.

Northampton Rebels had initially been accepted into Championship One but later withdrew. Former Widnes scrum-half Steven Myler had gone on record as welcoming the introduction of rugby league into the town, where he currently plays for rugby union outfit Northampton Saints, saying: "It can be very entertaining and it may appeal over the summer months, when the Saints are in off-season. Crossing over was more difficult than I thought it would be. The games are totally different but, having played both, I can honestly say that I love both codes."

Due to share Northampton Town's all-seater, 7,500 capacity stadium, the Rebels withdrew their application in August 2012. Chairman David Cardoza admitted that the new club would have had a negative impact on the football club and that it had become apparent that they did not have the personnel or infrastructure to make it work.

Elsewhere, during 2011 various chickens that had flown the Welsh coop in 2009, came home to roost. There had, in the intervening years, been much concern, not just in and around Widnes, about the manner in which Celtic Crusaders had been parachuted into Super League.

In a move which seemed to cast some doubt over the legitimacy and transparency of the licencing process the RFL announced, in July 2009, that they had sent a Task Force to Bridgend "to help [the club] meet the challenge of running a full-time operation" as they "have been experiencing difficulties due to the adverse economic climate".

While Crusaders owner Leighton Samuel reaffirmed his commitment to creating a Super League club in South Wales, observers throughout the sport were concerned by the RFL announcement that "we are determined to do everything we can to help them find additional investors. We are trying to establish a Super League club outside the traditional rugby league heartland." The deep involvement of the RFL with Celtic was seen by many of those observers to cast some doubt on the content and reliability of the accounts and projections submitted by the fledgling Welsh outfit.

This seemed to be at odds with the fact that Widnes were 'marked down' for not having a full year's accounts – the new company had only been trading for a few months when the application was submitted. Despite continuing to trade in the black, and the preparedness of the owner to lodge a personal £500,000 Bond with the RFL to ensure that the club would survive at least through the 2009-11 Licence period the Vikings' application had, as we know, been dismissed.

In addition, with the Crusaders having won only three of their 27 matches in their debut season in Super League, and suffering serious financial problems, eyebrows were raised even further when it was announced that six Australian players recruited by the club – including skipper Jace Van Dijk and top try scorer Tony Duggan – were to be deported for visa irregularities. The UK Border Agency had found that the players were playing illegally under 'working holiday' or 'student' visas between 2006 and 2008. Significantly during this period the club had gained promotion to Co-operative National League One – a pre-requisite to enable them to apply for a Super League Licence.

Subsequently in December 2009 Celtic Crusaders escaped legal proceedings but were fined £60,000 for their part in the fiasco.

The effect of these revelations was to underline the concerns, expressed at various times by both rugby league fans and commentators alike, that the Crusaders weren't ready for such a big step up. It is also reasonable to ask whether the club would have achieved the necessary National League One status without these players who were in the country illegally. These events only served to give a level of credence to the whispers around the game that the governing body were so intent on having a Welsh presence in Super League that a blind eye had been turned to any shortcomings in their operation and Licence application.

Over three years later the issue again hit the headlines as through the columns of the *League Express* former Crusaders star Tony Duggan claimed that both the club and RFL were fully aware of the visa situation. Duggan even claimed that the players were offered money in exchange for their silence when the 'scam' was exposed. Referring to the RFL he went as far as saying: "They approved our visas and approved the fact that we were on amateur contracts. They knew all about this right from the start and approved it all." In response the RFL stated that the UK Border Agency investigation was closed and that any remaining issues were with the players' employer – Crusaders.

While clubs throughout the game were undergoing their pre-season preparation the attention would not go away from the Crusaders. As a consequence of their financial problems and inability to build a fan base in South Wales, rumours began to leak out about a proposed takeover by Wrexham Football Club, and a potential move to the North Wales town just 30 minutes drive from Widnes and Warrington.

Arguments raged across the rugby league community about the acceptability of this proposed move as the Super League Licence was openly granted by the RFL on an 'expansionist ticket'. The comment from an RFL spokesman that "Moving home grounds is not against the terms of the Super League Licence and isn't without precedent," misses the point completely, I would suggest. To move over 150 miles, within 12 months, to the back door of the 'heartlands' of the game was surely a breach of the spirit of the Licence if not the letter. I would venture to suggest, however, that questions would have been asked if, say, Steve O'Connor had wanted to relocate the Vikings to Carlisle, which is a similar distance from the Cumbrian 'heartlands'.

Crusaders' assistant coach Kevin Ellis added to the debate when he declared his concerns to the *Glamorgan Gazette*: "I think it would be a tragedy and embarrassing if we moved to Wrexham as it's only 30 minutes away from Widnes. I think that would be the wrong thing to do as all the development work in schools and the community down here would be wasted."

It is also worthy of mention that from the early days the RFL were keen to point out that membership of Super League was by the award of a 'Licence' and not a 'Franchise'. While it is commonplace for Franchises to be 'sold on' without geographical restriction that is not normally the case with Licences. However, by mid-December 2009 the move was confirmed, and the transfer of ownership of the rugby club to Wrexham FC owner Geoff Moss completed. This saw the Licence in the hands of a company who had submitted no accounts, no business plan, no projections or any other material pertinent to the issue of that Licence.

Initially the move to North Wales had seemed to pay off, but just 12 months after re-locating the club was again in dire straits. While early-season attendances at Wrexham's Racecourse ground were higher than those experienced in South Wales they fell away alarmingly once the novelty value had worn off and only 1,495 turned up for the final home game of 2010.

Unsurprisingly things went from bad to worse for the Crusaders as they were forced into Administration in November of that year. While no Widnes fan, having lived through the uncertainty that that brings, would wish that on any other club, it did seem that this was an accident waiting to happen. Rubbing salt into the wound was the fact that the club were being pursued at the same time by a group of players for missing pension payments that hadn't been paid into an offshore fund in Guernsey as promised.

With the RFL thought to be a major creditor of the club the governing body sanctioned a deal which saw Ian Roberts and Geoff Moss buy back the club from the administrators. Rising from the ashes as Crusaders RL for the 2011 season, and with chairman Ian Roberts speaking confidently of the rehabilitation of the club and a promising future, the Welsh experiment was to founder yet again within months as the rugby league world gathered to witness the unveiling of the 13 clubs to join Widnes in Super League XVII.

In February 2011 another Super League club entered Administration when the board of directors of Wakefield Trinity Wildcats conceded defeat in their battle to save their club. As was the case with Widnes it was the threat of a winding up order being issued by HMRC (Her Majesty's Revenue and Customs), which if successful would have seen the 138-year-old club liquidated, that forced the hand of the Wildcats board.

With the RFL's 2008 assessment of Belle Vue as 'limited and old fashioned' no doubt still ringing in the ears of the Wakefield hierarchy this news could not have come at a worse time, with the next round of Super League Licences due to be awarded just six months later. In fact the combination of these factors immediately led to the Wildcats being installed as favourites to fall to the Championship in 2012.

Within days of entering Administration there was, however, talk of four potential buyers but ultimately the ailing club was rescued by Yorkshire businessman Andrew Glover. With the Crusaders and Wakefield clubs now continuing to operate, albeit under new ownership, this created an interesting scenario with regard to the scrutiny of accounts as part of the licensing process.

In 2008 it was stated that Widnes' inability to submit a full year's accounts – the new company had only been operating for a few months when the Bid was submitted – was a factor in not awarding the Vikings a Super League Licence. Three years down the line and the RFL were now faced with two clubs, inside the Super League clique, that were in that same position. As both clubs also had additional shortcomings the announcement on 26th July 2011 would have been extremely interesting if Crusaders hadn't baled out and Halifax's bid had been that little bit more robust.

Following these developments, and subsequently those at Bradford, there was a great debate about the validity of licensing and the optimum size of the Super League competition.

A handful of noisy chairmen, chief executives and journalists saw the failings of Crusaders, Wakefield and Bradford as proof positive that a) licensing didn't work and b) that the top tier should be reduced to 12, or even 10 teams.

The unfolding events at Odsal, fewer than 12 months after being granted a Licence for 2012-14, certainly added to the debate about the effectiveness and transparency of the licensing system. How could a club submit healthy accounts and business plans in support of their application and be in such a dire financial situation so quickly?

In awarding the Bulls a Grade B Licence the RFL had commented that the club had 'a strategy, tactical plan and targets to achieve improved commercial and financial performance', and that 'its business plan for the next three years will move it to a position of sustainability with good prospects for further growth'.

As the depth of the Bulls' financial problems became clearer the questions being asked across the game were: 'was proper due diligence carried out', and if so 'how could the findings apparently be dismissed?' Naturally no definitive answers were forthcoming.

With the iconic club staring extinction in the face unless an initial £500,000 was rapidly forthcoming appeals were issued for support. As Easter approached there were fears that the Good Friday match against Leeds would be the last at Odsal. With the assistance of benefactors such as Steve O'Connor and others, and with ex-players donating their memorabilia to the fighting fund, the club survived the first hurdle. Within 48 hours of the appeal being launched O'Connor had pledged £10,000 from his own pocket to the fund, and also donated the ticket income from the Bradford fans who had travelled to Widnes for the Easter Monday fixture.

Bradford chairman Peter Hood commented: "Steve rang me to offer his support for the situation we find ourselves in – but also to say he wanted to pledge an enormous sum of £10,000."

Having extended their deadline by a few days Bradford reached their initial target and by the middle of April were confident of raising the full £1 million, until in early June it became apparent that they actually needed £1.25 million to survive. The situation became so dire that within days of the Administrator taking over 16 staff were made redundant, including all the coaching staff. Subsequently Mick Potter and his staff returned to work, on a voluntary basis and, but for the 6 point penalty for entering administration, would have steered the Bulls into the play-offs.

Bradford's situation had been a cause for concern for some time before the Administrators stepped in. Matters came to a head when the club's bankers withdrew their overdraft facility following the sale of their major asset, Odsal stadium, to the RFL. While the sale allowed the club to repay a £700,000 loan from the governing body, it also meant that the bank would not cover the outstanding payment to HMRC. Faced with a potential winding-up order the club had announced on 27th March that it needed to raise £1 million to survive, with half of that sum needed within 10 days.

It soon became apparent however, that this was the tip of the iceberg and Bradford finally went into Administration on 26th June before, following some false dawns, being saved by local businessman Omar Khan on 1st September 2012.

The potential demise of one of the most successful clubs of the modern era certainly added fuel to the fire for those unconvinced about the licensing system. While I believe that there are merits in the system and its aims, there are certainly questions about how that process is managed. There were misgivings about how Celtic Crusaders met the criteria in

2008 but the stark reality of the Bradford Bulls case is that their financial plight was either completely missed in the due diligence process, or it was identified and subsequently ignored. Neither scenario casts the system or the RFL in a good light. On balance, for what it is worth, I personally favour the traditional system of promotion and relegation because it is totally transparent. Having said that it is also my view that with total transparency and strict management licensing can be a success.

Turning to the argument of the number of clubs in Super League I believe that is a totally separate issue from licensing and the financial management of individual clubs. To suggest that Crusaders, Wakefield and Bradford entering administration proves that there are too many clubs at the top is pure fantasy. That smacks of trying to find an argument to support a pre-conceived agenda.

While there are questions to be answered about the management of the licensing process, the system itself cannot be blamed for the problems experienced by those clubs. Those clubs found themselves in dire straits through their own mismanagement. No other reason. They would have found themselves in that situation if traditional promotion and relegation were still in place, and no matter how many teams were in Super League.

The sub-plot to the Bradford saga was a question of in which division they would compete in 2013. Strong, if not utterly convincing, arguments were put forward that they were too big a club, with too big a following, to be lost to Super League. Similarly there was also a significant level of support for the argument that the Bulls should be demoted to the Championship. While the former case appeared to be largely based on sentiment and a perceived loss of fans, and revenue to the game, the latter sought to emulate the 'sporting integrity' argument so recently employed by the Scottish football authorities in demoting Rangers to the bottom tier of their game.

Much to the annoyance of some of the more ambitious Championship clubs the RFL trod the middle ground by awarding Bradford a one-year probationary Super League Licence. The BBC reported RFL chief executive Nigel Wood as explaining: "This is a very positive development which provides stability for all the clubs in Super League and below. It allows the sport to approach next season with even greater confidence. The board deliberated long and hard and took into consideration the many views of the sport's various constituents before reaching a decision which we believe is in the best interests of the whole game."

Moving away from the contentious issue of licensing, the RFL again courted controversy during 2012 as they turned their attention to a review of the academy system as they sought the holy grail of a successful national team. Apparently the latest idea to enable us to catch up with our antipodean friends is to replace the successful youth programmes at our clubs with a more regionalised approach.

The proposal was that club academies would be disbanded and replaced with regional camps where the players would be groomed by the more powerful Super League clubs, and not by the local club that had spotted and nurtured them. I have yet to hear how these players would then be 'allocated' between the 14 top tier clubs. While success on the international stage is another laudable aim of the RFL this latest tinkering, or some may say meddling, by the governing body can only destabilise the professional game at its very roots. In both rounds of licensing which the RFL have overseen there has been a call for clubs to produce home-grown talent and provide, and demonstrate, a pathway to the first team. Indeed this was identified by the RFL as a weakness in Widnes' 2008 bid.

That, and the fact that Vikings chairman Steve O'Connor is a great believer in generating the club's future stars from within, led Widnes to overhaul their structures to ensure compliance with the RFL diktat, while at the same time improving their sustainability.

O'Connor laid down the challenge, initially to Stuart Wilkinson, and then Paul Cullen and Phil Finney to do just that. The work done over the years by them and their coaching staff put Denis Betts in the position where he could hand Super League debuts in 2012 to seven graduates of the Vikings' excellent Academy: Danny Craven, Paddy Flynn, Alex Gerrard, Tom Gilmore, Grant Gore, Anthony Mullally and Jack Owens. "We have invested a lot in these players," Cullen said. "We are proud that they have emerged and will eventually progress to be established Super League players for Widnes Vikings. That's the vision we have for them."

After the countless hours put in over the years Cullen and Finney would obviously hate to see the system founder on the rocks of this latest RFL proposal. Ex-England Coach Cullen's frustration was plain when he told Ian Cheveau, editor of the club's matchday programme:

"The challenges we as a club have had to face are the most difficult I have been involved in in my time in rugby league. The landscape has changed so much and we are fighting tooth and nail to keep hold of the thriving Academy set up that we have.

"There are some huge challenges that we are faced with in terms of the Academy structure at present. The goal posts are moving all the time in the fact that the RFL are consulting with all 14 Super League clubs about the prospect of having eight regional camps as opposed to Academies run by the clubs, and other potential changes to the Super League Academy Structure."

If these dramatic RFL proposals were implemented it could very easily be the thin end of the wedge where we go down the same road as cricket and award 'central contracts'. In years to come our best international players could be contracted to the RFL and only appear for their clubs on rare occasions. Imagine what that would do to match attendances and the consequential reduction in a variety of income streams for a sport so recently embarrassed by the financial failings of at least three Super League clubs.

Cullen continued: "When we came up to Super League we had to include eight home grown players as part of the Licence criteria. We had to include these players and we had no other choice. When other Super League clubs have been promoted, in what we know now as the yo-yo system, or have come up through a licensing process, they received special dispensation in this area. Our calls to the RFL for similar treatment were rejected and we have simply got on with it."

The club's highly respected director of rugby added: "All other clubs have been given dispensation to have more overseas players and less home grown to ease them into the top flight. We were denied access to precedents that were an accepted part of movement into Super League. We were forced to meet challenges that no other club coming into Super League has been asked to do.

"The RFL actually increased the number of 'Home Grown', and the reclassified 'Home Grown While There', categories you were required to name in your first team squad of 25 players. This was like fighting the Klitschko brothers with both hands tied behind your back.

"We have been out of the top flight for six years, so at £1.2 million per annum RFL investment to each club, we are £7.2 million behind other Super League clubs. We kept the

Academies and the Scholarships going and we could not have done that without Steve O'Connor's personal commitment to that area.

"We are fighting hard to keep what we have – we have a strong structure and we have a track record of developing players from within. We don't want them to go off to camps which will be run by the top Super League clubs.

"We want the players we are developing now to become fully fledged Widnes Vikings Super League players. There has been a great deal of time, effort and work that has gone into developing what in 2009 was just a concept. Now we have something that we are proud of and the players are coming through and that's testament to the structure and work that has gone in on all sides." The fact that the club have a custom built facility in the pipeline for the Academy set up only adds to the pain with the envisaged reduction in academy activity at club level.

At the time of writing I have learned that a re-vamped version of these proposals is indeed going ahead. Following an assessment process, which took place mid-season in 2012, the RFL issued a grade to each of the academies at each of the Super League clubs, excluding Catalan Dragons, and Sheffield Eagles, Featherstone Rovers and South Wales Scorpions. Of these Leeds, Wigan, St Helens, Warrington, Hull FC and Bradford (who were in the midst of their financial crisis) were graded 'Green' and awarded Regional Academy status. With the Scorpions being the sole club placed in the 'Red' category, Widnes were one of the nine remaining clubs granted 'Amber' status. The RFL assessment identified the Vikings Academy as having "a clear pathway that points to long-term sustainability" recognising the "positive influences of the youth team staff".

At the end of this process the RFL's plans were, surprisingly, dealt a blow when all six of the clubs awarded Regional Academy status rejected the proposals, opting instead to retain club-based academies.

The fall-out from that decision is that the RFL are implementing a 'Partnership Plan' between Super League clubs and those in the Championships, with Widnes forming an alliance with Workington Town. At the same time academy teams are to be restricted to under-16 and under-19 age groups while all other age groups are to be disbanded, and in addition no over-age players will be allowed.

With Super League clubs required to register a first team squad of 25 players, and only 17 of those playing in any one week, there is an obvious lack of match practice for the remaining eight players – and any other player on the club's books over the age of 19. To provide competitive action for these players each top flight club can now enter into a partnership agreement with a single club from the lower leagues. The RFL explained to me, at the time of writing, that it is expected that the parent club "can loan up to five or six players to its partner club, while still being able to place further players with other clubs".

At a time when the governing body is seeking to strengthen the game at international level it seems ironic that this latest move could have dire consequences at the lower end of the professional game. It is a natural consequence of this latest move that clubs outside Super League will reduce the numbers of their own contracted playing staff and severely weaken the pathway opportunities from the community game. The accidental silver lining will be the strengthening of BARLA and its representative team!

As it stands there is no talk of reducing the numbers of 'quota' players, at any level, to mitigate against this loss, so it seems self-evident that a lot of young British talent will be lost to the professional game. It would therefore seem that clubs in the Championships will be fielding teams where nearly half of the players are 'temporary imports', and running the risk of losing more of their local identity which, in all probability, will lead to a fall in support. As a consequence the RFL could well find their attention, and funds, diverted away from giving transfusions to ailing expansionist clubs in order to provide life-support to the game in the heartlands!

Unfortunately this is not the only recent intervention by the governing body which has affected the running of clubs. Again Paul Cullen explained: "Already we have seen changes to the reserve grade structure. It's changed from under-21s down to under-20s, with three overage players, then under-20s with five overage players. Now there is talk that it will be an under-23s team from 2013. We were forced to actually dismantle an under-23s team here at Widnes last season, so you can see that the landscape is changing in the game on a regular basis."

One thing is certain about the game of rugby league – it doesn't stay the same for long. Sadly sometimes the mantra appears to be 'If it isn't broken – fix it!"

CHAPTER TEN
Licenced to Thrill

The two weak spots identified by the RFL in the Vikings' 2008 bid for Super League status were the lasting stigma of Administration, and the need to boost the numbers of locally produced players coming through to the first team. The effects of the previous company going into Administration were always at the back of people's minds, but to be told that the club hadn't produced its own first team players in sufficient numbers was an unexpected blow. Salt was rubbed into the wound when it became apparent that rivals Salford were able to claim the credit for bringing through Richie Myler and Adam Sidlow, both of whom they signed from Widnes during the fall-out of Administration!

Over the next three years the club was able to clearly show that it was now being run in a businesslike fashion. Similarly, by the time the 2011 bid was handed in, the club could demonstrate the success of the youth development programme, under Head of Youth Performance Phil Finney. No fewer than 20 'home grown' players had progressed to the first team since Steve O'Connor took control of the club, with four of these players subsequently representing the club in Super League.

Everything about the new bid was centred on the key element of sustainability – as a business and as a rugby club. The management team had put together a business plan which, if adhered to, would see the club prosper and grow in the medium to long term. On the playing side the sustainability would not just come from winning trophies, but as Denis Betts explained to Alan Jackson of *Radio Merseyside* just weeks before the bid was submitted: "We want success on the field, but that can't just be seen as winning silverware, that has to be about developing youth."

This philosophy was underlined when his chairman, explaining the role of Paul Cullen as director of rugby, commented on the same programme that "we want a consistency right through so that we are all doing the same thing, so that we give the head coach of the first team the best possible players coming through our system".

So with the weak points from the 2008 bid addressed and a sustainable business plan in place Steve O'Connor told Alan Jackson: "I couldn't be any more relaxed about this process now. I've kept in touch with the Rugby League all the way through, I know that we've met all of their criteria and I'm absolutely certain that ours is the most sustainable business plan." A quietly confident O'Connor added: "It's not just about an application. That document that took three years to put together is our business plan. That's our business blueprint going forward and it shows that we've got targets that we have to hit. It's not about arriving at Super League and making up the numbers."

Although there still remained those nagging doubts at the back of some people's minds about the outcome of the second round of licensing, there was also a perceptible increase in confidence among many of those with Widnes' interests at heart. Much of the comment that had come out of RFL headquarters at Red Hall on the topic of Super League Licences seemed to point in only one direction – Widnes. Trade press and national journalists alike were soon of the opinion that Widnes were the outstanding candidates for a Licence come March 31st 2011.

Once the dust had settled on the massive disappointment of 2008 Widnes chairman Steve O'Connor had been consistently bullish about the club's prospects of success in 2011.

Speaking at the launch of the 2011 Bid in March 2010 a confident O'Connor said "We believe the organisation is in much better health than it was last time around. As much as we felt our application then was robust, we were very much in our infancy. Now we are able to demonstrate that we've got a sustainable future. We've got some real talent coming through and we've got some robust pathways to get our youngsters through to the first team.

"When our Super League application was turned down last time we were told it was because as a club we couldn't display a track record of stable and prudent management. When the applications for the next three-year period are submitted later this year we will be able to do that."

By the time that Bid document for the second round of Super League Licences had been submitted in early December 2010, the Vikings' chairman was not only confident of achieving Super League status, but was also determined that the club would not be just making up the numbers in the top tier. Speaking to the *Liverpool Echo* O'Connor observed that: "We've seen four or five clubs taking most of the honours in the last 15 years or so. There's no reason why Widnes couldn't be one of those clubs," adding "We're very confident we can be a force in years to come."

O'Connor, and the rest of us, were already aware that the RFL had committed to 'promoting' at least one Championship club to Super League for the Licence period 2012-14, subject to that club meeting the minimum criteria.

As we have already identified the first box that had to be 'ticked' by a Championship club was to have taken part in a Grand Final, or won the Northern Rail Cup, in 2009 or 2010. Clubs that had met that on-field criterion were also required to meet the following minimum criteria:

a)   have a stadium with an operational capacity of 10,000
b)   have a turnover of at least £1 million in the financial years ending in 2009 or 2010
c)   have an average attendance of at least 2,500 in 2009 or 2010

Studying the minimum criteria it is easy to understand how this time round Widnes found themselves cast in the slightly uneasy role of being most people's favourite to be granted a Licence. A cold, hard look at the facts showed that of the three applicants – Barrow and Halifax being the others – the Vikings were indeed the only club that seemed to meet all the criteria. In addition, during the three years since the unsuccessful Bid in 2008, the club had put down more solid foundations in all areas of its operation.

Clubs that met these minimum standards could then submit a formal application to the governing body which would be judged on a further set of criteria. As we have already seen those criteria were:

a)   Commercial, Marketing, Media and Community
b)   Facilities
c)   Finance
d)   Governance & Business Management
e)   Playing strength & Player performance Strategy

The RFL further explained that whereas in 2008 clubs were assessed and awarded points on reaching minimum standards, the 2011 process was based on meeting 'A' Grade Licence criteria. If a club met all of the 'A' Grade criteria it would naturally be awarded an 'A' Licence, while those whom the RFL felt could achieve that standard in three years time would be awarded a 'B' Licence. The complex issue of any remaining Licences ('C') would, according to the governing body, 'be issued to those clubs that the RFL board believes are the most suitable', taking into account:

a)   Extent to which each club helps meet the SLE Strategy and the strategic aims and objectives of the licensing process

b)   Historical activity of the clubs under consideration

c)   RFL's reasonable opinion as to future performance of the clubs under consideration.

The RFL had brought the issue of stadia to the forefront of the licensing debate on several occasions, and had written to those clubs most at risk. It was always unlikely that a club would be jettisoned just because of their ground, but as time moved on it became more likely that this issue could become a 'tie-breaker'. With most factions of the media suggesting that a Super League Licence was on its way to WA8 attention turned to a discussion about which of the current Super League cabal would lose out in favour of the Vikings.

Back in August 2010 Blake Solly, the RFL compliance manager, had informed a press briefing that a key part of the governing body's strategy was to 'maintain footholds in Wales, France and London'. That gave the clearest indication possible that Crusaders, Catalan Dragons and the then Harlequins were absolutely certain to retain their Licences. It seemed to imply that, no matter how unsuccessful those clubs were on or off the field, their Licences were almost guaranteed in perpetuity.

This declaration must surely have caused shockwaves in Wakefield, Castleford and Salford as it became the concensus of opinion that one of them would fall by the wayside. The one thing that these clubs had in common was that they were all seeking to build a new stadium, and despite the spin coming out to the contrary, none of them had planning consent in place at that time. It appeared then that it would all come down to a race to see who could have tangible evidence of a new stadium by July 2011.

With Salford having finally begun construction it became a battle between the two clubs resident within the boundaries of Wakefield Council. As the day of the announcement drew closer neither club was anywhere near breaking ground on their new home, as Castleford were held up by a lack of funding, while neighbours Wakefield were still waiting for the final nod on their planning application. Unless there was a catastrophe elsewhere the RFL would be faced with a very difficult decision.

It was against this background that the Vikings' bid was submitted and as Julie Gaskell said, once the bid was in there was nothing that anyone could do, except wait for the announcement on 31st March.

Although not part of the formal submission there was one last push to underline the case for Widnes winning that coveted Licence. In conjunction with the *Widnes Weekly News* the club launched a 'Back the Bid' campaign which saw supporters 'sign up' to the internet campaign to underline the depth of support for the club's return to Super League. In addition the profile of the club was boosted as 'Back the Bid' car stickers, free with any purchase from the club shop, became a common sight around Widnes, and beyond.

Chairman Steve O'Connor commented: "Any extra momentum we can gain by having *Weekly News* readers backing our bid can only build on our already strong Licence application and prove just how irresistible we are to the game."

While Denis Betts and Paul Cullen urged fans to back the bid and pass on their messages of support, chief executive Julie Gaskell added: "Despite being a relative newcomer to the sport, I have been staggered by just how much this club and the game itself means to its local community, and having the support of such a well-read local newspaper on our side is invaluable. We're hoping many readers will help our quest and sign up at this important time."

The campaign certainly demonstrated its worth as it got off to an excellent start with more than 1,000 fans signing up within the first two weeks. Non-internet users were later able to submit a cut-out coupon from the paper which eventually saw the total rise to a figure just under 4,000.

Looking back at the 2011 process it is fair to say that as a whole it didn't capture the imagination in the same way as in 2008. There was an overall impression of less hype and glamour surrounding this round of licensing, both centrally and locally, compared to the inaugural event three years earlier. This may have been due to the fact that the RFL, in a bid to give the chosen club more time to prepare for the step up, had chosen to announce only the successful Championship club at this time; the remaining 13 Licences would be announced in July.

Similarly it is true to say that the 2011 Widnes bid document and presentation was less glitzy in style than its forerunner, while still making a forceful but concise case for the club's admittance to Super League.

Days before the announcement Ms Gaskell commented: "We haven't taken any of this lightly. It's good that I wasn't around three years ago because it enabled me to look at it like any other piece of work. It wasn't an easy task but I can't think of anything that we could have failed in.

"I would be staggered if anything fell down on the stadium. We've done the youth development work, and Steve has done everything he said he would do."

Steve O'Connor was perhaps more descriptive in his language when he told *League Weekly* that he felt like an "expectant father" in the run up to 'D-Day'.

"You know there is nothing you can do about it you just have to wait. Inside, you are sure that everything is going to be alright, but there is always a little niggle in the back of your mind that there might be complications."

He, and his team, were confident that they had addressed the shortcomings of the 2008 bid, where a lack of youth development and the Administration issue were cited as reasons for failure by the RFL. "We believe our bid is far more comprehensive than it was last time, but we won't know until we watch the announcement on Sky."

In his last programme notes before D-Day the Vikings' chairman confirmed that "everything that could have been done has been done" and reassured fans that the business plan put forward was "deliverable, sustainable and robust". Emphasising Widnes' outstanding success in an area identified as key by the RFL – youth development – he commented: "We have invested a lot in developing our young players and this is an area of the criteria in which we are leading. Our bid highlights this and we can demonstrate that the youth system we have is a system that works." If anyone had any doubts the proof of that particular pudding was to be tasted during an injury plagued 2012 campaign.

Away from the club David Parr, chief executive of Halton Borough Council threw the full force of the local authority behind the bid by saying: "Widnes is a rugby league town, always has been, and Halton is a rugby league area. A successful Widnes Vikings team adds massive value to the community, and that's why Halton Council continues to support the Vikings and is continuing to support their bid for a Super League Licence."

Those of a nervous disposition may well have noticed that there was perhaps an unhappy parallel with 2008 as, from early morning, the Vikings faithful gathered at the stadium on the third anniversary of handing in that unsuccessful bid. However, the level of anticipation was so high that the club had sold all 700 tickets available for the stadium a week before the big announcement, while those who couldn't get a ticket gathered wherever they could to watch Richard Lewis deliver the verdict live on Sky Sports News.

For now they had to put their faith in O'Connor as he admitted that the club had benefitted from having longer to put this bid together, compared to the 2008 submission, and had learned valuable lessons from the previous exercise. He added: "We have worked long and hard over the three years since our last application and left no stone unturned in our bid to return this club to the elite competition. I'm extremely confident that we can succeed where we failed last time around."

In a similar vein Denis Betts pointed to the fact that the club had overcome challenges both on and off the pitch since the last round of Licence applications, adding: "It's clear to see the massive strides that have been made. It's an exciting time for the club, the town and its surrounding areas."

From early morning Sky Television were cranking up the suspense through regular features on the cases put forward by the three clubs involved, including the following calm but assured summary from Julie Gaskell: "We think we've got a robust business case, a good plan, strategy and vision. What we have created is vision and values that will be there in the club. I think there are a lot of very attractive things in there that aren't just ticking boxes, there are things that we've put in there as well."

At the stadium 'Voice of the Vikings' Gary McGrath had been talking to fans and officials in what he described as "an air of excitement and expectation, mixed with some fear and trepidation" as the countdown began.

Speaking to McGrath early on Julie Gaskell, happy not to have the memory from three years ago, described the atmosphere among the staff as "positive but nervous" while hoping that it would turn out to be a good day for everyone connected with the club. She added that a positive outcome would "mean a lot for everyone, it would put confidence in the town and for the club itself it will give us some energy and confidence", saying in reference to the bid handed in on 3rd December "I think we have done everything we can."

Admitting that "things are hotting up in the room now and it's getting very loud" Paul Cullen added: "everyone is on edge because we are so certain that we have done everything that needs to be done." The director of rugby underlined the importance of being the first team to 'tick the box' as that "allowed us to change tack slightly. Youth development is probably more important [than winning games]. It's about showing to Super League that Widnes want to bring something to the table, not simply take from it."

Feeling strongly that Widnes can add to Super League Cullen went on to say: "We're not one of those clubs that wants to attract Wigan here so we get a good crowd, we want to take a good crowd to Wigan. That's why other Super League teams want us in."

Former player and chairman Jim Mills was also in optimistic mood when he told McGrath: "I'm sure we are going to get in" before paying tribute to the work of chairman Steve O'Connor, and adding that the number of fans outside the stadium showed that a successful Widnes side will pull in great crowds in Super League. Mills' point about crowds was well made as many people commented that there were more fans at the stadium for the announcement than some clubs get for home games.

As I watched events unfold in the Bridge Suite I witnessed the level of expectancy rise in direct relationship to the growing number of people in the room and the passing of time towards 11.30am. Wherever you looked nails were being bitten amid the noise of incessant nervous chatter as we all sought to convince ourselves that all would be well this time – wouldn't it? The arrival of various television, radio and written media personnel only served to raise the level of tension and excitement still further in a room crammed with more 'expectant mothers and fathers'. All were hoping and praying that within a couple of hours they would have cause to 'wet the baby's head' along with its proud father Steve O'Connor.

With barely a minute to go Gary McGrath eloquently summed it up as follows: "The tension's building, everybody's excited, there's a mixture of hope and fear. I've never known anything like it. It'll be one sentence from Richard Lewis and the place will either explode in ecstacy or collapse in despair."

In common with the club office and the Social Club the Bridge Suite fell quiet as at 11.30am Richard Lewis began the address that would ultimately name the club that was to step up to Super League in 2012. After a pre-amble in which he praised the benefits of the licensing process he finally arrived at the point at which there was a collective holding of breath by groups of fans in Barrow and Halifax along with the hordes gathered at the Stobart Stadium. Lewis eventually got to the heart of the matter when he stated that "Halifax and Widnes both meet the required standards for Super League membership", while adding that Barrow had failed to meet those criteria.

With everybody waiting in silent anticipation Lewis continued: "After careful consideration the RFL Board has decided that the Super League Licence from 2012 will be awarded to…Widnes Vikings".

At the utterance of the word 'Widnes' the fans at the stadium allowed themselves to breathe again, amid a deafening roar, which was no doubt replicated in homes, offices and hostelries throughout the area and beyond.

It is highly unlikely that anyone present heard Lewis continue by saying: "on behalf of the RFL and Super League I congratulate Widnes Vikings who have made significant strides in the last three years. It reflects a huge amount of hard work by chairman Steve O'Connor, the directors and staff at the Stobart Stadium." Despite the RFL chairman's contention that it had been a "difficult decision" the Bid assessments of the two clubs, shown in Appendix IV, tell a different story.

After two minutes of hand-shakes, hugs and backslapping a jubilant, beaming O'Connor told Gary McGrath: "The hard work starts here. Trust me, after today we've got to be a much bigger organisation, but what a fabulous day. I think we'll find the whole town will be out today."

This was undoubtedly a fantastic day for Widnes fans, not only those lucky enough to be in the stadium or around the town, but for those living all over the world. Three years previously I had been in the club office during the announcement and you could cut the atmosphere with a knife, but after three long years of hard work by a lot of people behind the scenes, the atmosphere on this day was absolutely superb.

As the Vikings' best-known supporter, Pat Price, said: "I can't believe it. I've waited three years for this. It's been like Christmas Eve for me, waiting until half eleven to open my presents."

When I spoke to Clare O'Connor some months later she looked back to this momentous day and told me: "I was more nervous than in 2008, thinking surely they can't refuse us again. We've just got to do it this time. It was really exciting and an amazing atmosphere; the whole thing was fantastic." Describing the moment when Richard Lewis finally announced that Widnes had been successful Mrs O'Connor added: "It was the best feeling ever as the room erupted into cheering, screaming and hugging. I felt proud – not just for Steve – but for everyone at the club and the fans."

It was only after persuasion from David Parr that she accompanied husband Steve as he went to address the fans, and was therefore able to savour the moment and see how happy the fans were. "I was really proud hearing the fans chant his name and didn't want to leave, but I had to pick my son up from school. I was surprised how much it means to me. I really care – it matters."

Steve O'Connor summed up the emotion of the day when he said: "three years of anxiety were relieved in a couple of seconds" when Richard Lewis uttered the words 'Widnes Vikings'.

The man who had once said: "I don't know my [rugby league] history but I like to think I can influence the future" had certainly done that, and in turn made his own piece of history.

Richard Lewis, who admitted that the Vikings were "desperately close last time", paid further tribute to the Vikings by commenting that: "Widnes put in a terrifically strong application and I and the RFL board believe that they will be a fantastic addition to Super League", going on to add that: "Widnes are an ambitious, well run club, they've got stability" before stating perhaps significantly: "Steve O'Connor and the club have conducted themselves extremely well over the last three years."

Shortly after the news had sunk in with all concerned with Widnes Vikings a "very relieved" Steve O'Connor was cheered into the Bridge Suite to be interviewed on Sky Television. Admitting there were several people in the room who might challenge him for the title of the happiest man in Widnes, O'Connor commented that it was "really encouraging that the RFL saw the value of the robustness of the bid" and, signalling the amount of work ahead for everyone associated with the club, added: "The onus is on all of us to prove that we were right to be given the Licence. We certainly don't intend going into Super League to make up the numbers."

Paul Cullen added: "We've worked so hard behind the scenes to fend off two very strong bids from Barrow and Halifax. We feel for them because this club's been there, we know exactly how that feels, but the RFL have set out some tough criteria and we've met it."

Meanwhile director of player welfare Terry O'Connor described the news as "Huge. I'm a Widnes lad and very proud of where I come from, and I was in the side that was relegated in 2005. During my career I was very lucky to have played in big finals and top level international rugby, but this really is one of the biggest days of my life."

Later in the day the Vikings chairman took advantage of an appearance on *Boots 'N' All* to outline how Widnes would approach, and sustain, their return to the top flight. While the granting of the Licence was the culmination of three years hard work by everyone at the club, Steve O'Connor underlined that it was now the beginning of a much more difficult period. While the public gaze would naturally be on player recruitment there was also much work needed to be done to bring the off-field operation up to Super League standards, with a requirement to have certain posts filled which were not needed in the Championship.

O'Connor pointed out that the club had plans which they would start to implement immediately, both on and off the field, and were excited at the prospect. With regard to player recruitment he reaffirmed that the club would be making every effort to bring people to the club that "have the right values and approach to being a part of a successful organisation. We want players who will bring a legacy; help to develop the best kids that we've got. We want world class players playing at the Stobart next year, and ultimately we want world class Widnes lads playing for the club."

Within days further recognition of the work being done at Widnes came, perhaps surprisingly, in Mike Stephenson's regular column in *League Express*. Referring to the 'Brains Trust' at the Stobart stadium of Steve O'Connor, Terry O'Connor, Paul Cullen, and Denis Betts 'Stevo' commented: "It's a foursome that spells success, where corporate drive and finance meets rugby league experience and determination. I'm glad the boys at Red Hall have realised that, because it's the way to a secure future."

Having arrived in Super League Vikings fans naturally wanted to see marquee signings arriving at the Stobart Stadium, with some unreasonably expecting the chairman to personally foot the bill. But that is not what licensing, or Steve O'Connor, is about – the watchword for the resurgent club has always been 'sustainability'.

However, while admitting at this early stage that the club would be looking at all available players, and that agents were already in discussion with the club about potential signings, the Widnes chairman again reiterated that player recruitment had to be within a sustainable business plan. The club was evidently on an upward spiral and it had been made abundantly clear by O'Connor throughout the process that the club would live within its means in Super League.

It had been well documented that in the view of O'Connor, a long-time advocate of the licensing process, the long-term success of Widnes would need to be built on the success of the club's youth structure. With a much stronger supply line of young talent coming through than was the case three years previously, and now with the security of a three-year Licence, the club was well placed to establish themselves in the top flight.

Looking to the future O'Connor said: "We have to manage expectation in our club and make sure fans see that we really want to develop these young lads. They tell me they want to see Widnes lads playing for Widnes, but I'm sure, in a successful Widnes side.

"We've got some diamond players coming through the 18s, a couple of whom are still at school, but the Licence system gives us time to develop them. I think for 2013 -14 we've got the backbone of what will be a very impressive Widnes Vikings side."

Having achieved his committed aim of bringing Super League to Widnes it is fair to say that where the club went from there was very much in the hands of the fans. It is plain that Steve O'Connor has become a big fan of the game and the club, but his stay at the helm may have been longer than he envisaged when he first set out to save the club.

As he said in that *Boots 'N' All* interview: "Obviously I'm enjoying where we've got to so far but it is really about the fans. We need to make a connection and understand what the fans perspective is. They will be the determining factor about whether Widnes Vikings are a successful club." In a hint about a further announcement to come he added: "At the moment everybody is very upbeat and optimistic, and I'm looking to take advantage of that situation and see if we can use that as a springboard to develop our support, and that will start on Sunday against York." That announcement was of course the introduction of the innovative Viking Stronghold.

The size of the challenge that was just beginning became evident when the Vikings' owner said that the club needed to attract crowds of 10,000 at home matches in order to spend the full salary cap. He emphasised that the Vikings' would have to "triple our business plan, triple our turnover and triple our attendances. But we've got some great ideas."

But in the heady atmosphere that surrounded Widnes, talk of business plans and sustainability were put to one side as fans put every effort into celebrating the return of the Vikings. With both bars at the ground heaving with ecstatic supporters chants of 'Wid-nes, Wid-nes, Wid-nes' and 'there's only one Steve O'Connor' were occasionally punctuated with conversation, with talk of the tasty prospect of renewing derby battles with Warrington and taking on Wigan and St Helens in competitive action top of the agenda.

Speaking from the players' perspective Widnes-born skipper, Dave Allen, told the *Widnes Weekly News*: "There has been a lot of heartache and disappointment in recent years but now we have the opportunity to make the people of this town proud of their team once again." Allen, who was to miss only one Super League match in 2012, went on: "Each and every one of us wants to prove that we have what it takes to make it at the top level", adding that the only way we can do that is by being successful this season."

This theme was continued by Terry O'Connor when he told *Rugby League World* in June 2011: "Before the announcement you could see that a number of players were a bit edgy. They didn't know whether they would be given a chance to play in Super League, or have their jobs taken away from them. Now they've got the perfect opportunity to test themselves at the next level. But to do that they've got to perform at this level."

Reassuring as it was to hear Steve O'Connor tell Alan Jackson in December 2010 that he was excited to be around, he made a further commitment to the club in his programme notes just days after the Super League place was secured. It read: "I made a commitment to the fans three and a half years ago and I could easily walk away into the sunset now and say that we as a team have delivered, but I'm not going to do that as I'm enjoying it. I'm going to be here at the club seeking new challenges, and they don't come much bigger than Super League."

With Widnes Vikings assured of their Super League place there was still one final twist to come in the 2011 licensing story when the rugby league media reconvened at Old Trafford on 26th July. As they settled into their seats, with I suspect in many cases an obituary already written for Wakefield Trinity Wildcats, the rugby league world was taken aback at the news passed on by Richard Lewis.

At the eleventh hour Celtic Crusaders had informed the governing body that they could not continue to support a Super League operation and withdrew their application. One can only speculate at the reaction from within the RFL as a favoured expansion club had again been forced to throw in the towel due to financial problems.

There was however, a positive side to this and, it could be argued, a 'get out of jail free card' for the RFL as Wakefield were saved from the ignominy of 'relegation' to the Championship. Such had been the wealth of opinion stacked against Wakefield keeping their Licence that a William Hill spokesman had described the Wildcats exclusion from Super League as a "foregone conclusion".

Crusaders chairman Ian Roberts had said in November 2010, after buying back the club from the Administrators: "We are excited about the potential of Super League in north Wales and our business plan will enable us to go forward with renewed enthusiasm." This view was then supported, in February 2011, by chief executive Rod Findlay despite the club only attracting 2,615 fans to their opening home fixture of 2011. As late as June 2011 Findlay was quoted as saying: "Rugby league in north Wales has come a long way, and we are confident we can take it a lot further." Six weeks later the club had effectively folded, to be reborn as North Wales Crusaders in Championship One.

As with Paris St Germain before them, and London Broncos/Harlequins it proves that you cannot simply plant a group of players from an alien sport in a town and expect immediate acceptance and success.

In contrast things at Widnes were moving along nicely as the club prepared for its return to the top flight. By the end of July the 'Super League club in waiting' were already reporting a very encouraging response to the Viking Stronghold initiative, with numbers continuing to grow week on week. Meanwhile Paul Cullen and Denis Betts were starting to put together the 2012 squad with the signings of Ben Cross, Shaun Briscoe and Hep Cahill already secured.

Gradually further additions were made to the squad and as the new season approached the club had assembled a blend of experienced Super League players and home-grown talent. The question on everybody's mind was 'how will they fare in the top league'?

But before we turn our attention to the Vikings' return to the promised land I think it is appropriate to take one last look behind the scenes. Much, quite rightly, has been made in this book and elsewhere of the contributions of Steve O'Connor and his management team, and the coaching and playing staff, to the survival and progress of the club. But let's learn a bit more about some of the key backroom staff who ensure the smooth running of the club – or to borrow a phrase from Steve O'Connor's 'Business Person of the Year' acceptance speech – people who 'just get on with their job'.

Probably the best known of these is Widnes-born Paul Hansbury who joined the staff at the club 29 years ago at the age of 16. However, his first 'official' connection with the club had been in 1976 when he became the Chemics' first-ever mascot, for the 1976 Challenge Cup Final against St Helens, with the suit worn that day by the eight-year-old Hansbury now on display in the club Museum. Joining the club as assistant groundsman Hansbury would work all day on the pitch, including a spell under head groundsman Alan Tait, returning on Tuesday and Thursday evenings and Saturday mornings to ensure that everything was ready for the players training sessions and again on matchday. Looking back to those days Hansbury identified stark contrasts with today as he remembers "tackle bags being filled with sawdust and players training on the concrete under the stand and running up and down the steps if the pitch was wet".

Much has changed during the 29 years that Paul Hansbury has been working for Widnes Rugby League Club, not least that he is now responsible for a full-time first team squad and four part-time teams. In his early days at the club he was responsible for the players' training and match boots while the players looked after their own kit, whereas today it is the other way round. Similarly tackle bags have moved on from being filled with sawdust to a more high-tech product, and the humble 'kit-man' tag has been replaced with 'logistics manager'.

For a typical home match the duties of our logistics manager begin when he arrives at the ground three hours before kick-off to prepare each player's kit. However, it is not just a case of getting 17 shirts ready. In addition to warm-up kit and towels the Vikings' kit man has to have a full back-up kit ready in case of blood injuries, while also carrying a few numbered but 'un-named' spares in case a further change is necessary. Next on the list is putting out a selection of fruit, yoghurt and cereal bars, for those who want it, together with water and vitamin drinks, and generally attending to the players' needs. Having ensured that everything is ready for the players Hansbury's final pre-match job is to write out the team sheet and hand it in to the match officials.

In addition to his role at Widnes Hansbury has also carried out the kit-man job for both Ireland and Wales. With Irish family connections Hansbury was pleased to be approached by ex-Chemic Steve O'Neill and looked after the Irish squad for a period of six years, including the 2000 World Cup, while the Welsh job came about as a favour to Neil Kelly.

Asked to pick out personal highlights from his time at Widnes Hansbury opted for his last trip to Wembley as mascot, when the Chemics beat Wakefield Trinity to lift the Challenge Cup in 1979, closely followed by the World Club Championship success against Canberra Raiders 10 years later.

If you have telephoned the club over the last ten years the chances are that you have spoken to Janet Pheysey. Over that period Janet has often been the first port of call for a variety of enquiries from fans, myself included, but her real job is Football Secretary - a role which covers a myriad of vital elements to the day-to-day running of the club. Miss Pheysey's key responsibilities centre around compliance with RFL regulations, contracts, payroll, visa applications, while also monitoring the salary cap and arranging transport and accommodation for all the club's teams.

With regard to Visa applications Janet explains that, as sponsor, the club is responsible for applying to both the UK Border Agency and the RFL for permission to bring someone into the country. Once the UK Border Agency and the RFL have given the go-ahead it is then up to the player to complete the process with the appropriate embassy.

Miss Pheysey describes the biggest difference in her job since promotion to Super League as being the significant increase in the amount of regulatory compliance that is required. Like Paul Hansbury she will arrive at the stadium some three hours before kick-off and most of that time will be spent with the RFL's match commissioner "to ensure that the game takes place in a safe environment in accordance with RFL regulations". The long list of items to be checked, before the match is allowed to kick-off, ranges from the provision of medical equipment to the correct placement of advertising boards, and includes the mandatory presence of the video cameraman. In a similar vein Miss Pheysey is responsible for providing appropriate facilities for UKAD (UK Anti-Doping) staff on the occasions that they arrive at the stadium to carry out random drug-testing on matchdays.

Joining the Vikings in 2002 following 20 years service with ICI Janet has lived through some turbulent times at the club. Being both a fan and an employee of the club could perhaps cause a conflict when dealing with the 'highs' and 'lows' of life at Widnes Vikings, but Janet explained that the fan in her "switches off during the week and I return to work mode". Speaking to Ian Cheveau, editor of the matchday programme, she described her job as: "so busy that the days certainly fly by and are never boring. You get the chance to deal with people from all areas of Rugby League, Sky, the Home Office, to coaches and staff from other clubs both here and overseas. We have good working relationships with most clubs both in the Championship and Super League. It's not all competitive. Off the pitch, clubs can and do help each other out in lots of different ways."

Finally I spoke to the man behind the voice that so enthusiastically confirms the identity of Widnes' scorers during matches at the Stobart Stadium – Media and PR manager, Mark Naughton. Our matchday announcer began his working life as a nightclub DJ before moving on to hospital radio broadcasting in Warrington, where he combined his love of music with a strong desire to be involved in sport. Later 'head hunted' by Wire FM, initially as a rugby league commentator, Naughton became co-host, with Graham Lovett, of a new rugby league magazine show – the Super League Phone-in – following Widnes' elevation to Super League in 2002. Eight years later Naughton negotiated a permanent transfer to the Vikings.

Having worked on the corporate side for Widnes since 2004 he became the obvious choice to cover for Steve Roberts at a Player of the Year event, and became the regular 'MC' for future Supporters' Club functions. Subsequently when Pat Cluskey left the club Naughton was invited to fill the role of matchday announcer by Alex Bonney, while also helping out with the community department. In turn he took over as 'webmaster' when Bonney moved on, with responsibility for communicating with fans and stakeholders through the club's official website. With his media background Naughton set out to "paint pictures on there, add a bit of colour, a bit of life". Flattered to be given the role of Media and PR manager Naughton remains "a local lad having a craic and trying to put a bit back into the club that I've watched all my life".

While the main thrust of the media side of the job may be seen as building relationships and liaising with the local, trade and national press, the variety extends to dealing with the sports departments of local television broadcasters, in addition to rugby league's main outlet of Sky Sports. It is through Naughton's personable and pro-active style that he is able to keep "feeding little tit-bits" to these organisations in order to raise the club's profile and keep it in the public eye, with "stoking the fires and stimulating interest" during the Back the Bid campaign particularly key. In addition the public relations element sees Naughton as the first point of contact for both individuals and organisations that have, or are seeking to have an involvement with the club in one way or another. This can range from people seeking to join the Viking Stronghold to charitable organisations interested in a partnership with the club.

Asked to identify highlights of his days as a Widnes fan Naughton, Widnes born and bred, recalled his first Wembley trip in 1979, admitting to "being bitten by the bug ever since", and "being on board as a staff member when we got the thumbs up from the governing body. I had a big lump in my throat that day. It was absolutely top drawer".

CHAPTER ELEVEN
Back Where We Belong

Widnes' arrival in Super League signalled that Steve O'Connor had now met his initial target of returning the Vikings to the top tier of rugby league. Would he stay or would he go? Thankfully he had committed to stay and as the season beckoned all Widnes fans were hoping that new goals would be similarly set and achieved.

With the opening fixture just three weeks away it seemed that the local community was getting behind the club like never before. Widnes had attracted over 4,000 members to the new Viking Stronghold, which in old terminology meant that they had in excess of 4,000 season ticket holders when, in its entire history, the club had never sold more than 2,800 season tickets.

In a further boost director of marketing Brian O'Connor told the *Widnes Weekly News* that the club had sold nearly 2,000 replica shirts, adding: "There is a real buzz around the place at the moment. The response to both shirts [home and away] has been fantastic, and over Christmas the merchandise sales have been fantastic." In another new venture the club had included the name of every Viking Stronghold member in the design of the away shirt, "so the fans can buy their own little piece of Vikings history". While it is commonplace for fans to have the name of their favourite player on their replica shirt, this latest innovation saw the players carry the names of the fans into battle with them.

But no matter how successful the club was off the field it was results, or at least performances, on the pitch that would determine its success or failure in the eyes of the fans. Key to any immediate success would naturally be the recruitment of new players but, despite gaining their Licence in late March, Widnes were still tied to the anti-tampering deadline of September 1st. So was the early decision really of any benefit?

"No, it didn't help us at all" was the answer from Denis Betts when I spoke to him later in the season. The small pool of quality players available naturally wanted to join clubs where they thought they would be challenging for honours, and in any event I suspect, would be looking for salaries considerably in excess of what Widnes were prepared to pay. "It was very, very difficult and up until six months ago it was extremely difficult to get players" Betts added, also pointing out that "People have now seen the plans we have put in place; how the team plays; how it is organised and the discipline that is required to be part of this." With the progress during the second half of the season players' perceptions changed and Betts confirmed that Widnes "are now getting enquiries about players that want to come here, where initially you didn't see that as it was 'ground zero' and nobody knew what was going to happen. Staying true to our beliefs is starting to pay dividends."

With regard to recruitment the Vikings' head coach gave the following insight: "We look at recruitment, not just next year but the year after, looking at lads that are on contract now, when their contract runs out, and whether we see them as someone that can move us forward, or whether their time will come when that contract runs out. We can't make plans too far down the line as form can change. Things can also change year on year with what you've actually got to spend. It's a really fluid situation and our recruitment is built on what are our needs and how do we see our team playing."

As a new club entering Super League there was bound to be a large turnover in playing staff, but equally there was no way in which the club could afford, or indeed want, to bring in a whole new squad of experienced top flight players. In any event such a move would fly in the face of the declared policy of developing from within.

By the time the squad had been assembled there was a mix of experience and youth, old and new, with 15 players being retained from the 2011 Championship campaign, eight of whom were products of the club's youth policy.

First through the door were new arrivals Ben Cross and Hep Cahill, with Cross agreeing two separate deals on the same day! Currently on the books of Leeds Rhinos the highly experienced Australian Prop Forward had joined Wigan on loan for the remainder of 2011, while also penning a deal to link up with Widnes for their Super League return. Former Crusaders forward Cahill, who like Cross had played for Melbourne Storm, was seen by Denis Betts as bringing "a tremendous appetite and bags of unfulfilled potential" to the club.

Throughout the remainder of the close season there was a steady influx of further signings headed by Shaun Briscoe, Scott Moore, Jon Clarke, Patrick Ah Van and Cameron Phelps. England International Briscoe, who brought the experience gained from over 230 senior club games to Widnes, commented: "Widnes were really big in their day and I'm excited to be part of building them up again." The arrival of Moore, another England International, represented a massive step forward for the club, with Betts describing him as "one of the best hookers in Super League". Unfortunately by mid April the former St Helens player was released from his contract with immediate effect.

Gaining the signature of the powerful Ah Van, a proven try scorer in both the NRL and Super League, represented another key capture. Having finished 2011 as Bradford's top points scorer he repeated the feat with Widnes in 2012, becoming a firm fans' favourite in the process. The arrival of Phelps, delayed while he waited for his baby son's passport, was another welcome addition to the squad, especially in view of the growing injury crisis within the club. The versatile Australian, looking forward to getting in the team as soon as possible, commented: "I'm feeling good and alongside doing a heap of individual work I've also been training with Canberra Raiders' feeder-club which has certainly helped."

The unexpected departure of Moore threw extra responsibility and workload onto the shoulders of new skipper Jon Clarke. The signing of the ex-Warrington and Great Britain hooker, who had chalked up in excess of 320 games in a career which also took in Wigan and London Broncos, was described as a "massive coup" by Betts. Like Paul Cullen before him, Clarke had to deal with the 'baggage' of the Warrington tag before ultimately winning over his critics.

While it may be true that other signings didn't come with the 'star name' status that many fans craved, the majority went on to earn the respect of those fans. Familiar faces Ben Davies and Chris Dean made permanent returns to the Stobart Stadium having previously had successful loan spells with the club, while relative 'unknowns' Willie Isa, Rhys Hanbury, Lloyd White, and Frank Winterstein and Sione 'John' Kite added their various skills to the cause. In addition Stefan Marsh who had a brief loan spell at Widnes in 2010 returned on a season-long deal from Wigan.

As the injury crisis deepened the playing roster was beefed up by the services of Gareth O'Brien (Warrington), Joe Mellor (Wigan) and Paul McShane (Leeds Rhinos) at various times.

While the bulk of the players retained from 2011 had only experienced Championship rugby league there was nonetheless top flight experience provided by Dave Allen (Wigan), Steve Pickersgill (Warrington) and Simon Finnigan – with Finnigan having previously played in Super League for Salford, Bradford and Huddersfield following his three-year stint at the top with Widnes.

At the other end of the scale Academy products Danny Craven, Alex Gerrard, Grant Gore, Anthony Mullally and Jack Owens had limited experience of senior rugby, but were to accredit themselves well at Super League level, along with 2012 debutant Tom Gilmore.

Possibly the signing that had most excited the fans in the build up to the new season was ultimately the one that disappointed them most. Great hopes were placed on the shoulders of the mercurial Anthony Watts after his performance in a friendly at St Helens, but sadly his signing eventually turned out to be a gamble that failed. He had come to England to put his off-field problems behind him and make a fresh start, only to be struck down by a season-ending injury to his anterior cruciate ligament after 10 minutes of his competitive debut. Unhappily as time moved on his demons returned and, just a week after signing a new extended deal with the club, he was released.

In addition to Watts' injury Widnes' cause hadn't been helped when Thomas Coyle's season was wiped out with a fractured left tibia and fibula in another pre-season friendly. One of the smallest squads in Super League, in terms of depth, was already taking a battering. Worse was to come when Ben Kavanagh ruptured an achilles tendon against Salford which caused him to miss 22 matches before reappearing for the last three games of the season.

Other long-term injuries were picked up by vice-captain Shaun Briscoe, Simon Finnigan and Lloyd White. Briscoe became a long-term absentee when an adductor muscle came away from the bone, which led to him missing a run of 10 matches, only to pick up an injury to a pectoral muscle on his return which limited him to a total of eight appearances in 2012. Finnigan and White suffered their injuries in successive matches mid-season and were to spend the rest of the year on the treatment table. Finnigan fractured his fibula and ruptured ankle ligaments in the match at Castleford before White ruptured cruciate ligaments in the home match against the Catalans Dragons.

However, with the first match of the season just days away Denis Betts commented: "It seems like we've been waiting for this week for such a long time since we were awarded the Licence in March. The anticipation around the whole town has built a nervous energy among us all."

Eventually after all the hype of the build up Super League XVII was here, and Widnes Vikings were part of it – a new team, in a new league, on a new pitch. Chosen by Sky television to host the opening fixture of the new season, exactly four years on from the first match of the O'Connor era, the controversy that we all feared was only 80 minutes away.

The following pages summarise the 'highs and lows' of the Vikings return to Super League in the 2012 season, paying more attention, admittedly to the 'highs'.

With 8,120 fans inside the Stobart Stadium Widnes were roared onto the pitch as the adventure got under way. From the kick-off Hep Cahill made the first crunching tackle as he showed the home fans what to expect from him for the remainder of the season. However, the bubble was nearly burst as early as the second minute but Chris Dean and Danny Craven combined to put Ben Cockayne in touch a split second before he grounded the ball. In the eighth minute Widnes claimed the try that their play warranted. Gaining possession just inside the Wakefield half they drove forward until on the last tackle Danny

Craven took a pass from Scott Moore to dab a kick through the Wildcats' defence. The young full-back then beat Richie Mathers to the ball, just before it ran dead, to notch the first try of the season. Patrick Ah Van added the conversion. Widnes then dominated possession and position until Wakefield, on a rare excursion into Widnes territory scored through Ali Lauitiiti in the 21st minute. The remainder of the half was an end-to-end affair during which Frank Winterstein had a try denied by the Video Referee before Ah Van scored in the corner, just before the break, after the ball had moved through several pairs of hands to the winger.

The lead was short-lived as the visitors levelled matters in the first minute of the second half through Andy Raleigh. Willie Isa then became the second Widnes player to have a try chalked off by the Video Referee, but the Vikings reclaimed the lead in the 56th minute when Cahill charged down a kick to race 65 metres to score in the corner. With Ah Van missing his kick the Vikings led 14-10 and that was as good as it got for the home side as Wakefield took control of the game through tries from Mathers and Tim Smith. Peter Fox scored two late tries, while Ben Cross was in the sin bin, to give Wakefield a flattering winning margin.

Disappointing as the result was, the post-match debate centred largely on the new pitch, fanned by wild comments from some Wakefield players who had picked up some grazes. Richie Mathers, via Twitter, went as far as describing the pitch as "an absolute joke… no skin on elbows and knees, atrocious". However, teammate Tim Smith commented "I know a few boys got cuts and grazes but it was dry and fast, and players like that. I thought it was alright to be honest. I didn't find it any different at all with kicks. I thought it was good to play on, and there were no dramas for me."

Richard Agar, also seemed to take a much more pragmatic view than some of his players, when he conceded that "conditions on the night might have played a part". In fact similar, if not worse, injuries were picked up in the televised match at Salford the following evening. The common factor was that both matches were played with temperatures falling to minus 7 degrees Celsius.

The team that took the field for that first game back in the top flight was: Craven; Dean, Marsh, Isa, Ah Van; Clarke, Hanbury; Cross, Moore, Kavanagh, Winterstein, Allen, Cahill. Subs: White, Pickersgill, Haggerty, Mullally.

With the bubble of expectation and optimism burst, the visit to Huddersfield was hardly one to look forward to. To call it a one-sided affair was an understatement as the Vikings fell behind in the third minute and conceded a further 11 tries as they slumped to an embarrassing defeat by 66 points to 6.

This was followed by further home defeats at the hands of Salford City Reds and Leeds Rhinos before a fruitless trip to Hull KR where Widnes were 'nilled' by the home side who adapted to the arctic conditions much better than the visitors.

Five games – five defeats. The portents were not good when Wigan came to town in round six in front of a disappointing crowd of only 7,357. In the continued absence of Coyle, Watts, Moore (broken jaw) and Kavanagh, Widnes handed debuts to new recruits Cameron Phelps and John Kite, in addition to Gareth O'Brien who had arrived on loan from Warrington.

Coming on the back of that heavy defeat at Hull KR there weren't many people in the crowd who could see a home win, but that is exactly what they got. In a typically high-scoring match Widnes had fallen 18 points adrift of Wigan early in the second half before clinching a dramatic victory. The afternoon began badly for the Vikings as Wigan charged to an early 12-0 lead through tries from Gareth Hock and Harrison Hansen before Paddy

Flynn, the victim of a high tackle inside his own '20', reduced the arrears from the resultant attack. Widnes gained ground through Dave Allen and Steve Pickersgill before Shaun Briscoe joined the attack at pace and fed the ball to Stefan Marsh. As Marsh broke through the Wigan defence he passed inside but the supporting Briscoe could only juggle the ball, but managed to knock it backwards towards Flynn who gathered it to score from five metres.

Widnes fought to level the scores but in a hectic five minutes on the half-hour Wigan first broke away to regain their 12 point advantage, through Matthew Russell, before the Vikings notched two tries in as many minutes. The first of these came as the ball was moved at pace through Jon Clarke, Danny Craven, Gareth O'Brien, and Shaun Briscoe for Stefan Marsh to race through a gap in the visitors defence to score. Straight from the kick-off Widnes piled forward for Dave Allen to release Simon Finnigan on the Wigan '40', with the supporting Briscoe taking a pass from Finnigan to weave his way through the defence from 30 metres out to score under the posts. O'Brien's three conversions enabled the Vikings to go into the break at 18-18.

A Wigan purple patch early in the second half saw Brett Finch, Joe Mellor and Russell run in tries in a five minute period to make the score 36-18 in their favour. While the fans feared another rout the Vikings fought to get back into the game and gained a toe-hold in the 54th minute through Lloyd White. Having repelled another Wigan attack the Vikings moved deep into the opposition half with O'Brien being baulked five metres out. From the play the ball White darted through a gap to give the fans some hope. Within six minutes a resurgent Vikings had further narrowed the gap. Flynn fielding a kick on his own 10 metre line burst through five Wigan defenders to race 70 metres before being stopped. Two tackles later O'Brien, three metres out, fired a flat ball across the posts for Briscoe to collect and score the 100th try of his club career.

From the re-start Josh Charnley kicked the ball out 'on the full' and Widnes were immediately back on the attack. Moments later Frank Winterstein received the ball on the 10 metre line and twisted, turned and forced himself over the line, dragging three defenders with him. O'Brien's sixth goal of the afternoon made the score 36 apiece. With both sides giving everything for the victory it was Widnes who edged in front, with 10 minutes left on the clock, when Lloyd White put over a drop goal. However, it looked to be in vain when with four minutes remaining referee Robert Hicks misread a fumble by Michael McIlorum and awarded Wigan a penalty 40 metres out. As Charnley took an age to line up his kick, without the clock being stopped, it appeared that another defeat stared Widnes in the face, but he pushed his kick wide and short. Spirited defence saw Widnes survive and Briscoe joyfully kick the ball into the crowd as the hooter sounded.

Questions were asked after the game about Wigan coach Shaun Wane's team selection but he stood by his selection saying: "I'm absolutely gutted but the team I picked was totally capable of winning that game. We were poor, they were good."

An upbeat Denis Betts commented: "It's been hard to see the fans suffer but this was a top performance and now we have to try and maintain this high intensity. We all feel better but know wins aren't going to fall into our laps. We have to work hard."

The following week a more confident Widnes travelled back to Humberside only to return with the same net result as two weeks earlier. But in their next home game there was another bright dawn as they saw off fellow strugglers London Broncos and moved off the bottom of the table, albeit temporarily.

The side that showed seven changes from the defeat to Hull FC got off to the best possible start as they raced into a 12 point lead inside the first five minutes. The early scores came when Lloyd White shot over from dummy half and Chris Dean capitalised on a kick from Gareth O'Brien, but the Londoners pegged the Vikings back on 12 minutes when Luke Dorn touched down. By half-time Widnes had regained a 12 point lead through a try from Hanbury – set up by the returning Scott Moore – and a penalty from O'Brien. When a Ben Davies try – set up by Simon Finnigan – was converted early in the second half it looked as though Widnes would win at a canter but the Broncos fought back, aided by Ben Cross having another enforced 10 minute rest. Tries from Mark Bryant, Michael Witt and Liam Colbon squared matters at 24-24. Although another converted White try edged the home side in front again the visitors again levelled the scores through Tony Clubb's converted effort. Eventually Widnes came out on top as Willie Isa set up Cameron Phelps' first try for the club followed by another penalty from O'Brien.

After the match Denis Betts said: "We are making progress day in and day out, and hard work is the key. We are panicking a bit at times and losing some composure but, at the moment, are bouncing all over the place."

Unfortunately the team were still unable to put two results together, and immediately returned to losing ways when they travelled to the south of France the following week, returning home on the wrong end of a 76-6 scoreline. The only bright spot was John Kite's first try for the club.

Next up was the first competitive derby match with Warrington for several years. The Vikings, missing seven players through injury shocked everyone by roaring into an early lead, before falling away badly to suffer another big defeat.

Taking the game to Warrington Widnes were 12-0 up inside nine minutes through tries from Chris Dean and Dave Allen, both being converted by Patrick Ah Van. As early as the third minute Widnes had forced a goalline drop out which Cameron Phelps ran back to the 30 metre line, with Hep Cahill eventually stopped inches from the try line. From the play the ball Scott Moore fed Rhys Hanbury who quickly passed to Chris Dean who scored out wide. Within six minutes Widnes fans were delirious as the lead was extended. On the back of successive penalties conceded by Warrington John Kite was able to power forward to the 10 metre line. The ball was then played through Danny Craven and Hanbury for Dave Allen to run onto at pace and storm through a gap in the home defence.

Widnes more than held their own for the next 15 minutes but, once breached by Chris Bridge, they conceded three tries in seven minutes, through Bridge again and Chris Riley to go into the break trailing by six points. Early in the second half Widnes almost levelled matters when Hanbury did exceptionally well to force his way to the line only to drop the ball in the act of scoring. Shortly afterwards Warrington extended their lead through Brett Hodgson and as Widnes wilted under the pressure further tries from Ryan Atkins, Brad Dwyer and Riley (2) wrapped up the game.

Further league defeats came at the hands of Bradford Bulls at the Stobart Stadium followed by a mauling at St Helens, and a 36-12 reverse at Castleford. A relative bright spot came in this sequence when Widnes restricted St Helens to a two point winning margin in a Challenge Cup tie. Taking a third minute lead through Ah Van Widnes immediately conceded an equalising try from Josh Jones before Jonny Lomax and Rhys Hanbury traded tries. By half-time Saints had established a 28-10 lead which was cut by Lloyd White's early second half score before the visitors took control to build a lead of 40-16. However, Widnes fought back with further tries from Kurt Haggerty, Hep Cahill, Ah Van and White to bring the final score to 38-40.

Just six weeks after their heavy defeat in Perpignan Widnes played hosts to Catalan Dragons at the Stobart Stadium and went a long way towards redeeming themselves, eventually losing by the narrow margin of 34-42. The game started badly with the Dragons taking the lead in the second minute through Clint Greenshields and adding further scores through Leon Pryce and Vincent Duport by the quarter mark. Stefan Marsh, put in by Rhys Hanbury, reduced the arrears before a try by Joe Mellor – who had returned for another loan stint with the club – brought the Vikings within two points of the Frenchmen.

Louis Anderson then extended the visitors' lead only for it to be cancelled out by an 80 metre try from Hanbury after the hooter had sounded. Early in the second half Widnes hit the front for the first time when Chris Dean made the most of a storming break from Stefan Marsh. The tide then turned again when Jon Clarke was sin-binned on 52 minutes. While he was off the field both Lloyd White and Joe Mellor were stretchered off and Catalan bagged two tries through Anderson and Lopini Paea. With Clarke back on the pitch Widnes edged in front again through converted tries by Dave Allen and Ah Van, only for tries from Thomas Bosc and Scott Dureau to see the visitors home.

Again, after another defeat to Catalan Dragons, the next opponents were Warrington as Widnes moved on to take part in their first 'Magic Weekend'. Perhaps the least said about this performance the better as a totally out of sorts Vikings were blown away by their near neighbours.

Walking to the ground my wife and I were, in common with most Widnes fans, expecting the worst, not knowing that there was to be a silver lining waiting for us. We had had a chat with Brian O'Connor and Alex Bonney outside the ground during which Brian asked if I had my 'phone with me and to check if I could get a signal. "Someone might want to get in touch with you", he added pointedly. Failing to pick up on any possible significance in that remark we made our way to the car park to see the Stobart Super League trucks. It was then that all became clear as, like all Stronghold members, we received the text message announcing that the club had signed Kevin Brown. In view of what transpired later in the afternoon this was a very astute piece of timing.

Skipper Jon Clarke later commented: "It's a massive signing for us and I think it shows the commitment and foresight of the club", while head coach Denis Betts added: "It just shows our intentions. What we lack is composure, leadership and someone on the field who can actually control a game. That's why we went after Kevin and pushed really hard to get an Englishman in that position. He has got vast experience, is 27 years of age and has got the best years of his career in front of him."

For his part Brown explained that he was looking to move back to the North West saying: "I know what Denis Betts is all about and the set-up [at Widnes] is great. I'm looking forward to getting there, working hard and seeing if we can improve. A couple of clubs came in, but Widnes is the one I've chosen. Wigan was an option but I'm not sure how much of an option it was to Huddersfield." He added that "although some of the players are low on confidence, the game time some of the youngsters are getting will be good for them next year".

Ironically the next match for the Vikings was a home game against Brown's current employers, although Widnes' new signing was unavailable through suspension. He was, however, left in no doubt as to the feelings of the fans as he was applauded all the way up the steps of the North stand to take up a vantage point in the TV gantry along with his coach Nathan Brown.

Speaking to the club's website in September Brown commented that "Having spoken with Denis Betts, Paul Cullen and Steve O'Connor, I was tremendously impressed with what they already had in place such as the structures and facilities and what their plans were for the future. I knew that it was something I really wanted to be a part of and I'm excited and glad that I've joined the Vikings and I can't wait now to get started properly and meet the rest of the boys."

With regard to the facilities the new man added: "I'd never actually been over to the gym until after I had signed, so to say that I was blown away when I first saw it is a bit of an understatement. I mean no disrespect to any other clubs when I say this, but they would bend over backwards to have the type of facilities we have in place here at Widnes."

Of more immediate concern in May, however, was the current form of the team. And in that context there had been many cries from the terraces for Denis Betts and Paul Cullen to be replaced. Chairman Steve O'Connor admitted that he was disappointed with the club's league position but he reaffirmed both his commitment to the club and his confidence in Betts and Cullen. The chairman told the *Widnes Weekly News* that he believed that disciplinary problems and long-term injuries had contributed to a lack of form and consistency. He went on to add: "We had to make brave decisions to disconnect with two of our marquee players but at the end of the day we have a responsibility to look after our youngsters by setting certain standards of behaviour. We simply cannot have players at the club who will jeopardise their futures by setting a bad example. Denis and Paul were absolutely right to put their foot down. Maybe these things will weaken us in the short term, but they will certainly make us stronger going forward."

May also gave us the news that Anthony Mullally, whose contract was due to expire at the end of the season, had rejected several new contract offers from the club. This was undoubtedly a blow to the club who had invested in his future as he progressed through the academy set-up, and had arranged for him to spend the 2011 season in Australia.

Mullally, according to his agent, wished to test himself on the open market and Paul Cullen added: "Anthony Mullally has rejected a number of contract offers that we've made to him to improve and extend his current deal.

"We're disappointed he chooses to go on the open market. If Anthony wishes his future to be elsewhere we wish him well" and "we'll concentrate on those who want to be a part of the club long term".

The rumour mill had it that he would be on his way to Huddersfield in 2013, and so it subsequently proved. In the meantime he went on loan to Championship side Whitehaven making three appearances before injury brought his season to an early close.

Looking back to the opening match against Wakefield 'Mull' felt he played "ok" but conceded that "I let the occasion get to me". The prop forward also told me that while his most enjoyable game was the victory over Wigan, "being voted Man of the Match by the players after the home match against Leeds meant something special when your fellow players think you've done well".

Moving into June Widnes picked up only their third win of the season when they took on Kevin Brown's Huddersfield at the Stobart Stadium. The win, secured with a last minute try from Cameron Phelps, was also notable for the first try of Ben Cross's professional career, scored in his 125th appearance.

Widnes had taken the lead in the third minute when Patrick Ah Van took a pass from Paul McShane – making his debut on loan from Leeds – following a break by Rhys Hanbury, to score in the corner. The lead was increased just five minutes later when Hanbury ran onto an inch-perfect kick from Joe Mellor. Ah Van's conversion gave Widnes a 10-0 lead that was extended in the 11th minute when Cross was the first to react to a grubber kick from McShane bouncing free in the in-goal area to make that piece of personal history.

After Huddersfield replied through Dale Ferguson on the half-hour Steve Pickersgill was 'binned' by the referee. The visitors took full advantage as both David Fa'alogo and Danny Brough touched down to make the half-time score 16-12. Two early second half penalties from Ah Van gave Widnes an eight point lead before former Viking Scott Grix scored in the 67th minute. The conversion and two penalties by Brough put Huddersfield in the lead and set up the finale as the game entered the final minutes. With the final attack of the afternoon Hanbury put in a grubber which rebounded off the posts and the grateful Phelps dived on the ball to secure the win.

Commenting on Cross's first try Denis Betts said: "I've never seen anyone react like that in my life. It's his first professional try at about 64 years of age! Everyone was walking away and he was still jumping up and down hollering." Cross added: "Hopefully people can see there is more to my game than just scoring tries, but I won't lie, it was a fantastic feeling!"

Unfortunately, Widnes were again unable to follow up with a win in their next game – a vital four pointer at The Stoop against London Broncos. They seemed to be on their way to completing the double, and extending their lead over the Broncos when Cameron Phelps, 15 metres out, ran onto a pass from Jon Clarke to score with ease after only three minutes. Widnes then conceded a succession of penalties to hand the advantage to their opponents, who scored through Craig Gower. Six minutes from the break the Londoners took the lead through winger Omari Caro, but were unable to hold on as Frank Winterstein's powerful run on the hooter brought him his second try of the season and levelled the scores at 12-12.

The second half began in similar fashion to the first as Widnes gained possession from a knock-on inside the London '20', which saw Phelps gallop in for his second of the day. The lead was again only short-lived as Tony Clubb's converted try made it 18-18. The balance again tipped in favour of the Vikings when Winterstein completed his brace with another barn-storming run. With seven minutes remaining Broncos appeared to have levelled again but Shane Rodney failed to convert Dan Sarginson's try. So as the clocked ticked down – amid some controversy – Widnes were defending a two point lead going into the last minute. With the last play of the game Antonio Kaufusi ran through the Vikings defence to seal the win for the Londoners.

After a 16 day break the Vikings returned to action with the short trip to Wigan boosted by the return of Shaun Briscoe. This turned out to be another fruitless journey as Widnes left the DW Stadium still looking for that elusive away win after conceding 10 tries in a 54-12 defeat. Widnes' response came in the way of tries from Ben Cross and Joe Mellor with Patrick Ah Van converting both.

Days after this defeat Paul Cullen went on record as saying that despite the fact that the club found themselves at the foot of the Super League table they would not attempt to buy themselves out of trouble. "The critics are right," said the club's director of rugby, "this is not the strongest squad that Widnes have ever had, but it is the one we can afford."

He added: "Seeing what has happened to Bradford absolutely qualifies the stance that we have taken as a club. There are a number of models we could have followed, the

Crusaders being one and we know how that ended. The Bulls is another classic example that if you spend money you haven't got, and your business is unsustainable, then you end up in this situation."

For the next few matches Widnes gathered themselves to put in successive solid performances and picked up two wins and two narrow defeats. First they took on Castleford in a return at the Stobart Stadium running in seven tries to finish as comfortable winners by 40 points to 10, and climb off the bottom of the table again.

Again the Vikings got off to an excellent start when they capitalised on two consecutive penalties for Stefan Marsh to power over in the fourth minute. Jon Clarke had taken a quick play the ball under the posts and the ball passed through several hands before Marsh side-stepped the defence to score. Although Nick Youngquest replied for the visitors after 15 minutes Widnes recovered to take an 18-4 lead into the half-time break. Widnes' second try came when debutant Eamon O'Carroll dropped on a loose ball on halfway to set up a drive deep into Tigers territory in which John Kite featured twice before the ball eventually came out to Frank Winterstein who powered over from close range. Just before the break Marsh collected a weak goalline drop out to set up another attack. Ben Davies helped to drive the ball forward before taking a short ball from Clarke to score by the posts.

A revitalised Castleford came out after the break but they were knocked out of their stride by two Widnes tries within the space of five minutes. First, after a strong drive by Winterstein, Paul McShane darted between two defenders on the line to go over from dummy half to register his first Widnes try before Joe Mellor, on the end of a flowing cross-field move dummied his way past three defenders to score. Stuart Jones then intervened to grab a consolation effort for the Tigers before O'Carroll managed to get his fingertips to McShane's grubber in-goal to score on his debut. The final score of the game came eight minutes from time when Rhys Hanbury tormented the Castleford defence before playing in Patrick Ah Van.

Their next outing saw the Vikings take on St Helens in a game that was to end in controversy. Attempting to gain revenge for the narrow Challenge Cup defeat, and the 62 point hammering the following week, Widnes eventually fell by a single point as the match finished 23-24. After an error-strewn opening 30 minutes, during which Stefan Marsh and Rhys Hanbury had gone close, Sia Soliola pounced to open the scoring when Hanbury failed to collect a kick on his own line. Within minutes Saints' Tom Makinson returned the favour when he allowed a kick downfield to bounce, giving Chris Dean the opportunity to flick the ball to Patrick Ah Van who raced clear to score.

Within 15 minutes of the re-start Widnes had edged in front for the first time by 14 points to 12. The first try of the second half had come from Jon Wilkin, but two tries in the space of four minutes put the Vikings ahead. First Mellor took a quick tap penalty to play in Hanbury who picked out a run from Dean for the centre to score against his former club. In a controversial decision the touch judges declared that Hanbury's conversion attempt had failed, although those sat behind the kick were convinced that it had indeed gone over. In the next set Dean and Hanbury combined to put Ah Van through for his second of the afternoon, although Saints replied through Michael Shenton. However, four minutes later the Vikings bounced back again as Ah Van completed his hat-trick with a 90 metre interception try and tied the scores at 18-18.

With only seven minutes remaining Hanbury put over a drop goal, and Jon Clarke and Hanbury created a try for Cameron Phelps, as Widnes entered the final three minutes with a five point lead. They held out until Lee Gaskell converted Josh Jones' try with the last kick of the match.

In reference to the touch judge's decision to disallow Hanbury's conversion a bitterly disappointed Denis Betts said after the game: "We won that game – even though it doesn't look like it in the papers" adding "It was a great game. We're starting to reap some rewards now."

Next up was a trip to Salford's new stadium which finally resulted in the first away win of the season as Widnes put in a commanding display to overpower their hosts by 46 points to 8. For once everything seemed to go in the Vikings favour, even the decisions of the officials.

After a messy opening spell with defences on top Widnes finally broke the deadlock after 24 minutes, when John Kite made a strong 20 metre run into the Salford 10 metre zone. The ball was quickly played through Paul McShane, Rhys Hanbury and Frank Winterstein who slipped an exquisite inside pass to Cameron Phelps who scored under the posts. Within three minutes Widnes had increased their lead after McShane, Joe Mellor and Hanbury passed the ball along the 10 metre line for Phelps to put Ah Van over in the corner. Two further tries put the Vikings firmly in control at half-time. The first came as a result of a chip over the defence by McShane which Ah Van raced onto to again score by the corner flag. Just before the hooter sounded Phelps gathered a kick and fed Hanbury deep inside his own '40' and the scrum half outpaced the Salford defence to score. His faultless kicking gave Widnes a 24-0 lead at the break.

After repelling early pressure from Salford, Widnes extended their lead in the 48th minute when McShane burrowed past three defenders from dummy half. Widnes were straight back on the attack from the kick-off and Hanbury, receiving the ball just inside his own half burst through the centre of the Salford defence before passing to Phelps who ran in from 15 metres to bag his second of the night. With only a further 60 seconds on the clock Hanbury had done it again. Receiving the ball 75 metres from the Salford line he again outstripped the defence to score what was becoming a trademark try in the corner. All that remained was for Salford to gain consolation tries through Ashley Gibson and Danny Williams, as Widnes eased off, before Danny Craven had the final say with a 70 metre interception try six minutes from time.

After the match Denis Betts paid tribute to the defensive effort saying: "Our determination not to let Salford cross our line was outstanding. We have had some really good performances recently and we showed great composure." Of Man of the Match Hanbury the head coach added: "Rhys was outstanding. He showed phenomenal pace and went round some very quick players for his tries. His confidence is high and he is pretty special."

A much more confident band of supporters gathered at the Stobart Stadium for the next match against Hull KR, but were to be disappointed by another narrow defeat, despite taking a first minute lead when Stefan Marsh put Joe Mellor over. The lead was short-lived as tries from Michael Dobson, former Widnes target Ryan O'Hara and Josh Hodgson gave the visitors a 12 point lead over the home side who had already lost Ben Cross and Mellor. Struggling under the growing influence of Dobson and Blake Green Widnes would have fallen further behind but for Stefan Marsh chasing back to thwart David Hodgson. With the game already in danger of getting away from the Vikings the last play of the half saw Marsh reduce the arrears to 8-18 after taking a cleverly worked pass from Jack Owens.

Despite playing the second half with only 14 players (Steve Pickersgill failed to appear after the break) Widnes started brightly with Kurt Haggerty taking advantage of a fumble by the Rovers defence to stroll in under the posts, with Hanbury claiming his first 'extras' of the day. The tries continued to come as Dobson put Ben Galea in followed by a bizarre reply from Danny Craven. Having put up a high, spiralling bomb Craven was first to react, when Willie Isa hacked the ball further forward, and outpaced the defence to collect and score. Hanbury's conversion from the touchline brought Widnes within two points of Rovers. Although Hanbury chased down a kick from Patrick Ah Van to make it a two point game with seven minutes remaining Rovers finished the game off with a try from Louis Sheriff three minutes from time.

Putting the defeat in context Denis Betts said: "We had 14 fit players out there after losing Ben Cross and Joe Mellor in the first 10 minutes, and Steve Pickersgill. To be in it right to the death with 14 blokes, I'm really proud of them. It was a brave effort."

Beaten but not bowed Widnes then went on the road for games at Bradford and Leeds, losing a close game against the Bulls before returning to Yorkshire to be soundly beaten by the Rhinos. Played in poor conditions Denis Betts felt that the Bradford game was closer than the 38-26 score suggested, as his team ran in five tries, but were undone by some poor discipline. Widnes established a 12-0 lead inside the first 10 minutes through former Bull Patrick Ah Van and Ben Davies, but that was pulled back to six when Michael Platt was the beneficiary of a penalty for obstruction. Danny Craven, taking a pass from Stefan Marsh, responded with a try from 35 metres having sold an outrageous dummy to Karl Pryce on the way, only to see tries from Brett Kearney and Shaun Ainscough establish a 22-16 lead. A Rhys Hanbury try on the hooter reduced the deficit to two points at the break, but the hosts had established a match-winning lead just after the hour through tries from L'Estrange and Platt. With Patrick Ah Van's try cancelled out by Ainscough's second the home side hung on for the win.

If the scoreline flattered Bradford that could not be said of Leeds six days later as they romped home scoring 12 tries in the process. The home side scorched into an early 18 point lead before Stefan Marsh got Widnes back into the game, albeit briefly. An excellent off-load from Frank Winterstein allowed Danny Craven and Cameron Phelps to set up the chance for Marsh. Leeds responded with three further tries before Winterstein got himself on the scoresheet after Rhys Hanbury's pace got him away from the home defence. But on the stroke of half-time Leeds scored again to make it 40-12 at half-time.

Widnes took the fight to Leeds after the break and Phelps, aided by Dave Allen, and Marsh following good work by Willie Isa, restored some respectability to the score. However, during Kurt Haggerty's 'binning' Leeds ran in three tries followed by two further late efforts to make the final score 68-24.

Returning to the familiar surroundings of the Stobart Stadium the Vikings bounced back to the impressive form they had shown in the weeks before their trips over the Pennines. With a wealth of experience returning to the side they were more than a match for a Hull FC outfit who were chasing a top four finish, while Widnes were seeking a win to catch London Broncos and Castleford at the foot of the table. In addition to the returning Shaun Briscoe, Jon Clarke, Ben Kavanagh and Paul McShane, Paddy Flynn finally made his 100th appearance for the club.

When Hull took the lead through Jordan Turner in the eighth minute I doubt that anybody in the ground would have predicted the final outcome. But just five minutes later

Widnes had levelled through Willie Isa, who had already had one effort ruled out by the video referee. Hep Cahill regained possession, after the Hull defence failed to deal with a Craven bomb, but was stopped just short of the line. The Vikings then swept from right to left via the hands of Craven, Rhys Hanbury, Cameron Phelps and Shaun Briscoe for Isa to dive into the corner to score his first try of the season. Two minutes later Flynn, on his landmark appearance, put Widnes in front after Hull had been caught offside at the re-start. Widnes drove down the centre before Craven switched the ball to his right where Briscoe raced through in support and put the winger over in the corner. From the kick-off Briscoe turned sinner as he knocked on to gift possession to Hull just 10 metres out and Joe Westerman made Widnes pay. As half-time approached Briscoe redeemed himself, with Frank Winterstein also crossing to make the score 20-10 at the break. With a penalty taking Widnes deep into Hull territory the ball eventually came to Hanbury who put a grubber into the in-goal area. Briscoe, first to react, caught the ball between his knees before rolling over to ground it. From the kick-off Widnes moved up to their 40 metre line and Phelps dabbed a neat kick through the opposition defence. Isa collected the ball, made ground and laid it off to the supporting Winterstein who ran in from 40 metres to score on the hooter.

Widnes came out after the break firing on all cylinders and within five minutes had gained a 20 point lead. It was Craven who got the scoreboard moving after just three minutes when Hull fumbled the ball on their 30 metre line. The half-back was first to react, kicked the loose ball forward, and gathered to touch down. Two minutes later the points were secured after Hull knocked on deep in their own half. Widnes immediately drove forward and Phelps, with three defenders pulling him to the ground, got a marvellous off-load away to Hanbury who sped down the touchline before passing to Isa, who had cut inside, for the winger to claim his second try of the afternoon. Hanbury 0/2 and Craven 2/3 handed the kicking responsibilities to McShane who knocked over the first of three conversions.

A try from Aaron Heremaia interrupted proceedings in the 56th minute but Widnes dug in and scored two further tries late on. Hull again turned over possession on their 20 metre line and Widnes steadily moved forward before McShane fed Hanbury from dummy half and the Vikings scrum-half passed back inside for Briscoe to complete a brace against his former club. Two minutes later, as both teams took it in turns to lose possession on halfway, Craven took control and passed to Hanbury who took the direct route to score under the posts and complete a comprehensive victory.

While Peter Gentle admitted his side were "disgraceful" Denis Betts praised the contribution of Briscoe, adding: "He gives us experience and talk." The Vikings' head coach continued: "We stuck to our task and we got in their faces and forced them into errors. Hull could not break us down and we can take a lot out of that performance."

In their final away match of the season Widnes were matched against Wakefield, the team who had spoilt the party back in February. Not for the first time this season the Vikings were to let an early lead slip away. That lead came in the sixth minute courtesy of Rhys Hanbury after an exchange of short passes with Frank Winterstein, just inside their own half, set him free to race to the line and fend off a last ditch challenge from Richie Mathers. The lead lasted only five minutes as Wakefield made the most of a penalty to advance to the Widnes 30 metre line. On the last tackle of the set the ball was played to Kyle Amor who made a diagonal run through the Widnes defence to score from 10 metres out. In a scrappy half Widnes went back on the attack and, with Hanbury pulling the strings in another impressive outing, they came close to regaining the lead almost immediately through Willie

Isa. However, it was Hanbury who had the last say of the first half when he took a short pass from Winterstein on the 40 metre line, raced into the Wakefield half, chipped the pedestrian Mathers and collected the ball to sprint to the line. Paul McShane missed the conversion and Widnes led 10-6 at half-time.

With little improvement in the play after the break it was Mathers who levelled matters. As the game came alive there were tries either side of the hour mark, with Paddy Flynn giving Widnes the lead, thanks to Dave Allen's pass cutting out two defenders to put Flynn over in the corner. Ali Lauitiiti replied for the hosts to level matters at 18-18 and with 18 minutes left set up an exciting finale. With Widnes pushing for the win a somewhat harsh penalty was awarded against Flynn in the 68th minute, and to compound the issue James Child sent the winger to the sin bin. Paul Sykes stroked the ball over to give his side a two point lead. Flynn's 'binning' was made all the more remarkable three minutes later when Lee Smith blatantly pushed Cameron Phelps off his feet as he attempted to play the ball. Amazingly Smith stayed on the pitch, but Hanbury levelled matters again with a penalty from 40 metres with eight minutes remaining. In their next set Wakefield's Danny Kirmond went over in the corner to clinch the match.

While the win all-but clinched the Wildcats place in the play-offs, the defeat consigned Widnes to the wooden spoon, unless they could beat Warrington on the last day.

Widnes went into the match having won only one of their last five matches but took another early lead when Jon Clarke's short pass put Frank Winterstein over in the corner, with Rhys Hanbury converting from the touchline. This was yet another short-lived lead as on 10 minutes Warrington had levelled when Lee Briers converted Micky Higham's try. Paddy Flynn was working overtime to prevent further scores but Rhys Williams further extended the lead, as Chris Riley, Stefan Ratchford and David Solomona piled on the agony to give the visitors a 22-6 half-time lead. Riley claimed his second straight after the break before Paul McShane grabbed a second for the Vikings but, injured in the process, had to leave the pitch. Warrington were scoring at will and Chris Hill and Higham added further tries before Rhys Hanbury scored the Vikings final try of 2012 in front of 8,617 fans – the biggest crowd of the season. The last word went to Warrington as Ryan Atkins and Paul Wood added further tries.

In a slightly subdued atmosphere the Viking Stronghold Player of the Season event was held, in the Marquee Suite at the stadium, a couple of hours after the hooter brought down the curtain on a mixed season. Despite suffering the heartache of missing virtually all of the season Ben Kavanagh's work with the Valhalla Foundation gained him recognition with the 'Foundation Community Award', while the seamless transition from part-time professional in the Championship to full-time Super League player earned the Young Player of the Season award for Danny Craven.

Hep Cahill, who by most people's reckoning had had a storming season scooped both the Player of the Season and the Players' Player of the Season awards, presented by head coach Denis Betts. Runner-up to Cahill was Rhys Hanbury, who may well have laid the ghost of the No.7 shirt, with top scorer Patrick Ah Van recognised, in third place, for his efforts throughout the season.

To sum up 2012 it was plainly an inconsistent season, but one in which significant progress had been made. There were some dark days in the first half of the year with the occasional highlight but, with the odd exception, the performances in the second half of the year were much more promising.

At the outset pundits were saying that Widnes would finish bottom, with some even suggesting that they would not win a single match. Yes, they did finish bottom of the pile but, with just a little bit of the rub of the green in any one of four or five matches, they would have finished at least one place higher. Throughout the year they had attracted negative comments, from one quarter in particular, about their suitability for Super League. Those comments, which simply showed a lack of understanding of the basis of the licensing system, were certainly laid to rest by some of the results and performances in the second half of the season.

To put the Vikings' season in context it should be compared to the other clubs who have either been given a wild card entry to Super League, or 'promoted' via the licensing system. Catalan Dragons' debut season in 2006 saw them gain eight victories, while in 2009 Crusaders bagged just three wins in their first season at the top level. It should be remembered that both of these clubs were afforded then, and for some time, a highly inflated number of 'overseas' players in their ranks – a facility not made available to Widnes.

Speaking to Denis Betts as the season drew to a close he assessed the year as follows: "We stayed true to ourselves. We've taken some hits on the chin, and we've kept moving forward. There were certain aspects of certain games where we under-performed but overall we've performed as well as we possibly can at times; we could have got another couple of wins – losing in the last seconds at London and losing by one point to St Helens. With those two possible wins we could be sitting on 16 points and in a strong position for finishing 11th or 12th which would have been an overachievement for this year.

"With two games to come I've got to assess what other people's perceptions are. If we finish 12th or 13th then it's been a success for their perception of a team that has come from basically an amateur environment to a full-time environment. Inwardly I'd say that we've grown, we've got better and we are developing along the right lines."

The head coach added significantly: "I know for a fact that we lost the game here against Salford where we underperformed massively because I dropped three players for disciplinary reasons. That affected us on that day [but] I think that decision on my part made us stronger throughout the year."

To get a players' perspective I spoke to Shaun Briscoe and Jack Owens at the end of the season. Briscoe explained that "at the start of the season everyone had sat down as a group and agreed that it [the coming season] was not about points. It was about the progression of the team and club as a whole."

The England International admitted that while "we did have opportunities to finish a bit higher" he considered 2012 to be "a successful season when you look at where we started and the progression made. We'll be looking for the same again next year – more progression and to improve week on week."

On a personal level the full-back added that when you join a new club "you want to do your best and show the fans what you can do. I was really disappointed as I've never missed as many games through injury." During the season he was restricted to eight appearances having initially suffered a serious groin injury, where the adductor muscle came away from the bone, and a torn pectoral muscle during his comeback game against Wigan at the DW stadium.

Unsurprisingly Briscoe described being injured as the worst part of the game, adding that he finds watching "an absolute killer". However, he did recognise that "having several key players out at once is one of those things, but it gave youngsters like Danny Craven, Jack Owens and Alex Gerrard opportunities to shine".

At the other end of the experience scale Jack Owens, an England Under-18 International, didn't know what to expect at the start of year. "I hadn't set myself any particular targets, I was just looking to play well for the under-20s, and would be happy if I got a chance in the first team."

Naturally when the time came Owens was "happy to be making my Super League debut and tried to keep focused over the weekend". He had been told before training on the Saturday morning that Cameron Phelps was injured and that he would be playing against Bradford in the Easter Monday fixture.

Owens considered that his Super League debut "went well although I finished on the losing side. It felt good to get a taste of Super League" adding "the nerves didn't hit me until I walked out for the kick-off, but when I got a touch of the ball I felt ok".

Looking forward to 2013 Owens told me that his aim is "to play well for the under-19s, get more powerful, and take my chance when it comes," while helping the younger players in the same way that he has benefitted from Shaun Briscoe's advice.

While there were undoubtedly some very dark days in 2012 the players that remain will have learned and gained a lot from the experience, not least the young ones that have just broken into the squad. It is a compliment to the club that seven products of the Vikings' highly regarded academy structure represented the club at Super League level. If that production line continues, blended with a nucleus of experienced professionals, 2013 and beyond should indeed be happy days for everybody associated with the club.

Widnes Vikings are undoubtedly back where they belong, but if they are to progress further and re-live the glory days of the past everyone needs to play their part. Let's hope that, starting with 2013, more and more people get behind the club because, to paraphrase Steve O'Connor, the more people there are on the river bank the better chance we have of catching some big fish.

Appendices

Appendix I

Following the meeting with member clubs on 8th April 1995 the RFL announced the following structure for the sport from the Summer of 1996.

Super League
Bradford Northern
Halifax
Leeds
St Helens
Wigan
Calder   (Castleford, Wakefield, Featherstone)
Cheshire   (Warrington, Widnes)
Cumbria   (Barrow, Carlisle, Workington, Whitehaven)
Humberside   (Hull, Hull Kingston Rovers)
Manchester   (Oldham, Salford)
South Yorkshire   (Doncaster, Sheffield)
London
Paris St Germain
Toulouse

First Division
Batley
Bramley
Dewsbury
Highfield
Huddersfield
Hunslet
Keighley
Leigh
Rochdale
Ryedale-York
Swinton

plus a new Welsh club to be based in Cardiff

Appendix II

The RFL announced the following revised structure on 30th April 1995:

Super League
Bradford Northern
Castleford
Halifax
Leeds
London
Oldham
Paris St Germain
St Helens
Sheffield
Warrington
Wigan
Workington

First Division	Second Division
Batley	Barrow
Dewsbury	Bramley
Featherstone	Carlisle
Huddersfield	Chorley
Hull	Highfield
Keighley	Hull KR
Rochdale	Hunslet
Salford	Leigh
Wakefield	Ryedale-York
Whitehaven	Swinton
Widnes	

Appendix III

RFL assessments of the inaugural 2008 Super League Licence Applications.

BRADFORD BULLS
The Coral Stand offers good hospitality but the remainder of the stadium requires improvement and there are some development plans. The club has historic and projected profits and operates without the need for shareholder support. The club is known for its game day experience and has positive brand alignment to national partners. Attendances are not as high as in previous seasons, however, the club remains one of the most well supported. Excellent Super League results over the years are backed by a strong playing department, although the club appears to have a slight overseas reliance.

CATALANS DRAGONS
Gilbert Brutus represents a sound functional stadium with further investment planned over the next 12 months. Although there are differences in the formalised game day operations between the countries, the match day experience is positive for supporters. The financial information regarding projections was not as detailed as it could have been and the club has been reliant on shareholder input. A Challenge Cup Final appearance helped the financial position and further capital injection is planned. As was anticipated, the club's crowds and merchandising have improved considerably over the three year period from a low base before the introduction into Super League. The commercial plan appears reasonable but would have benefitted from further evidence. On the playing side, the first team are producing good results and are introducing more French trained players. The club needs to advance its fledgling youth development processes. Commercial success and increased player pool prove that the introduction of a French club into Super League has been vindicated.

CASTLEFORD TIGERS
While well maintained, the ground is limited and old fashioned. However, the club recognise this and has relatively advanced plans for a new stadium. Financial projections are based on the new ground, although there is evidence of a Plan B. The club is well managed financially with limited external borrowings and/or shareholder funds. The club has produced a holistic commercial plan, has a record of commercial achievement and achieves strong support even when relegated. The club's reasonable playing infrastructure has been hurt by the yo-yoing between Super League and National League. The club has maintained youth pathways but has not always been able to secure the best local talent.

CELTIC CRUSADERS
While well maintained, the ground is limited and old fashioned but there is a commitment to immediately enhance the current facilities. In the medium term the club recognises the need to develop a new facility and appears to be working with the local public agencies to deliver this. As with any new venture, financial projections are more subjective but the club has demonstrated financial stability during its progress through the National Leagues. The club has built good relationships with commercial partners and TV channel S4C offers exciting opportunities. There is supportive independent market research for Super League

in South Wales, although inevitably this can only be fully tested by the club's actual participation in the competition. The playing infrastructure is very good in places but the club is understandably at the early stages with its scholarship and academy teams.

FEATHERSTONE ROVERS
While the stadium is well maintained and of a good standard for the National Leagues it would require further investment to achieve Super League minimum standards. The club's finances appear stable from the information provided. The club has a good community programme and has secured some positive and creative media coverage in the last year. However, the club faces competition for crowds from current Super League clubs within the area. The assessment of the club's playing strength would have been enhanced by the submission of further evidence. There is a player pathway framework but this would require further investment before it would be considered to be of Super League standard.

HALIFAX RLFC
The club has previously made a good contribution to Super League but is significantly restrained by the incomplete nature of their stadium. This makes financial projections and marketing plans difficult to produce with any degree of certainty. Player development structures would require further investment before they could be considered of a Super League standard. However, the club's first team performances are consistently at the higher end of National League 1 over recent seasons.

HARLEQUINS RL
The Stoop provides good facilities across the board. The club relies on significant shareholder support and is seeking additional investment. Crowds have fluctuated and the club is looking to increase attendances on the back of stability in a good stadium. The recently appointed new management is tapping into a large catchment area and making the most of a robust community programme. The club has been reasonably successful in Super League and has a well resourced playing department. There are emerging local players but the club's juniors are not yet regularly attracting national honours.

HUDDERSFIELD GIANTS
The stadium is an excellent 13-year-old facility despite the absence of some facilities that a new build might have. The club has a dependency on shareholder support and will need to deliver on a strong commercial plan to achieve the projected increases in turnover and profitability. Attendances have improved significantly since a Challenge Cup Final appearance and with the recruitment of key commercial and marketing staff. The club has invested in the first team and will need to ensure that scholarship and academy structures are sufficient to produce Club Trained players.

HULL FC
The club plays in an excellent stadium and has high attendances. The club is well organised in all areas of marketing – particularly its community and Customer Relationship Management programmes – and is commercially strong. The club has historic and projected profits and operates with little external financial input. Despite a recent dip in playing form this season the club achieves high marks in most areas of playing strength.

HULL KINGSTON ROVERS
This is the club's second year in Super League and it is showing strong potential. The club has invested significantly in improving its facilities, much of which is behind the scenes. Further significant developments are planned. This commendable investment has required, and will continue to require, strong financial management. The club's commercial plan is well thought through and logical and its community work is achieving results. The assessment of the club's player performance strategy would have been enhanced by the submission of further evidence, particularly with Academy Reserves but there is a growing infrastructure since promotion to Super League.

LEEDS RHINOS
An example of an older stadium that has had significant improvements, with more planned. The club has historic and projected profits and strong net assets. Commercially the club has produced good results and they achieve high attendances. The club's playing record speaks for itself and the club is producing quality Club Trained players.

LEIGH CENTURIONS
The new stadium is close to opening. Inspection of the current site, together with a review of the current plans, suggests that it will be an excellent facility. The new stadium provides the basis on which the club might develop into a strong candidate for Super League by developing its existing structures in a number of areas. Recruitment will need to take place to help deliver the good, reasoned commercial plan. The club has strong historic and predicted shareholder reliance. Evidence was provided of investment in youth production, which would require further strengthening to achieve Super League standards.

SALFORD CITY REDS
While well maintained, the ground is limited and old fashioned. However, the club recognise this and has relatively advanced plans for a new stadium and are on site. The Willows offers good corporate facilities and disabled facilities. Despite previous relegations from Super League the club has a long history of financial stability. The club's commercial and marketing plans appear well developed and will allow them to make use of a new stadium and access to the Salford and Manchester conurbations. The club's player performance strategy is very diligent in every area and there is a strong infrastructure although the club currently struggle with under-16 player development.

ST HELENS
The ground is an old and tired stadium. However, a new stadium is planned and has recently secured planning permission. The club's financial position and commercial activities are constrained by the current stadium. Financial plans are based around a new facility. The club is a market leader in merchandise. On the playing side, the club has a strong infrastructure and again are market leaders in junior production.

TOULOUSE OLYMPIQUE
The club would offer geographic expansion and independent market research shows some support for Super League in Toulouse. Despite the club's commendable commitment to player production there is a concern that it has a limited supply of Super League standard

player talent in the area. The club has established strong business links and is well placed for commercial development, although the club would need to work hard to meet its financial projections. The application proposed using two quality facilities while the club's own ground was being redeveloped.

WAKEFIELD TRINITY WILDCATS

While well maintained, the ground is limited and old fashioned. However, the club recognise this and have plans for a new stadium. These are not as far advanced as might be the case despite projected occupation by 2010 and evidence of a Plan B would have been beneficial. There is good progress within community development and attendances are improving. Evidence of specific commercial measurable targets with the commercial strategy would have assisted. There has been a recent improvement on the pitch and increased investment in the playing department. Youth development works reasonably well and pre-16 players are attracting national honours but the club has not always been able to retain the best local talent.

WARRINGTON WOLVES

The club plays in a quality new stadium which in all but one or two aspects is excellent. Further ground improvements are planned and although financial projections are challenging, the club has a good record in this area. The club has strong sponsorship packages and a good commercial plan. The club has performed reasonably well in Super League and has invested well in its playing infrastructure and now needs to start contesting major finals and semi-finals. At this stage it is not yet developing Club Trained internationals.

WIDNES VIKINGS

The stadium is an appropriate size and well appointed following significant investment in recent years. The club has been in the difficult position of seeking to take into account the club's historical attendance and playing records but naturally distancing itself from the previous regime's financial record. The current company has only been in existence for a few months following insolvency in October 2007. Early indications are that under new ownership the club has made very good progress so far and has attracted good sponsors and the support of the local authority. The club has maintained a reasonable playing infrastructure despite being in the National League but this would require further investment to ensure that they could be competitive in Super League particularly within Club Trained rules.

WIGAN WARRIORS

The club is playing in an excellent stadium and attracts good attendances. There is currently some reliance on the new majority shareholder. The club has strong commercial plans and is a market leader in many aspects of marketing and commercial activity. The club has had what it will view as disappointing Super League results in recent seasons and now seems to be making use of its excellent playing infrastructure. The club achieves national honours at scholarship level and has expressed commitment to converting more into the first team squad.

Appendix IV

March 2011 Licence Application summaries issued by the RFL

HALIFAX RLFC

Halifax RLFC submitted an application with insufficient detail in their marketing, media or commercial plans. The club business plan was inadequate, figures presented by the club as the budget and performance forecasts for the 2012-14 Licence period were speculative and the club did not provide sufficient information for KPMG to complete their assessment procedures. While the club has an excellent community program, a good facility and has recently strengthened its board and player performance system, the club fell below the standards expected of a Super League club. Grade C.

WIDNES VIKINGS

Widnes Vikings provided a detailed application containing marketing, management, financial and operational plans to ensure the club would make a significant contribution to the Super League if granted a Licence. The crowd, commercial and sponsorship targets set out in the application are ambitious; however, with further staff additions to complement the talented staff currently in post and a measure of on-field success, the targets are achievable. Widnes's current stadium and plans for a new training facility show the club has developed, and continues to develop, a high quality infrastructure. Widnes have committed to a full Super League player pathway, currently operates an accredited Academy and Scholarship and engages closely with Service Area Programmes and training groups for talented young players. Grade C.

Summaries were not produced for Barrow Raiders, who failed to meet the criteria, and Crusaders, who withdrew their application.

Appendix V

Results 2008

Date	Opponent	Venue	Score	Att
3rd February	Blackpool Panthers – NRC	A	4-38	905
10th February	Leigh Centurions – NRC	H	8-15	4,032
24th February	Leigh Centurions – NRC	A	10-20	3,615
27th February	Barrow Raiders – NRC	H	78-0	3,472
2nd March	Blackpool Panthers – NRC	H	60-12	3,169
9th March	Skirlaugh – CCC3	H	60-18	4,510
16th March	Barrow Raiders – NRC	A	16-24	1,413
21st March	Batley Bulldogs	A	28-23	1,091
24th March	Leigh Centurions	H	30-12	4,722
30th March	Whitehaven RLFC	H	32-28	3,596
6th April	Sheffield Eagles – NRC	H	44-8	2,262
11th April	Salford City Reds	A	16-16	6,143
20th April	Doncaster – CCC4	A	38-12	1,541
27th April	Celtic Crusaders	H	14-16	4,201
6th May	Dewsbury Rams	A	29-22	1,434
11th May	Hull FC – CCC5	H	18-32	4,102
18th May	Sheffield Eagles	H	30-22	3,891
24th May	Celtic Crusaders – NRC	A	18-50	1,750
1st June	Featherstone Rovers	A	22-34	1,910
8th June	Halifax RLFC	H	30-40	3,971
19th June	Salford City Reds	H	20-18	8,189
26th June	Celtic Crusaders	A	6-38	3,595
11th July	Batley Bulldogs	H	34-22	4,079
20th July	Halifax RLFC	A	26-26	2,561
27th July	Dewsbury Rams	H	40-0	4,082
3rd August	Leigh Centurions	A	24-33	3,089
10th August	Featherstone Rovers	H	30-20	3,924
14th August	Sheffield Eagles	A	26-20	1,823
24th August	Whitehaven RLFC	A	16-20	2,104
4th September	Halifax RLFC – P/off	A	16-32	1,913

Appearances 2008

	App	T	G	D/G	Pts
Sam Barlow	6	2	0	0	8
Bob Beswick	30	6	0	1	25
Adam Bowman	4	0	0	0	0
Jason Crookes	11	5	0	0	20
Chris Dean	10	4	0	0	16
Gavin Dodd	30	15	28	0	116
Dayne Donoghue	15	2	0	0	8
Rob Draper	15	5	0	0	20
John Duffy	26	4	0	0	16
Adel Fellous	6	0	0	0	0
Richard Fletcher	14	3	8	0	28
Paddy Flynn	5	4	0	0	16
Tommy Gallagher	14	2	0	0	8
Jim Gannon	30	7	0	0	28
Dean Gaskell	28	16	0	0	64
Shane Grady	15	3	0	0	12
Ian Hardman	29	10	0	0	40
Tim Hartley	16	7	55	0	138
Danny Hill	21	11	0	0	44
Ben Kavanagh	21	2	0	0	8
Martin McLoughlin	2	0	0	0	0
Iain Morrison	28	4	0	0	16
Gareth Morton	6	1	0	0	4
Paul Noone	17	2	0	0	8
Michael Ostick	7	0	0	0	0
Lee Paterson	27	14	0	0	56
Stephen Roper	13	1	0	0	4
Josh Simm	2	0	0	0	0
Mark Smith	22	3	0	0	12
Matty Smith	10	3	0	0	12
Danny Speakman	2	0	0	0	0
Matt Strong	4	1	0	0	4
Steve Tyrer	10	7	36	0	100
Scott Yates	13	6	1	0	26

Results 2009

Date	Opponent	Venue	Score	Att
8th February	Barrow Raiders – NRC	A	4-12	1,563
13th February	Oldham – NRC	H	20-22	2,783
21st February	Gateshead – NRC	H	40-18	3,001
1st March	Blackpool – NRC	A	46-16	864
7th March	Saddleworth – CCC-3	H	88-0	1,786
12th March	Toulouse Olympique	H	70-0	5,071
19th March	Halifax	A	14-24	3,274
28th March	Sheffield Eagles	H	28-20	3,181
3rd April	Halifax – CCC-4	A	16-20	3,204
10th April	Leigh Centurions	H	8-10	4,354
13th April	Doncaster	A	24-18	831
17th April	Batley Bulldogs	H	40-18	2,901
26th April	Sheffield Eagles	A	22-20	1,231
1st May	Barrow Raiders	H	6-27	3,290
7th May	Whitehaven	A	22-26	2,102
14th May	Leigh Centurions	A	16-23	2,556
23rd May	Gateshead Thunder	H	46-30	5,236
31st May	Batley Bulldogs	A	34-40	1,089
6th June	York City Knights – NRC	H	44-18	1,650
13th June	Featherstone Rovers	H	46-22	3,278
21st June	Halifax – NRC – S/F	A	27-22	3,972
4th July	Doncaster	H	78-4	3,453
12th July	Barrow – NRC Final	N	34-18	8,720
19th July	Gateshead Thunder	A	18-34	717
25th July	Toulouse Olympique	A	32-24	3,206
31st July	Halifax	H	42-16	4,039
9th August	Featherstone Rovers	A	29-34	2,125
13th August	Barrow Raiders	A	16-38	3,050
22nd August	Whitehaven	H	58-10	3,275
10th September	Whitehaven – P/off	H	26-21	2,375
18th September	Featherstone – P/off	H	24-32	3,296

Appearances 2009

	App	T	G	D/G	Pts
Stephen Bannister	4	3	1	0	14
Gavin Dodd	30	12	19	0	86
Lee Doran	29	8	0	0	32
John Duffy	23	6	0	0	24
Richard Fletcher	19	10	1	0	42
Paddy Flynn	25	20	0	0	80
Jim Gannon	30	8	0	0	32
Dean Gaskell	20	7	0	0	28
Shane Grady	13	4	0	0	16
Jonny Grayshon	9	3	0	0	12
Craig Hall	5	1	31	1	67
Tim Hartley	18	5	56	0	132
Dave Houghton	4	0	0	0	0
Ben Kavanagh	31	3	0	0	12
Toa Kohe Love	16	11	0	0	44
Danny Mills	2	0	0	0	0
Iain Morrison	11	5	0	0	20
Antony Mullally	1	0	0	0	0
Michael Ostick	27	3	0	0	12
Lee Paterson	6	0	0	0	0
Kevin Penny	11	11	0	0	44
Steve Pickersgill	11	1	0	0	4
Brett Robinson	0	0	0	0	0
Josh Simm	16	0	0	0	0
Mark Smith	30	7	0	1	29
Matt Strong	3	2	0	0	8
Anthony Thackeray	30	15	0	0	60
Dean Thompson	0	0	0	0	0
Sam Thompson	11	2	0	0	8
Steve Tyrer	3	0	5	0	10
Richard Varkulis	30	14	0	0	56
James Webster	30	8	0	0	32
Loz Wildbore	14	5	0	0	20
Scott Yates	12	6	35	0	94

Results 2010

Date	Opponent	Venue	Score	Att
2nd February	Gateshead Thunder – NRC	H	50-6	2,200
7th February	Batley Bulldogs – NRC	A	30-30	1,004
14th February	Barrow Raiders – NRC	H	22-20	3,432
21st February	Swinton Lions – NRC	A	12-36	816
28th February	Keighley Cougars	H	72-10	2,777
9th March	Wigan St Judes – CCC-3	H	64-12	1,622
14th March	Sheffield Eagles	A	30-44	1,085
18th March	Halifax	H	28-30	3,286
28th March	Dewsbury Rams	A	30-36	1,499
5th April	Whitehaven	H	48-18	3,033
10th April	Toulouse	H	38-42	2,793
22nd April	Lezignan – CCC – 4	H	44-24	1,349
25th April	Batley Bulldogs	A	24-32	1,046
30th April	Featherstone Rovers	H	8-9	3,448
8th May	Wigan Warriors – CCC – 5	H	10-64	5,504
13th May	Leigh Centurions	A	30-16	3,392
23rd May	Batley Bulldogs	H	16-35	2,780
3rd June	Barrow Raiders – NRC Q/F	H	26-12	1,718
13th June	Barrow Raiders	H	20-24	2,958
20th June	Keighley Cougars – NRC S/F	A	18-48	1,686
27th June	Featherstone Rovers	A	30-22	1,776
1st July	Whitehaven	A	4-40	1,580
11th July	Dewsbury Rams	H	27-26	2,715
18th July	Batley Bulldogs – NRC Final	N	25-24	8,138
25th July	Leigh Centurions	H	18-38	3,356
29th July	Halifax	A	30-16	2,707
7th August	Toulouse	A	30-44	983
12th August	Sheffield Eagles	H	30-10	2,659
18th August	Barrow Raiders	A	14-32	1,328
22nd August	Keighley Cougars	A	24-32	1,173
5th September	Barrow Raiders – P/off	A	38-0	2,434

Appearances 2010

	App	T	G	D/G	Pts
Shaun Ainscough	10	8	0	0	32
Dave Allen	17	8	0	0	32
Alex Brown	1	1	0	0	4
Thomas Coyle	20	8	0	1	33
Danny Craven	8	5	23	0	66
Ben Davies	17	3	0	0	12
Chris Dean	1	2	0	0	8
Lee Doran	29	5	0	0	20
Liam Farrell	6	3	0	0	12
Paddy Flynn	25	11	0	0	44
James Ford	12	6	0	0	24
Jim Gannon	27	4	0	0	16
Matt Gardner	29	12	0	0	48
Dean Gaskell	13	5	0	0	20
Alex Gerrard	2	0	0	0	0
Chris Gerrard	28	9	0	0	36
Shane Grady	26	13	101	0	254
Gareth Haggerty	8	1	0	0	4
Kurt Haggerty	9	2	2	0	12
Daniel Heckenberg	9	0	0	0	0
Dave Houghton	23	3	0	0	12
Danny Hulme	6	3	0	0	12
Chaz I'Anson	1	0	0	0	0
Jordan James	6	0	0	0	0
Ben Kavanagh	31	5	0	0	20
Tom Kelly	11	0	0	0	0
Toa Kohe Love	13	4	0	0	16
Chris Lunt	1	0	0	0	0
Stefan Marsh	3	3	0	0	12
Antony Mullally	0	0	0	0	0
Kirk Netherton	14	4	0	0	16
Steve Pickersgill	9	2	0	0	8
Greg Scott	1	0	0	0	0
Jack Smith	1	0	0	0	0
Mark Smith	22	4	0	0	16
Matt Strong	8	1	0	0	4
Anthony Thackeray	30	24	1	0	98
Dean Thompson	3	3	0	0	12
Richard Varkulis	22	10	0	0	40
James Webster	13	2	0	0	8
Scott Yates	12	5	1	0	22

Results 2011

Date	Opponent	Venue	Score	Att
6th February	London Skolars – NRC	A	18-62	643
12th February	Toulouse Olympique – NRC	H	44-28	2,376
20th February	Rochdale Hornets – NRC	H	50-10	3,155
26th February	Featherstone Rovers – NRC	A	16-22	1,719
6th March	Siddal – CCC-3	A	6-54	951
13th March	Sheffield Eagles	A	16-44	1,831
20th March	Hunslet Hawks	H	10-18	3,023
27th March	Leigh Centurions	A	54-16	3,198
3rd April	York City Knights	H	76-12	4,087
7th April	Leigh Centurions – NRC Q/F	A	50-18	2,737
17th April	Batley Bulldogs	A	32-12	1,101
21st April	Halifax	H	47-36	3,669
25th April	Barrow Raiders	A	30-12	1,965
28th April	Toulouse Olympique	H	26-12	3,601
8th May	London Skolars – CCC-4	A	18-62	415
15th May	Dewsbury Rams	A	34-34	1,083
21st May	Hull FC – CCC-5	H	26-50	3,387
26th May	Barrow Raiders	H	42-14	3,331
12th June	York City Knights	A	18-22	1,172
26th June	Sheffield Eagles	H	38-24	4,027
3rd July	Hunslet Hawks	A	22-24	1,101
10th July	Dewsbury Rams	H	36-22	4,030
23rd July	Toulouse Olympique	A	16-30	1,157
31st July	Batley Bulldogs	H	24-22	3,873
7th August	Leigh Centurions	H	18-24	4,732
11th August	Halifax	A	26-24	2,090
17th August	Featherstone Rovers	A	56-16	2,021
4th September	Featherstone Rovers	H	4-44	5,021
9th September	Sheffield Eagles – P/off	A	36-20	564

Appearances 2011

	App	T	G	D/G	Pts
Dave Allen	25	9	0	0	36
Alex Brown	0	0	0	0	0
James Coyle	6	0	0	0	0
Thomas Coyle	29	5	0	0	20
Danny Craven	9	8	12	0	56
Dom Crosby	13	3	0	0	12
Simon Finnigan	22	9	0	0	36
Paddy Flynn	26	14	0	0	56
James Ford	4	0	0	0	0
Gareth Frodsham	1	0	0	0	0
Matt Gardner	25	3	0	0	12
Dean Gaskell	12	3	0	0	12
Alex Gerrard	0	0	0	0	0
Chris Gerrard	8	1	0	0	4
Thomas Gilmore	0	0	0	0	0
Grant Gore	4	2	0	0	8
Shane Grady	21	4	2	0	20
Gareth Haggerty	0	0	0	0	0
Kurt Haggerty	18	4	7	0	30
Daniel Heckenberg	9	0	0	0	0
Dave Houghton	3	0	0	0	0
Danny Hulme	11	8	0	0	32
Chaz I'Anson	21	4	0	1	17
Ben Kavanagh	27	8	0	0	32
Tom Kelly	0	0	0	0	0
Macgraff Leuluai	24	8	0	0	32
Chris Lunt	5	1	0	0	4
Joe Mellor	14	7	0	0	28
Antony Mullally	0	0	0	0	0
Kirk Netherton	9	3	0	0	12
Jack Owens	2	1	0	0	4
Kevin Penny	11	5	0	0	20
Steve Pickersgill	24	2	0	0	8
Tangi Ropati	22	8	1	0	34
Greg Scott	0	0	0	0	0
Danny Sculthorpe	11	0	0	0	0
Jack Smith	0	0	0	0	0
Anthony Thackeray	10	9	0	0	36
Logan Tomkins	14	5	0	0	20
Ste Tyrer	25	23	106	0	304
Richard Varkulis	27	7	0	0	28
Lewis Whitty	0	0	0	0	0

Results 2012

Date	Opponent	Venue	Score	Att
3rd February	Wakefield Trinity Wildcats	H	14-32	8,120
12th February	Huddersfield Giants	A	6-66	8,,869
19th February	Salford City Reds	H	18-38	5,053
26th February	Leeds Rhinos	H	16-44	6,046
4th March	Hull KR	A	0-36	7,423
11th March	Wigan Warriors	H	37-36	7,357
18th March	Hull FC	A	10-58	10,705
25th March	London Broncos	H	38-30	5,635
31st March	Catalan Dragons	A	6-76	9,156
5th April	Warrington Wolves	A	12-46	12,042
9th April	Bradford Bulls	H	4-38	5,687
14th April	St Helens – CCC4	H	38-40	3,069
20th April	St Helens	A	0-62	14,243
7th May	Castleford Tigers	A	12-36	5,580
20th May	Catalan Dragons	H	34-42	4,684
26th May	Warrington Wolves	N	4-68	30,763
3rd June	Huddersfield Giants	H	26-22	4,644
9th June	London Broncos	A	24-28	2,117
25th June	Wigan Warriors	A	12-54	13,445
2nd July	Castleford Tigers	H	40-10	4,501
8th July	St Helens	H	23-24	7,023
20th July	Salford City Reds	A	8-46	5,196
29th July	Hull KR	H	26-32	5,325
5th August	Bradford Bulls	A	38-26	10,261
10th August	Leeds Rhinos	A	68-24	13,326
19th August	Hull FC	H	42-16	5,008
2nd September	Wakefield Trinity Wildcats	A	22-18	8,234
9th September	Warrington Wolves	H	14-52	8,617

Appearances 2012

	App	T	G	D/G	Pts
Patrick Ah Van	20	16	34	0	132
Dave Allen	26	2	0	0	8
Shaun Briscoe	8	4	0	0	16
Alex Brown	0	0	0	0	0
Hep Cahill	25	2	0	0	8
Jon Clarke	19	0	0	0	0
Thomas Coyle	0	0	0	0	0
Danny Craven	18	5	2	0	24
Ben Cross	21	2	0	0	8
Ben Davies	24	3	0	0	12
Chris Dean	20	4	0	0	16
Simon Finnigan	10	0	0	0	0
Paddy Flynn	21	9	0	0	36
Alex Gerrard	8	0	0	0	0
Thomas Gilmore	1	0	0	0	0
Grant Gore	1	0	0	0	0
Kurt Haggerty	15	3	0	0	12
Rhys Hanbury	25	14	25	1	107
Willie Isa	27	2	0	0	8
Ben Kavanagh	6	0	0	0	0
Sione Kite	15	1	0	0	4
Macgraff Leuluai	11	0	0	0	0
Paul McShane	11	3	4	0	20
Stefan Marsh	20	7	0	0	28
Joe Mellor	11	4	0	0	16
Scott Moore	6	0	0	0	0
Antony Mullally	10	0	0	0	0
Gareth O'Brien	4	0	15	0	30
Eamon O'Carroll	3	1	0	0	4
Jack Owens	4	0	0	0	0
Cameron Phelps	20	8	0	0	32
Steve Pickersgill	23	0	0	0	0
Anthony Watts	1	0	0	0	0
Lloyd White	15	5	0	1	21
Frank Winterstein	27	7	0	0	28

'Blackpool to Super League' in 100 games

The top-ranked five players in each of four categories are:

Appearances	App	T	G	D/G	Pts
Ben Kavanagh	91	12	0	0	48
Jim Gannon	87	19	0	0	76
Mark Smith	74	14	0	1	57
Anthony Thackeray	67	46	1	0	182
Dean Gaskell	66	30	0	0	120
Tries					
Anthony Thackeray	67	46	1	0	182
Paddy Flynn	60	38	0	0	152
Dean Gaskell	66	30	0	0	120
Gavin Dodd	60	27	47	0	202
Richard Varkulis	59	25	0	0	100
Goals					
Tim Hartley	34	12	111	0	270
Shane Grady	60	22	101	0	290
Steve Tyrer	18	16	74	0	212
Gavin Dodd	60	27	47	0	202
Scott Yates	37	17	37	0	142
Total Points					
Shane Grady	60	22	101	0	290
Tim Hartley	34	12	111	0	270
Steve Tyrer	18	16	74	0	212
Gavin Dodd	60	27	47	0	202
Anthony Thackeray	67	46	1	0	182

ND - #0241 - 270225 - C8 - 234/156/12 - PB - 9781780912028 - Gloss Lamination